Nelson's Annual

Preacher's Sourcebook

Nelson's Annual
Preacher's Sourcebook
2016

THOMAS NELSON
Since 1798

NASHVILLE   DALLAS   MEXICO CITY   RIO DE JANEIRO

Published in Nashville, Tennessee, by Thomas Nelson. Thomas Nelson is a registered trademark of HarperCollins Christian Publishing.

Typesetting by Kevin A. Wilson, Upper Case Textual Services, Lawrence, Massachusetts.

Thomas Nelson titles may be purchased in bulk for educational, business, fund-raising, or sales promotional use. For information, please e-mail SpecialMarkets@ThomasNelson.com.

Unless otherwise noted, Scripture quotations are taken from THE NEW KING JAMES VERSION, © 1982 by Thomas Nelson, Inc. Used by permission. All rights reserved.

Scripture quotations marked ESV are from THE ENGLISH STANDARD VERSION. © 2001 by Crossway Bibles, a division of Good News Publishers.

Scripture quotations marked NASB are from NEW AMERICAN STANDARD BIBLE®, © The Lockman Foundation 1960, 1962, 1963, 1968, 1971, 1972, 1973, 1975, 1977, 1995. Used by permission.

Scripture quotations marked NIV are from the HOLY BIBLE, NEW INTERNATIONAL VERSION®, NIV® Copyright ©1973, 1978, 1984, 2011 by Biblica, Inc.® Used by permission. All rights reserved worldwide.

Some Scripture quotations are noted from *The Message* by Eugene H. Peterson. © 1993, 1994, 1995, 1996, 2000. Used by permission of NavPress Publishing Group. All rights reserved.

[9780718041830]

Printed in the United States of America

15 16 17 18 19 20[RRD] 6 5 4 3 2

Contents

On the Road to the Cross

The Implications of the Cross and Resurrection

God's Family Plan

To the Ends of the Earth

Let Freedom Ring

Growing in Christ

The Community of the Committed

The Harvest Is Plentiful

The Attitude of Gratitude

Give Me Jesus This Christmas

Special Occasion Registries

Introduction

I have heard people remark that their church year consists of fifty-two unconnected sermons on disjointed themes. Being the son of a pastor and a pastor myself, I think this critique is largely unfounded. Nonetheless, busy pastors desire to improve the quality, freshness, and variety of their pulpit ministry.

Early in my ministry I attended a young Timothy conference where one of the speakers challenged me to pray and plan through my preaching ministry a year in advance. I was privileged to pastor a rapidly growing church and thus knew that weekly preparation time was sometimes difficult to find. I took his advice to heart and carved out a week early in the calendar year to get away from the office for a few days and look at the coming year in terms of the major Christian holidays, the needs of the church, and major biblical truths that needed exposition. I found myself drawn to short sermon series of four to eight weeks in duration—time long enough to fully develop a topic, yet short enough to keep interest at a high level.

We have chosen to organize this preaching resource book with attention to major events of the calendar year. The sermon series are all a month long. In most cases you will have the benefit of two contributors each month who have prepared sermons on the theme selected for that month. We have not attempted to provide full manuscripts but have chosen to give the reader two expanded outlines, one approximately twice the size of the other. These expanded outlines will allow you to personalize the message to fit your own preaching style and congregational needs. As you pray and plan with this tool at your side, you may find that one message sparks your interest and better suits the need of the moment. You also may choose to use both sermons weekly in different services.

The contributors are men from varying size congregations who have proven to be effective pastors and effective preachers. I am honored that they have given of their time and energy to join me in this pastor's annual. They have done so because they desire to be of service to fellow pastors. You will enjoy the unique insights of two or three preachers each month. The exception is March and December, when I have asked the contributing author to provide the entire month of preaching to help adequately prepare the congregation to consider the birth, death, and resurrection of our Lord.

This book is dedicated to pastors who desire to declare the Word of Truth with integrity and power. It is our prayer that it will prove to be a resource that will minister to you as you minister to those whom God has put in your charge.

Contributors

John R. Adolph
Senior Pastor
Antioch Missionary Baptist, Beaumont, Texas

J. Kie Bowman
Senior Pastor
Hyde Park Baptist Church, Austin, Texas

Marcus A. Buckley
Senior Pastor
Riverside Baptist Church, Greer, South Carolina

H. B. Charles Jr.
Senior Pastor
Shiloh Metropolitan Baptist, Jacksonville, Florida

Stephen Cutchins
Pastor of Worship
Hyde Park Baptist Church, Austin, Texas

Rick Ezell
Senior Pastor
First Baptist Church, Greer, South Carolina

Rick Fisher
Vice President
Blackaby Ministries, Jonesboro, Georgia

Tim Hawks
Senior Pastor
Hill Country Bible Church, Austin, Texas

Ken Hemphill

President of Auxano Press and Director of Center for Church
Planting and Revitalization
North Greenville University, Tigerville, South Carolina

Andy Lewis

Senior Pastor
Mitchell Road Presbyterian Church, Greenville, South Carolina

Walter Malone Jr.

Senior Pastor
Canaan Christian Church, Louisville, Kentucky

Larry Steven McDonald

Director of Doctor of Ministry Program
North Greenville University, Tigerville, South Carolina

Alex McFarland

President of Truth for a New Generation Apologetics Ministries
and Director of Christian Worldview and Apologetics
North Greenville University, Tigerville, South Carolina

D. Allen McWhite Sr.

Professor of Missions
North Greenville University, Tigerville, South Carolina

Ryan Pack

Senior Pastor
First Baptist Church North, Augusta, South Carolina

Ryan Rush

Senior Pastor
Kingsland Baptist Church, Katy, Texas

Steve Scoggins

Senior Pastor
First Baptist Church, Hendersonville, North Carolina

Gary L. Shultz Jr.

Senior Pastor

First Baptist Church, Fulton, Missouri

Ralph West

Senior Pastor

Church Without Walls, Houston, Texas

Ken Wilson

Teaching Pastor

Fellowship Bible Church, Conway, Arkansas

Don Wilton

Senior Pastor

First Baptist Church, Spartanburg, South Carolina

Rob Wilton

Lead Pastor

Vintage Church, New Orleans, Louisiana

John L. Yeats

Executive Director

Missouri Baptist Convention

JANUARY

God Makes Everything New

Date: January 3

Suggested Title: Cleansing and Keeping Clean

Scripture: Psalm 139:23–24

Contributor: John L. Yeats

Full Sermon Outline

Introduction

Have you noticed the health department signs in every public restroom? They indicate a seriousness about people, especially employees, washing their hands. Washing hands is a good hygienic discipline.

God makes everything new and fresh. If followers of Christ are to experience the fresh dynamic of God's work within, we must learn early in our Christian walk that there must be times of cleansing, or we discover the sadness of powerlessness. We need to daily experience the washing of our hearts.

Cleansing

Cleansing takes time because we are all prone to deny or minimize our own sins. How often have we prayed, "Lord, whatever is wrong in my life, please show me." Then we endure a ten second pause and move on to verbalizing our list of requests. It would be better if we prayed, "Lord, how shallow I am. Please forgive me," and then spent time confessing our wayward attitudes and hardness of heart.

Greg Frizzell says it this way: "Mark this well! The depth and power of your prayer life will never be greater than the depth of your daily confession and cleansing."[1]

Keeping Clean

Once we start experiencing God's cleansing, the individual question becomes, "What steps can I take to keep my heart clean?" Life is filled with plenty of moral distractions and intellectual traps to lure us away from a pure heart. The old processes of the flesh are still with us and will be until we leave these bodies. That's why it is important that we endeavor to stay clean. If we don't, it won't take long before our shields are down and the enemy entices us to believe the lies of the world.

We need to build some key practices into our lives to keep us true to our confession and our walk with God. Practicing the following keys does not justify us—or make us guiltless before God. Only through repentance and faith in the complete work of the Lord Jesus Christ do we find our relationship with our God.

Scripture-Based Actions

Consider practicing these Scripture-based actions to stay pure of heart and to avoid even the appearance of the old ways of the flesh.

1. Act like who you are in Christ (1 Cor. 6:9–11, 20; 1 Peter 1:18–19).

Remember, as a follower of Christ, you are not your own; you were bought with a price, and that was the precious blood of Jesus. This means that we surrender our rights to Him. Everything we know about walking with Him is revealed in the Word of God. If the Scriptures speak directly about something, that settles it. If we are unclear, then we ask for wisdom.

Surrendered rights is central to our identity as a devoted follower of Christ. We too often indulge ourselves in wickedness because we convince ourselves we have a right to it. Scripture gives us several lists of wicked behaviors. When believers practice those, it means they are choosing their own rights instead of a life of full surrender to Lord Jesus. Let us focus our lives on being who we are in Christ and take the initiative to reveal who Christ is through us in every sphere of life.

2. Run from temptation (1 Tim. 6:11; 2 Tim. 2:22).

Running is an activity. Being passive about temptation sets a person up for failure. If a believer spends enough time alone with temptation, the enemy can have a field day. That's one of the dangers of computers for believers and their family members. Believers must take the initiative to remove temptations and place safeguards by inviting accountability.

3. Be honest—no one is above temptation; pride will trap you (James 4:6).

The dumbest thing about the old flesh is the thinking that we can overcome things with our best efforts. Americans have a way of exalting self-reliance—making a god of our abilities. This is delusional thinking. Self-reliance can easily become the trap of the enemy, and pride becomes a stronghold. "God resists the proud, but gives grace to the humble."

4. Remember those who morally failed (2 Tim. 3:6–9).

One report of someone's moral failure is too many. We must be in prayer for the believers who have lost their witness due to impropriety. The landscape for too many families is littered with broken relationships precipitated by moral failure.

5. Take your spiritual pulse each hour (Col. 3: 1–17).

Many people are wearing digital devices to monitor their physical health. Wouldn't it be something if we had a tracking device that monitored our hungering and thirsting for God? Pause and take a breath and whisper to the Lord, "Am I revealing your glory with my words and attitudes?"

6. Thou shalt not touch—avoid casual touching of the opposite sex (1 Cor. 7:1–2).

Even casual touching can create unfulfilled expectations. We must respect one another and know the boundaries that will keep us from harm.

7. Guard the window of your mind (Matt. 5:28).

Pay attention to what you do with your eyes. It's simple: if you look with lust, you sin. By being alert to what we are looking at and thinking, we are guarding the window of the mind.

8. Treat every moment as a witness for Christ (Matt. 28:19–20; Acts 1:8; Col. 1:27).

Every moment is an opportunity to reveal His glory by practicing His presence. This one thing is so simple and so powerful. It alone keeps believers focused on their purpose in life. If we stay on mission, we are fortified to resist the subtleness of temptation.

Conclusion

Remember, it is the potential for believers to live a life of spiritual and moral cleanliness. The way of God is for us to experience His Holy Spirit permeating every area of our life so that He is Lord of all. Will we choose to cooperate with His work in us and through us?

Note

1. Gregory R. Frizzell, *How to Develop a Powerful Prayer Life* (Fulton, KY: Master Design, 2000), 54.

Date: January 3

Suggested Title: Irreducible Principles for a New Year

Scripture: Psalm 145

Contributor: John L. Yeats

Sermon Starter

Introduction

We usually take for granted what we have until we don't have it anymore. Once a great moral force in the world, the North American culture seems headed toward the trash pile of former great civilizations. What irreducible principles guide the followers of Christ to being light in a culture growing dark?

1. We know attributes of the only true and living God (vv. 1–9).

In a pluralistic society, no one ideology takes precedence over another. But what if the reality of the living God is not comparable to mere human ideations? Our modern ideas about God are at best pitiful. We tend to reduce His greatness and majesty down to a few lines in a chorus. Our thinking of Him as our buddy or our copilot or our friend on the seashore is way below the dignity of the God who spoke and the world came to be.

2. The Word of God remains the standard (vv.10–13).

If we reduce the Scriptures to the ten suggestions or to simply another appreciated holy book, we miss the reality of what the Word of God is. The Scriptures are the revealed heart of God who loves people and desires their highest good. His promises are true for all history and for all mankind.

The practice of the biblical standard is not always perfect, but cultures that embrace nonbiblical behavior as their relative standard are littered with broken relationships, disease, incest, polygamy, and horrific abuse of women. Rejection of the Word of God for family life results in a culture paying a high, unsustainable price for their choices.

3. Jesus must be Lord of all (vv. 14–16).

In societies dominated by secular thought, the citizens are required to constantly juggle the various spheres of life irrespective of other spheres. Each sphere has its own set of individualistic moral parameters.

The irreducible Lordship of Christ principle demonstrates the integration that redemption offers (Rom. 14:7–8). This principle transforms the little "g" god of our little universe to a part of the royal family of the King of kings. Our appropriate response is to surrender to the Lord Jesus in all things.

4. The believer's identity is secure (vv. 17–20).

In a pluralistic culture, the level of rejection is huge. You would think that classical tolerance would be normative in a pluralistic society, but that doesn't work when major players in the culture are militant. If we die to our own identity to live in Him, the rejections of this world may kill our bodies, but they can't touch our mission, our purpose in life. The collapse of the culture can never stop our Great Commission purpose!

Conclusion (v. 21)

When the gods of this world begin to fall down, the populace runs toward authentic answers to escape the collapse of the culture. When the collapse comes, all we need to do is point them to Jesus and pronounce "the praise of the Lord."

Date: January 10

Suggested Title: God's Agenda for a New Year

Scripture: 2 Timothy 1:5–7

Contributor: John L. Yeats

Full Sermon Outline

Introduction

In this the last epistle of Paul, you read about a young, discouraged man who desperately needed his mentor to impart wise counsel. In the context of a valley of discouragement, the Lord uses the apostle Paul to speak into young Timothy words of affirmation and principle—words that endure throughout generations. The entire book is laced with power phrases that remind us that God is at work to do something new in our lives.

Most often the work God chooses to do is preceded by months, if not years or decades of preparation. There were people who went before us who had a vision burning in their hearts for a great new work of God.

One example is Joel, a young church planter in Montreal. According to many missiologists, Montreal is the most unreached city in North America. Masses walked out of organized religion and vacated church buildings after the Catholic church priesthood scandal. However, while it is still embryonic, there seems to be a movement of God among evangelicals in the city.

Church planters are quick to point to prayer as the reason young adults are moving toward God once again. "We stand on the shoulders of others who have gone before us," Joel said. "My dad was one of those who prayed and fasted for a movement of God. When I was a small child, I watched him kneel beside his bed and cry out to God. I asked him why he didn't go someplace more comfortable." His dad's answer was that when Joel was older, he would understand why he knelt and prayed. "It was not until after I was twenty-three that I understood spiritual warfare is hard work," Joel said.

While church planters are working in darkness and brokenness, they are finding a spiritual hunger exists with people in Montreal, and truth is satisfaction to the craving soul. On their knees, the people who have for decades called on the Lord find new strength to persevere and claim a city for Christ.

The Place to Start Is Prayer

It may take decades to see results, but the most important strategy for reaching lost people and impacting a culture must begin with bended knees and humbled hearts calling out to the Lord who desires to transform lives.

When we are discouraged and our faith seems weak, the place to begin is prayer and especially intercession for lost people. Remember, it is the will of God that people be redeemed: "The Lord is not slack concerning His promise, as some count slackness, but is longsuffering toward us, not willing that any should perish but that all should come to repentance" (2 Pet. 3:9).

The Passionate Pursuit Is Prayer

What is God most passionate about? While He certainly loves His bride, His passion is for those who are lost. He knows their destination. Unless there is a remnant of faithful people who care about lost people like He does, there is no hope. Do we pursue what He loves or what we love the most?

We have discovered just about every method to persuade people to come to our churches, and yet they do not come. Could it be there is a vast difference between what God values most and what many American churches are doing? While He is focused on the lost, are we are too heavily vested in programs and ministries that simply gratify ourselves?

"But lost people are different than we are," you might say. True. They are probably about as different as we were to the generation before us.

Styles change. The truth of the transforming gospel does not. That's why to reach people with different values, different languages, different worldviews, different skin colors, different ages, we must humble our lives and yield our selfish flesh to the Lord Jesus. Instead of looking for a silver bullet to help our church's organizational processes, let us stay humbled before Him in prayer until God's love for lost people floods our hearts and renews our minds (Rom. 12:1–2).

The Penetrating Strategy Is Prayer

There are lost people in every city of our state, every town, every village, every neighborhood, every apartment complex, and every institution. With each government guideline or court ruling, it seems that our capacity to openly share the gospel is evaporating and eroding. We must recapture the most important element in God's strategy for pushing back the darkness and bringing light to the lost. That strategic, rudimentary process is intercessory prayer. Can you imagine the impact of two believers calling out for months to God for one person who needs to receive Christ?

Conclusion

These are the most urgent days in human history. Such days require extraordinary measures like interrupted to-do lists, death to our insecurities or fears, and brokenheartedness over the spiritual condition of a coworker, a neighbor, a fellow student, or a relative. The God who makes all things new has an agenda. It is prayer! He is working in the lives of believers all over the globe to bring His people to a renewed urgency for prayer and intercession for the lost. He has made this year as an opportunity for you to join Him.

Date: January 10

Suggested Title: Urgent Practices for a New Year

Scripture: Romans 1:18–25, focus v. 20

Contributor: John L. Yeats

Sermon Starter

Introduction

In the first century, Vesuvius erupted spewing volcanic ash into the air. Within minutes, the hot molten glasslike particles rushed into the city of Pompeii. This picturesque Roman city was completely buried by twenty-four to thirty feet of the volcanic debris in a matter of minutes.

Archaeologists have unearthed the city to make some amazing discoveries. Pompeii could have been described as "developed." They had a freshwater system, paved streets, a civic spa, and representative government where the magistrates provided entitlement-type services to sway the vote their direction.

In a city such as this, some people (if not most) embraced a boutique faith where an individual charted his or her personal belief without regard for what God said. There was no sense of urgency to prepare for a face-to-face with God. They thought life was good and secure.

But everything changed that fateful day in AD 79. The impact of the forces of nature overwhelmed the people's lives, and nothing more could be done to diminish their fate. In a matter of seconds, thousands stood before God. All of the sincere beliefs in sensual gods and economic security were worthless.

Life can change in seconds. We live with the reality that we are seconds from a physician's phone call, an accident, a natural event, or a terrorist attack. We can do our best to create a sense of security, but the frailty of life hasn't changed. Consequently, the importance of believers sharing the gospel with the lost is of infinite value.

What Believers Must Do

1. Get personal.

Every believer should know the name of at least one person who needs to know Jesus. Ask yourself, "Who do I want to see surrender to Christ this year?"

2. Pray for souls "here."

There is nothing as satisfying as calling out to God about something He really desires. The Word of God reveals that He is "not willing that any should perish but that all should come to repentance" (2 Pet. 3:9). The Holy Spirit knows every person in your sphere of influence. Purposefully stand in the gap for each person you know by name.

3. Pray for souls "there."

Missionary work is a long-term commitment to impact a culture with the gospel. Like never before in history, missionaries need your intercession so they can stand in the midst of spiritual darkness to proclaim the amazing life-changing truths about Jesus Christ.

4. Prepare to share.

If you don't know how, learn a method to tell the stories of Jesus in normal conversation.

Conclusion

World affairs are in such turmoil, and the sense of security that once permeated North America has evaporated. Not to recognize this reality is to live in denial; a sense of urgency should flourish in the hearts of Christ followers. In desperate times, people are more attentive to the voice of God articulated by the authentic follower of Christ. What person do you know who needs to know Jesus?

Date: January 17

Suggested Title: Enough Already!

Scripture: Ezekiel 9:8–10

Contributor: John L. Yeats

Full Sermon Outline

Introduction

One day in heaven, we may find ourselves speaking with an engaging character who introduces himself as Ezekiel and asks, "What did you think about my book?" Our response might be, "Book?" Or, we might be tempted to say, "Zeke, ol' buddy, I found it kinda hard to read; it didn't really fit with the American scene. It really didn't connect with me spiritually." But whether we connect with it or not, the book of Ezekiel is part of God's Word and it is exactly accurate.

When you study Ezekiel, you must understand the concept of the "Inviability of Jerusalem." This cultural concept went something like this: Prophets told the people Jerusalem was God's chosen city. God would bless Jerusalem. And the Messiah would come to the city. Because of this, a fatalistic view developed that because they were chosen, they could do no wrong. Repentance was unnecessary. So they participated in all kinds of evil, idolatry, and sensuality, and there wasn't a penalty. After all, Jerusalem was blessed. They believed there was no way that God would judge Jerusalem. But God did judge Jerusalem—severely. It's as if God said, "Enough already!"

Now listen to the voices in our culture and our national leaders—listen as they attempt to convince us of the power and might of our nation. The truth is that our nation is powerful, but not all-powerful; our nation is great, but not all glorious; our nation is strong, but not the mightiest. The Lord, our God who reigns, is Lord of all—He alone is El Shaddai.

If God would judge His beloved Jerusalem, why would He not judge the United States or any nation for that matter?

What was so bad in Jerusalem for God to say that He had forsaken the land? What things would God have Ezekiel itemize that would not be tolerated by God in any nation or empire?

1. The shedding of innocent blood

In Jerusalem, false, naturalistic religions had infiltrated the culture. Some of these beliefs called for the sacrifice of children. This practice was at first viewed as horrific. But eventually, a mind-set crept into the psyche of the culture that it would be better to sacrifice the little ones than for them to experience all the hell in this life.

In summer 2012, a picture went viral on the internet of a Chinese woman whose lifeless baby lay by her side. Family planning officials coerced termination of the seven-month pregnancy since the woman and her husband had violated the Chinese one-child rule. And while there were comments of anger on websites and blogs at the forced termination, there wasn't an international outcry for justice for this child and this family. Why were people in the United States not bombarding their officials with public outcry for the innocent? The answer: it seems this practice is not as horrific as it once was to our culture.

America, the blood of sixty million plus innocent children is on our hands! The God of this world today is the same God who judged His beloved Jerusalem because of the shedding of innocent blood.

2. The perversion of the population

More than one historical scholar describes this time in Jerusalem's history as comparable to Sodom and Gomorrah, which was known as the sensuous cesspool of ancient times. Compare that to our times. Billy Graham wrote that his wife, Ruth Graham, said to him after reading a draft of a book he was writing that, "If God doesn't punish America, He'll have to apologize to Sodom and Gomorrah."[1]

There are many who believe there are multiple forms of marriage, and others who desire complete freedom for erotic sexual expressions. They believe that the biblical perspective is antiquated and irrelevant. Followers of Christ hold there is a standard for sexuality and marriage and family. The standard is the Word of God, not man or the Supreme Court.

Men and women of God with convictional faith should not be consuming vile, hedonistic words or images. That's why men and women must stand up against the sewage of the internet that spews into our homes and businesses. It is time for people of God to stand up for the truth because we belong to the Lord and because we love our families.

Sexual sins are not like other sins. While sex in the context of a monogamous, heterosexual marriage is a wonderful thing, any form of sexual activity outside of that experience is sin. It gratifies the flesh and is a sin against your body and your loved ones.

Our culture has become so perverted in our thinking that we accept what was immoral and illegal only twenty years ago and think that is normal. But while we may move the standard of what is normal, God's standards for holiness are constant.

3. The rejection of God's reality

Verse 9 of the scripture in Ezekiel says, "For they say, 'the LORD has forsaken the Land, and the LORD does not see!'" That is another way of saying that the Lord is irrelevant. They refused to see the handiwork of God and said to themselves, "I can do what I want, when I want, because God doesn't exist; and if He did exist, He doesn't care."

Even though there is an attempt to write the faith of our nation's heritage out of state-approved textbooks, that doesn't diminish His reality. God is for real, He will not be ignored, and no nation can stand against His fury.

Conclusion

So what are the takeaways? Let the Scripture guide us in 1 Corinthians 16: 13–14:

1. This is the day to live wholeheartedly as a devoted follower of Jesus.
2. Stand on your biblical convictions.
3. Communicate the truth in love, even to those who reject our God.

Note

1. Billy Graham, "Billy Graham: My Heart Aches for America," Billy Graham Evangelistic Association, July 19, 2012, http://billygraham.org/story/billy-graham-my-heart-aches-for-america/.

Date: January 17

Suggested Title: Who Will Stand for Righteousness?

Scripture: Psalm 94

Contributor: John L. Yeats

Sermon Starter

Introduction

I wish I could tell you that the consequences of America's immoral choices by the generation of lawmakers in 1973 would not be visited on our children and our children's children. But I fear abortion has become the central outgrowth of just how morally corrupt our thinking is as a nation.

Where are the righteous ones? That kind of question is asked in this passage of Scripture. These simple truths about our Lord will give us a word of renewed hope and strength in a culture that devalues life.

1. The Lord knows those who are His (vv. 17–19).

Apart from God's work of saving grace, we would all be pursuers of evil. But God's grace has saved us to the uttermost (1 Cor. 6:9–11).

Because the gospel is the transformation of self-centered lives to consciences hungry for what is of value to our Heavenly Father, we are not the same as we were before. That is an evidence of secured salvation (v. 14).

2. Those who do evil are not exempt from His lordship (v. 20).

Just because something is legal does not make it moral. Abortion may be allowed by the law, but it is a violation of God's purposes.

Some of you have been hurt directly by evil people. Some have been hurt by evil secondhand and the destructive choices people make. Why doesn't God simply "take out" evildoers?

  a. We must remember Romans 3:23: "For all have sinned."

  b. God's great love of people means free moral choice is never violated. If He were to violate it for one, He would have to dismiss loving us all.

  c. Every knee will bow. The final chapter of history is conceptualized in Philippians 2:10–11.

Evil is a travesty when the law protects it. Abortion is an obvious evil protected by law. The violations of religious liberty in the public square, specifically the state education system, are gross injustices. And, prejudice toward the things that are unchangeable with an individual's beliefs or heritage is a sad commentary on our moral degradation. However, remember, the Lord is Lord even over those who do evil.

3. The Lord is the defender (v. 22).

  a. The Lord is the defender of innocent babies in heaven. In 2 Samuel 12:23, David's word captures the heart of a just God who protects the innocent.

  b. The Lord is the defender of those who come to the aid of the innocent. Examples:

   • William Wilberforce serves as an illustration of a statesman who worked tirelessly to abolish slavery.

   • Allied Forces freed people from the oppression of the Axis powers in World War II.

  c. The Lord is the defender of those who courageously take an unwed mom into their home, adopt a child in the name of Jesus, or volunteer at a crisis pregnancy center.

Conclusion

A rhetorical question is asked in verse 16. It is a question that echoes through the centuries and decades to this generation. Who will stand for His righteousness in this generation?

Date: January 24

Suggested Title: Prayer 101

Scripture: Matthew 6:9–13

Contributor: Ryan Pack

Full Sermon Outline

Introduction

Every college freshman knows that the academic journey begins with the 101 courses. In each discipline, a 101 class is required to provide basic knowledge. These introductory classes teach the groundwork that is the prerequisite for higher levels of learning. Without the foundational understanding of a subject, a student may wrestle with grasping the deeper principles taught in the next levels of their education.

Likewise, Jesus knew that His followers would need a basic framework for prayer so they could build a vibrant prayer life on the strong foundation commonly known as the Lord's Prayer. As a matter of fact, since the disciples saw the powerful impact of prayer in Jesus' life, they requested an introductory course in prayer: "Lord, teach us to pray" (Luke 11:1). Because of the time they spent in close proximity to Jesus, they were able to observe all aspects of His life and actions. It is interesting that even though they observed Jesus perform miracles, teach with authority, and draw crowds, they were most impressed by His prayer life. Therefore, they wanted a class on prayer.

Perhaps you find yourself longing for a stronger faith. Maybe you feel like your prayers aren't getting anywhere. You wonder if you are praying the right way—or if God is even listening to your requests. Simply knowing how to pray can give you confidence and open your eyes to the joy of talking to God and hearing from Him. Let's take a seat in the classroom of Jesus as He teaches Prayer 101 in Matthew 6:9–13.

Reverence (v. 9)

Too often our prayers begin with our laundry list of issues. God wants to hear our concerns, but Jesus taught the starting point of prayer is the awe of God. We revere God because He is our Father. God is not some distant deity but instead is our personal Father. Additionally we learn that God has a heavenly, eternal perspective of our earthly problems. Jesus prays, "hallowed be Your name," conveying to us the holiness of God. This verse is teaching us that the starting block of our prayer is the majesty, holiness, and size of our God—not the size of our problems. To put it in the simplest of terms, our prayers should begin with "Wow is God" rather than "Woe is me."

Release (v. 10)

Before we come to God with our requests, we must first come with the proper motive. If we were to listen closely to many of our prayers, it would sound as if we were attempting to twist the arm of God. In other words, we often try to tell God what to do rather than submit to His sovereign will. Jesus knew that letting go would be a problem for His followers, so He exhorts us to cry out for God's will to come to earth and be done just as He planned. If we are going to walk in faith, we must pray in faith. Real faith is when we release everything to God. We don't pray to push our agenda on God but to surrender to His.

Request (v. 11)

After we have worshipped God and let go of our desires, we are then in a place to bring our needs to God. It is a humbling concept that Almighty God has invited us to come to Him with our requests. Numerous times in the Gospels Jesus invites us to ask. He teaches us in this model prayer to ask God to provide for our daily needs. Please note the emphasis on the word *daily*. God knows just what you need. He knows that you have detailed, daily requirements to function. Just as provisions in life for a young child are delivered through a parent, our faith journey is at its best when we learn to depend on God every day.

Repentance (v.12)

The next step in Jesus' lesson on prayer is forgiveness. We are instructed to ask God to forgive our debts. Isn't this a word picture we all understand? Debt becomes a weight in our lives that holds us back. It makes us slaves to our debtors. The only way to experience victory from the debt of sin is to come to the one who is able to free us from it. First John 1:9 says, "If we confess our sins, He is faithful and just to forgive us our sins and to cleanse us from all unrighteousness." The word *confess* means to agree. Do you agree with God about the sin in your life? Are you regularly bringing your sins to God?

Once a person has experienced the forgiveness of sins through the gift of God's grace, then our response is to pass it along to others. Jesus teaches that we should forgive our debtors. Many are in bondage because they refuse to forgive another person. Forgiven people forgive others as well.

Realignment (v. 13)

If your car has ever lost its front-end alignment, you know that it has a tendency to drift off course. It becomes a struggle to keep it between the lines. We live daily with an enemy that desires to move us off course. Jesus reminds us to call down God's power to lead us in the right direction and keep us away from evil. Of course, God never leads us into sin. This would be against what the Bible clearly teaches. But it is imperative that Christians acknowledge the battle of temptation and take precautions through prayer.

Conclusion

Jesus closes this prayer lesson with the declaration, "For Yours is the kingdom and the power and the glory forever. Amen (v. 13)." Our prayers should end the same way our prayers start: praising God! Regardless of how the prayer is answered, a maturing believer knows that the foundation of prayer is the greatness of God and surrender to His kingdom.

Date: January 24

Suggested Title: Praying Over Burdens

Scripture: Nehemiah 1:4–11

Contributor: Ryan Pack

Sermon Starter

Introduction

A simple definition of the word *burden* is "something that is carried." Throughout modern-day Christendom, ministries have been launched because of a God-given burden that was carried by an individual. For example, Billy Graham's burden for evangelism continues to impact the world through the Billy Graham Evangelistic Association, and James Dobson's burden for the family birthed the ministry of Focus on the Family. How should you respond to a burden God has placed on your heart? The life of Nehemiah provides us with a guide for praying through burdens. Nehemiah himself became overwhelmed when he learned about the destruction in Jerusalem. He immediately sought God through prayer and fasting.

1. He started with praise (v. 5).

Just as Jesus taught opening our prayers with praise in the Lord's Prayer, we find this pattern also modeled this way. Nehemiah begins his prayer focused on the attributes of God. Fight the natural tendency to begin with worry or a laundry list of details. Simply begin with praise to the one who holds every burden.

2. He continued with persistence (v. 6).

Nehemiah prayed day and night. God-given burdens become realities when they have time to marinate. Meals from a slow cooker taste better than food from the microwave. Don't underestimate the power behind extended time to fully absorb God's will for your life. Persistence blesses us with clarity. Don't let *busy* bury your burden!

3. He confessed the problem (vv. 6–7).

Be sure to include yourself in prayers of confession. Passing blame to others will never unlock the burden. Nehemiah admits, "Both my father's house and I have sinned." There is more power behind a pure heart than that of pointing fingers.

4. He claimed the promise (vv. 8–9).

Nehemiah simply claims the promise God has already given. Claiming God's Word will anchor the burden in the heart of God. Remember that a burden from God is God's burden. He owns it but trusts you to manage it.

5. He ended with availability (v. 11).

It's not uncommon for a burden to fade away because no one steps up to the plate. A person may have a word from the Lord but lacks the initiative to see it accomplished. Too often we wait for someone else to do it. Nehemiah personally got involved by making himself available. He actually prayed for God to leverage his position with the king to move the burden forward.

Conclusion

As the book of Nehemiah continues, we read about the opposition and challenges his burden faced. Left exposed, his burden could have been defeated. There's no doubt wrapping the burden in prayer from the beginning and continuing in prayer through the journey provided the needed protection. Do you have a burden you are carrying? If so, follow the example of Nehemiah and start "praying before the God of heaven" (Neh. 1:4).

Date: January 31

Suggested Title: Praying for Others

Scripture: Colossians 1:9–12

Contributor: Ryan Pack

Full Sermon Outline

Introduction

Picture this scenario being played out in church parking lots each week. A friend stops you just before you open the door to your car. She begins telling you about a difficult situation in her life. Then you respond by saying, "I will be praying for you." You get in your car, start the engine, head to lunch, and forget all about your promise to pray for this friend. Or you do remember to pray but are embarrassed by the fact that you really don't know how to pray for others.

We know the power of prayer. We are encouraged when others pray for us. Deep down inside we desire to lift up effective prayers on behalf of others. In Paul's letter to the Colossians we discover that not only did he pray without ceasing but also he prayed specifically for others.

We Should Pray for Others
1. To be filled with God's will (v. 9)

Paul writes this letter to the believers in Colossae in part to combat heresy in the church. The issue at hand was the mixture of humanistic philosophies and other strains of religion that were being intermingled with the teachings in the church. Therefore, Paul prays specifically that believers would be "filled with the knowledge of His will in all wisdom and spiritual understanding."

Now fast-forward to our day. A major issue in the modern-day church is the clarity of God's Word being muddied with thoughts or trends in society. One tactic of the enemy is confusion. We must pray for one another to be filled only with the wisdom of God's will. Please note the importance of the word *filled*. Too many people live life *empty* instead of *filled*. We often use the phrase, "I'm running on fumes." However, God never intended for us to barely survive with our gauge on E. Paul knows that victorious living happens when we are filled with godly wisdom.

2. To walk in God's ways (v. 10)

Next Paul prays for the daily walk of believers. Our thoughts, attitudes, and choices are either moving us toward God or away from God. Specifically, Paul prays for others to walk:

a. Worthily. The first part of Paul's prayer is for godly knowledge, but now he prays for others to put that knowledge into practice. Walking in a manner that pleases God means that we make life decisions based on the spiritual wisdom that comes from God rather than man. Each step should be in alignment with God's ways.

b. Fruitfully. Many believers become discouraged when they never see any fruit from their efforts. Paul teaches us to ask God for fruitfulness in the lives of brothers and sisters in Christ. Can you imagine the greater impact the church could have if we were asking for one another to bear fruit?

c. Maturely. The latter statement in verse 10 is that others would increase "in the knowledge of God." Wouldn't you love for someone to pray that you would know God more? When we are at a crossroads in life, the answer is always going to be more of God. The more we know about God the sweeter our relationship becomes with God.

3. To be strengthened by God's power (vv. 11–12)

Weakness is a common problem for Christians. We can easily become weary physically, spiritually, emotionally, and mentally. Demanding schedules, overextended finances, and the struggle to keep our head above water wears us down. Paul's request is for the faithful in Christ to be "strengthened with all might, according to His glorious power." You can take a deep breath of release over some really good news in this verse: strength is not based on your power! The Bible tells us that our ability to function is according to His power. According to Paul, this God-given power enables us to be:

a. Patient. It is important to note that Paul uses two different words when referring to patience. This first word means having patience toward things or circumstances. There are times in life when the main issue draining our energy is in relation to a situation that is beyond our control. These moments in life take patience. Part of your intercession for others should include support for circumstances that may be weighing them down.

b. Long-suffering. In the Greek this word refers to patience toward people. If your current challenge isn't related to a circumstance, then it is most likely associated with a person. Paul knew that we would need strength to endure in situations dealing with circumstances and people. You will enhance your prayer for others when you ask God to grant them the necessary strength to hang on one more day according to His power.

c. Thankful. When life becomes overwhelming, it is easy to become bitter. Often this attitude of ingratitude can cause us to forget the larger picture and only focus inward. Paul concludes this prayer with the reminder to be thankful because of what God has done. God allows us to share in His inheritance. This is a prayer to take our eyes off of the momentary troubles and see the eternal perspective. Don't ever forget the vast resources and power you have as a child of God!

Conclusion

Can you imagine how different your life would be if someone was continually praying this prayer for you? Life is too short and there is too much power available through prayer to overlook this privilege of praying for others.

Date: January 31

Suggested Title: Prayer of Restoration

Scripture: Psalm 51

Contributor: Ryan Pack

Sermon Starter

Introduction

There's an episode of *America's Funniest Home Videos* where a preschool-aged child is covered in chocolate, the walls around him are covered in chocolate, and his baby brother is covered in the same chocolate. With the video camera running, the mother asks the boy, "Have you been eating chocolate?" The child shakes his head and answers no. While that is funny, it's true that part of the sin nature is the desire to hide even though our guilt is clear. David sinned with Bathsheba, attempted to cover up the sin, and then came to his senses by admitting his failures. Psalm 51 provides a road to restoration we can all use to come clean and get a new start.

1. Appeal to God's attributes (vv. 1–2).

There are times we won't approach someone because we fear the response. David approaches God with confidence by appealing to:

- God's loving-kindness
- God's tender mercies
- God's cleansing power

2. Admit your sin (vv. 3–6).

After a season of trying to cover up sin, David now comes completely clean with God. Notice the detail of his confession:

- The weight of the sin (v. 3—It is always before him.)

- The size of the sin (v. 4—He sinned against Bathsheba and Uriah but ultimately has rebelled against Almighty God.)
- The source of the sin (v. 5—We are born sinners [Rom. 3:23].)
- The truth about sin (v. 6—God's truth and wisdom is the standard; His truth must be the foundation of our heart and soul.)

3. Ask for restoration (vv. 7–11).

David's life and heart were a mess. He needed a total overhaul of his soul that only God could perform. Just as stained-glass windows are broken pieces of glass made into something beautiful, God takes our mess and makes a masterpiece. Here are the elements of restoration David requested:

- Forgiveness (v. 7)
- Rejoicing (v. 8)
- Clean heart (v.10)
- Steadfast spirit (v. 10)
- Renewed intimacy (v. 11)
- Joy of salvation (v. 12)
- Willing spirit (v. 12)

4. Act on your new freedom (vv. 13–19).

Why would we request a fresh move of God in our life only to return to the same habits? A changed life means changed actions! David now desires to:

- Point others toward God (v. 13—Changed lives want to change other lives.)
- Praise God for the victory (v. 14–15)
- Provide proper sacrifices (v. 16–17—The best offering we can bring to God is ourselves.)

Conclusion

Since the mess the preschooler made with the chocolate covered the walls, carpet, and furniture, there was no way he would be able to clean it up on his own. The only solution to recovering from his mess was to get outside help. In the same way, our sin cannot be addressed by our own efforts. Only through the work of God can we ever be made whole. Go ahead and admit that you've been hiding the chocolate. God will take care of the cleanup!

FEBRUARY

God Is Love

Date: February 7

Suggested Title: God's Mind Is Made Up, He Loves You!

Scripture: Romans 8:38–39

Contributor: John R. Adolph

Full Sermon Outline

Introduction

June 30, 2011, was a beautiful day. It was so pretty that one tourist in our nation's capital said, "God kissed it with His love." There was not a cloud in the sky, the air was clean, and the sun did not just shine on the thirtieth; it smiled. The warm embrace of a summer day brought thousands of tourists to the district. The sun would soon set, and Washington, DC, nightlife would wake up like a newborn baby ready to stay up and play for the rest of the evening. There was a huge private party on the rooftop of the W Hotel. By 10:00 p.m., it bore the party noise of a vibrant social event filled with prosperous people who were having a great time.

By 11:00 p.m., the entire scene would take a horrific turn for the worse. A woman's body lay covered with a white sheet near the front of the hotel. One report from the rooftop was that she had walked over to the fence guarding the edge of the building, climbed over it, and stepped off the edge to her death. The scene was roped off in CSI-like fashion; DC police were everywhere, and unsubstantiated reports from the crowd were that the woman had just told her friend that no one loved her, not even God.

Such a death is painful proof that people still do not understand the fact that God's love is real. More importantly, it is a reminder to the Christian church that our message to the world is simple and needs to be proclaimed repeatedly: God loves you.

When the apostle Paul writes to the church in Rome, he presents the greatest Christian apology ever written to the center of the then-known world. Paul makes it clear that he is bold for the sake of the gospel (Rom. 1:16), that the depravity of humanity is our problem (Rom. 3:23), that the redemptive plan of God is to save us by grace alone, through faith alone, in Christ alone (Rom. 6:23), and that God's love for us is real and will never fade nor change (Rom. 5:8). The words of Romans 8:38–39 are replete and clear to this fact, for Paul wrote, "I am persuaded, that neither death, nor life, nor angels, nor principalities, nor powers, nor things present, nor things to come, nor height, nor depth, nor any other creature, shall be able to separate us from the love of God, which is in Christ Jesus our Lord" (Rom. 8:38–39 KJV).

The Human Condition Does Not Change It

From verses 38–39, we gain insight on God's love that is overwhelming and life-changing. Paul makes it clear that the human condition does not change God's love for you. A close study of Romans 8 reveals a personal progression for the apostle as he brings his doctrinal argument to a climax. In verse 18 he says, "For I reckon"; in verse 28 he states, "And we know"; and in verse 38 he moves boldly to "For I am persuaded." The reason for the apostle's boldness is that he knew God's love personally. Paul could recall God loving him enough not to destroy him on the Damascus Road (Acts 9) and being loving enough to graciously spare his life and use him as an apostle called out of due season. When Paul says "neither death nor life," he means that no condition between these two spectrums can turn God's love off. The human condition does not change the fact that God loves you. God has never seen a person He did not love. From the worst of sinners to the greatest of saints, dead or alive, God loves us all.

Demons Cannot Restrain It

Not only does the human condition not change it, but neither can demons restrain it. God loves you in the presence of the adversary. Paul says, "nor angels, nor principalities, nor powers." The angels here are not good angels but fallen angels that work in conjunction with principalities and powers of this world against believers who are in Christ. What they do is work to lure believers into sin through temptation. They work at causing Christians to fall so that in a fallen state, a believer feels unlovable and a sinner feels unsavable. However, here is the gospel truth: you can be demonically possessed, and the Lord of heaven will still love you. We know this to be true from Mark 5:1–11. Jesus meets a man in the tombs tormented by demons, and He cares enough to save, heal, deliver, and use him for His glory. Here is some great news: when God decided to love you, not even the devil in hell could change God's mind about you.

Time and Dimensions Cannot Contain It

God's love for you is so pronounced that time and dimensions cannot contain it. Paul says, "nor things present nor things to come, nor height nor depth, nor any other creature." What he is saying is no present or future circumstance will keep God from loving you. In short, God loves you, and there is nothing that you can do about it. The reason why you cannot do anything about it is that you had nothing to do with it. God has made a decision to love you, and His mind is made up. Nothing can turn His love off, nothing can make His love cease, and nothing will ever cause Him not to love you deeply and personally.

Conclusion

A person not thinking or feeling that God loves him or her is wrong. Hear the words of God through Paul and receive God's love, feel God's love, sense God's love, know God's love, take God's love, remember God's love, and embrace God's love. God loves you!

Date: February 7

Suggested Title: His Love Made the Difference

Scripture: Romans 5:8

Contributor: John R. Adolph

Sermon Starter

Introduction

Born and raised in the swamplands of Louisiana, the young man started drinking and using drugs at an early age. When he turned fourteen years old, his family moved to New Orleans, and he remained there until Hurricane Katrina struck the Gulf Coast in August 2005. He was trapped on his roof in the Lower Ninth Ward with his wife, twin girls, and mother-in-law when the levy broke. His entire family perished, but while hanging on to an antenna of a house that was underwater, he whispered to God, "God, if you are there, spare me, and I promise I will live for you forever." He waited several hours and just before the sun could set, a huge Coast Guard boat carrying people to safety spotted him. The boat had room for only one more passenger, and when the Coast Guard operator took him by the hand to place him on board, he said to him, "My friend, God must really love you!"

This man has shared his story around the world, and with it comes the conversion sentiment that God's love made the difference. In Romans 5:8 Paul echoes a similiar thought when he says, "But God commendeth his love toward us, in that, while we were yet sinners, Christ died for us" (KJV). Oftentimes people think that human good is what provokes the Lord to love us. However, such is just not the case. If God's love can make the difference in the life of this man from the swamplands of Louisiana, it can be the difference maker in the life of anyone. The love of God makes the difference in several ways. Let us consider a few observations from the text together.

1. His love is always the turning point.

God's love has the power to turn everything around. When Paul says, "But God," it presents a moment in time when the Lord of heaven does something for fallen humanity that we could never do for ourselves.

2. His love always touches.

When Paul says God "commendeth his love toward us," it is the picture of broken pieces in a potter's house being placed together to make a masterpiece at the master's touch. This is what God's love does for us. He takes broken pieces and makes a masterpiece.

3. His love is always right on time.

God has a holy habit of showing up when all hope seems lost. The beauty of this verse is seen in the words, "While we were yet sinners, Christ died for us." Christ did not wait on us to get right with God. That would never happen, so He became us to save us; and He did it while we were in sin. Now that is love!

Conclusion

The love of God is a life changer. It left the man from Louisiana a changed man and will do the same thing for you.

Date: February 14

Suggested Title: He Loves Me, He Loves Me, He Loves Me!

Scripture: 1 John 4:10

Contributor: John R. Adolph

Full Sermon Outline

Introduction

Rogers Park is a gorgeous little recreational facility located on the corner of Gladys and Dowlen in the city of Beaumont, Texas. It is a beautiful spring day and children have covered this park like sprinkles on a cupcake. It is a perfect day for the playtime of fifth graders who need to burn off some energy, and they are burning it in grand fashion. Some are running and jumping, while others are sliding and screaming, and the masses are waiting for their chance at the swing just to see whose feet can go the highest.

While the line for the swing is long and others race around the park in training to become one of America's next Olympic medal hopefuls, there are two fifth-grade girls just taking a stroll picking up clovers from the ground. Each time one grabs one, her face is filled with excitement. If you could eavesdrop on their conversation it would sound like this from the little girl wearing a pink shirt: "He loves me, he loves me not, he loves me, he loves me not." However, the little girl wearing denim has a completely different approach. When she grabs her clover she says, "He loves me, He loves me, He loves me." Finally, after several episodes like this, the girl wearing pink says to her clover-picking companion, "You're not playing fair." To which her friend in denim replies, "Sure I am. It is just that we are talking about different people. You are plucking your leaves thinking about a guy, but every time I pluck one, I think about God. There is never a time that He does not love me."

As we explore 1 John 4:10 together, one principle should remain paramount as it pertains to John's writing: that God loves us. John says, "Herein is love, not that we loved God, but that he loved us, and sent his Son to be the propitiation for our sins" (1 John 4:10 KJV). This verse contains some wonderful portraits regarding God that make His love for us impossible to miss. Let us consider each of them.

1. Consider the portrait of our human inadequacy.

Here is the greatest news ever: God does not love us because we love Him. In fact, our love is filled with human error, which makes our love flawed. However, God's love is perfect. John's phrase "herein is love" could better be translated, "this is where you find real love." Real love started with God, and it will end with God. God is the source of all love, the force of real love, and the course of any love. There is no love anywhere without God.

There is a rich comparison and contrast found in the first segment of the verse. God's love for us is expressed in the phrase "herein is love," and our love for Him is "not that we loved God." John compares God's love to our love. God's love is real, our love is relative. His love is complete, and our love is partial. His love is eternal, and our love is temporal. His love is pure, and our love is tainted. His love continues when our love has stopped. His love succeeds where our love fails. His love is sufficient, and our love at best is inadequate. The blessing of this comparison is found in the fact that even when our love is found weak, fledgling, and nonexistent, God still loves us.

2. Consider the portrait of God's divine ability.

The ability of God should keep you in awe! God is an able God. He is able to create something from nothing. He is able to save, heal, deliver, strengthen, and restore. However, this text gives us something even deeper and richer regarding God's ability. God has the divine capacity and ability to love the unlovable. When John says "but that he loved us," he means that God has made a decision regarding you, and you cannot change His mind or alter His thoughts.

There is the story of a man who was blessed to father five sons. All of them were raised in a Christian home with a working mother and father. They were given every opportunity in life to succeed, and four of them did, but the youngest son struggled immensely. While incarcerated, the youngest boy wrote his father a letter asking to come home and start over, but he feared his father's rejection. In the letter, the son told his father to tie a yellow ribbon around the mailbox if he still loved him. When his son turned the corner there was not just one ribbon around the mailbox, but there was a yellow ribbon hanging from every tree, from the bumper of the station wagon, and one in his father's hand! That yellow ribbon said, "I still love you!" Just as this man still loved his son who had fallen and failed, God still loves each of us!

3. Consider the portrait of the Lord's sufficiency.

Imagine for a moment that you are living on death row awaiting your day to die. All of a sudden, the judge appears at your cell and says, "You are free to go!" As you walk out with the judge, you notice another man walking into your cell. You then ask the judge, "Who is that guy?" To which the judge replies, "He is the man that is going to take your place. And he is not just any man. That man is my son!" When John says, "sent his Son to be the propitiation for our sins," this is exactly what it means: Jesus Christ was our all-sufficient substitute that fateful day at the cross.

Conclusion

The little girl in denim at the park had it right. When we consider God's love for us, we have to conclude as she did, "He loves me, He loves me, He loves me!"

Date: February 14

Suggested Title: I'm Certain That He Loves Me!

Scripture: 1 Peter 5:7

Contributor: John R. Adolph

Full Sermon Outline

Introduction

Once while in worship, a very conservative, refined, pristine woman asked to share her testimony with the congregation. She approached the podium and addressed the congregation using the oratory of a highly educated woman. Her poise was noticeable, and her pitch, tone, and voice were splendid. However, as she spoke, tears began rolling down her face like rivers. This stately woman told the entire church that she had been convinced that God no longer loved her or her family. She said that she had seen years of unparalleled blessings from the Lord, but the last year had been one tragedy after another. Her husband of thirty-one years passed suddenly from a brain aneurysm, her only son was killed in a tragic car accident while returning to college, and she had been diagnosed with breast cancer. It was all just too much for her to bear alone. She had felt forsaken by God and abandoned.

To put an end to it all, she said that she started plotting and planning her own demise. She planned her suicide so that it would look like an accident in order for her family and relatives to collect her life insurance without any question. She reasoned that her family and relatives could live comfortably, and she would be out of her misery. She told the church that before she left home to take her own life she gave the Lord just one more chance to prove that He still cared about her. There on her nightstand was a Bible. She told God, "If you still love me, prove it right now." She opened her Bible, and the pages fell to 1 Peter 5:7: "Casting all your care upon him; for he careth for you" (KJV).

She heard God's voice in this one verse that spoke loudly to her heart regarding God's love for her. She concluded her testimony with these words: "I may not know everything, but I am for certain that He loves me."

His Love Carries Your Load

When Peter says, "Casting all your care upon him," he means casting all of your worries finally upon the Lord. There is a catch here. If you keep some of them, you must keep all of them. Cast them all or keep them all.

His Love Is Attached to His Loyalty

The place for your concerns, worries, tribulations, and trials is "upon him." The Him in the passage is not stated specifically. The Him in this passage is reserved for those who know Him, love Him, and trust Him. This Him for Peter is Jesus Christ, Son of the living God!

His Love Is Built to Last a Lifetime

"He careth for you." The word *care* here is *melo*. It is a picture of a husband's care for his wife. God says, in short: I am obligated to take care of you for the rest of your life, and My love for you will never fail.

Date: February 21

Suggested Title: This Prayer Is for You

Scripture: Philippians 1:9–11

Contributor: Walter Malone Jr.

Full Sermon Outline

Introduction

The epistle to the Philippians is one of the most spiritually intimate and loving letters that we read in the New Testament records. The apostle Paul wrote this letter with spiritual passion to a congregation that was dear to his heart. Paul gave birth to the church at Philippi during his second missionary journey. He opens this epistle expressing his gratitude and appreciation for their partnership in ministry and assures them that what God starts He will finish. And then he expresses this wonderful prayer for spiritual formation.

> And this I pray, that your love may abound still more and more in knowledge and all discernment, that you may approve the things that are excellent, that you may be sincere and without offense till the day of Christ, being filled with the fruits of righteousness which are by Jesus Christ, to the glory and praise of God. (Phil. 1:9–11)

Paul had a passion for the spiritual development of the believers whom he had led to Christ. This passion was not only manifested in his preaching and teaching, but it was also revealed in his prayer life.

Consider how this was revealed and expressed in other epistles.

- "Therefore I also, after I heard of your faith in the Lord Jesus and your love for all the saints, do not cease to give thanks for you, making mention of you in my prayers" (Eph. 1:15–16).

- "For this reason we also, since the day we heard it, do not cease to pray for you, and to ask that you may be filled with the knowledge of His will in all wisdom and spiritual understanding" (Col. 1:9).
- "We give thanks to God always for you all, making mention of you in our prayers" (1 Thess. 1:2). The primary focus of Paul's prayer was on the spiritual welfare of others.

One of the true indicators of a Christian's level of spiritual maturity is his or her prayer life. Real prayer does not flow from external requirements, but from internal passion—it flows from our relationship with God.

Relationship to Text

There are five specific things for which Paul diligently prayed on behalf of the Philippians: their spiritual progress in love, excellence, integrity, good works, and glorifying God. Here, we will explore the first three of these things.

1. Spiritual progress in love (v. 9)

Knowledge in verse 9 does not mean primarily a grasp of the facts about something or someone. Yes, we should know as much as we can about the Bible. We must read and study the Scriptures. Paul's prayer is not that we accumulate more facts but that we enter more deeply into a personal relationship with Christ, knowing more and more about who Christ is and what He can be to us.

The word *discernment* indicates perception or discrimination, the ability to make moral decisions. Our hard decisions in life are not usually between what is clearly good and what is clearly bad. More often we struggle between what is good and what is better.

2. Excellence (v. 10)

Excellence means thinking and living biblically. Excellence means that we desire to live our lives according to God's will and in a manner that pleases Him. Christians who live at the highest level of dedication and consecration to God are persons who live with spiritual focus. This is why we are encouraged to have the mind of Christ.

The word *sincere* carries the idea of testing something by sunlight. In ancient Rome fine pottery was relatively thin and fragile and often developed cracks while being shaped in the fire. Dishonest shops would fill the cracks with a hard, dark wax, which would be concealed when the object was painted or glazed. However when a customer would take the pottery outside and hold it up in the sunlight, the cracks would be revealed. Honest dealers would often stamp their products "sine cera" (without wax) as a guarantee of high quality.

In 2 Corinthians 4:7 we are told, "But we have this treasure in earthen vessels, that the excellence of the power may be of God and not of us." As the people of God, even when we come into a saving relationship with Christ, we recognize that there are cracks in our earthen vessels. There are shortcomings and issues in our lives. And when we consider our lives under the light of the Word of God, we begin to see where we need to grow and develop spiritually in our relationship with God. The experience of salvation includes justification, sanctification, and glorification. Sanctification is the continual process where God works in the cracks in our lives.

3. Integrity (v. 11)

Once we come into a saving relationship with God through Christ, God comes to live in our lives in the person of the Holy Spirit. It is the Spirit of God within us that enables us to be filled with the fruit of righteousness. In and of ourselves we could never live in holiness or with spiritual integrity. In Romans 8:12–14 the apostle Paul says to us, "Therefore, brethren, we are debtors—not to the flesh, to live according to the flesh. For if you live according to the flesh you will die; but if by the Spirit you put to death the deeds of the body, you will live. For as many as are led by the Spirit of God, these are sons of God."

Conclusion

All of us have been recipients of the prayers of other people who have brought us before the Lord. As we grow in the discipline of prayer, let us be mindful to cover others in prayer.

Date: February 21

Suggested Title: God Loves Me and God Loves You

Scripture: John 1:1, 14

Contributor: Walter Malone Jr.

Full Sermon Outline

Introduction

Within the Bible, the four books that comprise what we call the Gospels—Matthew, Mark, Luke, and John—speak to us primarily about the life and ministry of Jesus Christ. John wrote his Gospel to present Jesus as the eternal Logos. Jesus is the Word that became flesh.

Relationship to Text

In the prologue of his Gospel, John speaks to us about what we call in theological terms a high christology and a low christology. A high christology affirms the deity of Christ. It declares that Jesus is God. "In the beginning was the Word, and the Word was with God, and the Word was God. He was in the beginning with God" (John 1:1–2). The life of Christ does not begin in Bethlehem. He was with God in the beginning. Jesus was in the beginning because He is part of the Godhead. On the other hand, a low christology affirms the humanity of Christ. It declares that God in Christ left precincts of glory and made Himself subject to our lowly estate. It says that Jesus walked the dusty streets of Palestine, and He did so as One who was both God and man at the same time: "And the Word became flesh and dwelt among us, and we beheld His glory, the glory as of the only begotten of the Father, full of grace and truth" (John 1:14).

It is without question that God loves us, for He sent His Son into the world for no other reason than to save us from our sins. God sent Jesus into the world to make us whole. Jesus came as Savior, but He also came as sample copy of how to live as a child of God. He came as Deliverer, but He also came to demonstrate how to live with vision and victory.

1. In Jesus we see a God of purpose (John 3:16).

Jesus was not an accidental Christ. He was sent into the world with divine intention to carry out a purpose. As Christians, God has saved us for a purpose. We are to be His representatives in the world (2 Cor. 5:20).

2. In Jesus we see a God of transformation (Mark 5:1–20).

God is willing and able to change any person's life no matter what their situation might be.

3. In Jesus we see a God of power (Mark 9:1–13).

God purposes for us to live as His disciples with power. The purpose for us living with power is to expand the kingdom of God.

Conclusion

Knowing that God loves us is the most assuring knowledge we can live with. While there are many things that we don't know or understand concerning the nature and being of God, we know with certainty that God loves us! The love of God sustains us.

Date: February 28

Suggested Title: It's Done

Scripture: Philippians 1:6

Contributor: Walter Malone Jr.

Full Sermon Outline

Introduction

The epistle to the church at Philippi is one of the most intimate and personal letters written by the hand of Paul that we read in the New Testament records. The apostle Paul has several epistles that are a part of biblical revelation. Some were written to churches and some to individuals, but none is more passionate and expressive in love than this letter that he wrote to the church at Philippi.

The theme of this epistle has to do with the divine joy that becomes the birthright of every believer in Christ. Biblical joy is the settled conviction that God who is sovereign controls the events of life for our good and for His glory. For unlike happiness, God's joy is not based on external circumstances. We consider that happiness is an attitude of satisfaction or delight based upon external circumstances beyond one's control. In this light, happiness cannot be planned or programmed. It is experienced only if and when circumstances are favorable. It is therefore elusive and uncertain. And I think all of us could testify that we live in a world well acquainted with despair, depression, disappointment, dissatisfaction, and a longing for lasting happiness that often never comes to pass.

However, God's joy is so rooted and grounded in our relationship with Him that it becomes an internal disposition that is not predicated on the external context of one's life. A gospel song put it like this: "This joy that I have, the world didn't give it to me; and the world can't take it away!"

When Paul wrote this letter to the church at Philippi, he was probably a prisoner in Rome. This letter gave Paul the opportunity to express his love and appreciation for the Christians at Philippi, to share with them his situation and contentment in Christ, and to address some problems in the church. And it is in this sixth verse that Paul said something that was encouraging and insightful not only for the Philippians but also for every child of God when he declared, "Being confident of this very thing, that He who has begun a good work in you will complete it until the day of Jesus Christ." This verse in *The Message* Bible reads like this: "There has never been the slightest doubt in my mind that the God who started this great work in you would keep at it and bring it to a flourishing finish on the very day Christ Jesus appears."

Relationship to Text

Here Paul speaks of what theologians have called "the divine initiative." God is the doer, the initiator, and the actor in our affairs. We are the responders, the receivers, and the recipients of His action. Throughout the Bible we see the revelation that God is the initiator. For examples just consider episodes in the lives of Abraham, Jacob, and Moses. And even in the life of the apostle Paul, who could never forget the day he had seen and experienced Christ's transforming revelation on the road to Damascus. He was on his way with letters to arrest those who were committed to Christ when he got arrested himself by Christ. And the man who had been a butcher would become a brother. The man who had been an antagonist of the faith would become an apostle of the faith. It would be the apostle Paul who would go all over Asia Minor declaring the glorious gospel of Jesus Christ.

Have you ever considered the implications of what it means for God to be the initiator, the doer, and the actor in the affairs of life? Here are the implications:

1. It is to affirm the truth that it is God who is doing a good work through us.

When Paul wrote to the church at Ephesus, he put it like this: "For by grace you have been saved through faith, and that not of yourselves; it is the gift of God, not of works, lest anyone should boast. For we are His workmanship, created in Christ Jesus for good works, which God prepared beforehand that we should walk in them" (Eph. 2:8–10). A simple way of stating this is that we should always remember that we are saved by God's grace and not by our goodness.

2. It is to recognize the fact that God uses other people to help give shape to our spiritual formation.

What God is working out in our lives, He is doing so in relationship to the church. God's good work is not done in a vacuum; it is accomplished in the fellowship of believers. This is why we are told in the book of Hebrews, "And let us consider one another in order to stir up love and good works, not forsaking the assembling of ourselves together, as is the manner of some, but exhorting one another, and so much the more as you see the Day approaching" (Heb. 10:24–25).

3. It is to live knowing that we have the assurance that God is sovereign, and whatever difficulties and dilemmas we may face, our victory is guaranteed.

The trials and tribulations in our lives and the struggles and sorrows we have been challenged by are not indicators that God has forsaken us or reneged on His promises in our lives. Suffering, struggle, and sacrifice are parts of the Christian pilgrimage. For don't you recall that Jesus said, "In the world you will have tribulation; but be of good cheer, I have overcome the world" (John 16:33).

Conclusion

What God starts He finishes. We can live with the confidence that God has a plan and purpose that He is working out in our lives for our good and for His glory!

Date: February 28

Suggested Title: It's a New Day for Me

Scripture: Ephesians 2:1–6

Contributor: Walter Malone Jr.

Sermon Starter

Introduction

Every time I mount the pulpit I stand to declare the glorious gospel of Jesus Christ. With conviction and confidence I want people to know that God is willing and able to save, heal, and deliver them from the sin and shame that has characterized their lives. I want people who feel that things could never turn around to know that it doesn't matter how devastating and deplorable a life has been. God will meet them where they are.

But He won't leave them where He found them.

For being saved means that one has come into a personal relationship with God wherein a transformation has taken place in his or her heart. And out of this inner transformation of heart, mind, and spirit one begins to live a new life of vision and victory.

Throughout the Bible there are scriptures that attest to this eternal truth (Isa. 1:18, Jer. 29:11–13, John 3:16, Rom. 8:1).

Relationship to Text

In chapter 1 of Ephesians, Paul described our spiritual possessions in Christ, and now in chapter 2 he speaks of our spiritual position in Christ. With clarity and conviction the apostle declares that we have been taken out of a great graveyard of sin and placed into the throne room of glory. Paul gives us, as it were, a contrast: from death to life, from hell to heaven, from bondage to freedom, from pessimism to optimism.

1. Everyone is dead without Christ (vv. 1–3).

This text is a stirring reminder of how horrendous and horrific our lives were without Christ. For the idea of death in this text is not a figure of speech. Paul means that we were absolutely dead. Everyone is dead apart from Christ. It may appear that people around us are so very much alive; however, without Christ they are simply walking dead. In particular verses 2–3 inform us that those who are spiritually dead are under the sway of the world, the devil, and the flesh.

2. Our spiritual position must be in Christ (vv. 4–6).

The person without Christ is not sick; they are dead. They do not need resuscitation; they need resurrection (Ezek. 37:1–3).

Paul spoke with clarity about the excruciating and painful predicament of our position when we were separated from God in Christ. But he did not want that scathing reality to be isolated from the glorious hope of deliverance (key phrase: "But God").

Paul spoke to us about the predicament of our past, but now he speaks to us about the possibilities of our present and future life in Christ. God's answer to death is resurrection. Christians are those who have already been made alive.

Conclusion

As Christians all of us are in the process of becoming. We may not be all that we ought to be, but thank God we are not what we used to be. By the grace of God every day we are emerging into new people in Christ!

MARCH

On the Road to the Cross

Date: March 6

Suggested Title: The Way of the Cross—From the Garden to the Garden

Scripture: Genesis 2:8; John 19:41; Revelation 21:3

Contributor: Don Wilton

Full Sermon Outline

Introduction

God gives all people the grand picture in and through His Word of the hope we have for the forgiveness of sin and reconciliation with a holy and righteous God through the person and work of the Lord Jesus Christ. God has a grand plan for the salvation of all people. This grand picture in His Word takes us from the garden of Eden to the Garden of Gethsemane, and as we reflect on God's Word we will clearly see our story in His story. This picture is the reality of where we all are. It is a beautiful picture at times, a horrid picture at times, and a hopeful picture in the final analysis—all because God loved us so much that He gave His only Son to come to this earth and die on a cruel Roman cross. He died so that all who would believe in His name would receive eternal life and spend all time and eternity back in the garden with our Savior forever.

God's Story Shows Us Three Pictures
1. People living with God in God's presence (Gen. 2:8)

The story of the creation of man at the hand of God is quite marvelous. Many have tried to explain this away and even more have, at the very least, tried to reduce man's development from the need to eat of the leaves of a tree to the gradual desire for "evolving" man to "have the monkey" taken out of him so that he could satisfy his appetite on the grass below. The eventual cross of Christ finds its "roots," not in man's evolution, but in God's wondrous creation. God created man in His image, and this means three things:

- Man was created to look like God.
- Man was created to love like God.
- Man was created to live with God.

In the opening verses of Genesis this is the picture we see. Adam and Eve lived with God in an exclusive and God-purposed way. They fellowshipped together, and man enjoyed the abundance of all God had made available to him. But something terrible happened.

2. People living without God in God's presence (Gen. 3:23)

This is a sad and very tragic picture. The devil came along and deceived Adam and Eve into thinking that God would, in some way, accommodate any form of sin and disobedience. They took the bait. They ate of the fruit of the tree that God had expressly told them not to eat. The consequences were immediate. God cast them out of the garden. God did not go anywhere, but their sin now separated them from Him in every way. They could no longer have any fellowship with Him. This separation meant three things:

- Man could no longer look like God.
- Man could no longer love like God.
- Man could no longer live with God.

The wages of sin certainly meant death. Sin now caused man to die slowly in his physical appearance. Sin now caused man to hate his fellow man and make war against him at every possible instance. Sin now caused man to be separated from a holy and righteous God for all time and for all eternity.

This sin problem was catastrophic for man in every way. He had nowhere to run and hide. He had nowhere to turn for help. He had no future in his life of living, and he had no hope whatsoever beyond the grave. Sin had robbed this man of everything good, and sin had sentenced him to a life of hard labor and hopeless endeavor. He had nowhere to turn and no one to help him. His very looks died before his eyes, and the love that came from his heart was temporary and subject to the ebb and flow of his emotion. He was, in fact, totally lost. To make matters even worse, this man could not help himself from sinning as he became a sinner "by nature and by choice." And as much as man loved his little children, nothing could prevent them from suffering the same fate.

This is why Jesus died on a cross and went from the Garden of Gethsemane to the Garden Tomb (John 19:41). This is the means by which God showed His love to us, "in that while we were yet sinners, Christ died for us" (Rom. 5:8). The death, burial, and resurrection of Jesus shows us this beautiful picture. It brings us to this third point.

3. People living with God forever in God's presence (Rev. 21:1–4)

This is the greatest picture ever. Consider what the Bible is teaching us. At the end of the age there will be a new heaven and a new earth. The old heaven and earth, the one we read about in Genesis and the one we live in today, will be gone. There will be no more separation between the two. God will come down from heaven up there and make His home on earth down here. This will be His "dwelling place" forever. It will be with us and for us. It will be a totally perfect place. And our citizenship in this beautiful place is all made possible because God loved us so much that He sent His only Son to die for us. Sounds like the garden to me.

Conclusion

To live forever in God's presence, sinful man must turn from his sin and trust fully in Christ.

Date: March 6

Suggested Title: The Way of the Cross—Totally Secure

Scripture: Psalm 16

Contributor: Don Wilton

Sermon Starter

Introduction

Our world is in turmoil. There are so many wars going on and so many rumors of wars. ISIS, Al-Qaeda, and other terrorists make us all fearful. However, we can have courage in our hearts when we consider all that God has done for us in and through the Lord Jesus Christ on the cross. The psalmist really had it right when he said in Psalm 62:7: "The rock of my strength, and my refuge, is in God." The sixteenth psalm is another in which he comes right out and asks: "Preserve me, O God" (v. 1), or as we would say, "Please keep me safe, O God." It is the cry of the human heart lost in sin and degradation. Without Christ we are nothing and we have no hope of forgiveness and certainly no hope of eternal life. And so the psalmist gives us a beautiful picture as he looks ahead to the cross and the empty tomb.

The Psalmist's Picture
1. Total dependency on the love of God (vv. 1–4)

    a. Because He takes me into His refuge (v. 1)
    b. Because He covers me with His goodness (v. 2)

What this tells us is that God's plan for our salvation through Jesus is the very means by which we can be held in His arms and covered in His goodness. This happens through the imputed righteousness of Christ that is conferred on all who believe in His name.

2. Total security in the plans of God (vv. 5–8)

    a. Because He secures me in my salvation (v. 6)
    b. Because He secures me in my assignments (vv. 5, 6)

The plans the Lord has for us are all made possible through the death, burial, and resurrection of the Lord Jesus Christ. Here the psalmist reminds us of the security we can all have when we put our faith and trust in Jesus. When we do, Jesus not only gives us a "good inheritance" in and through our salvation, but He also gives us assignments that fall in "pleasant places." How can anything be more fantastic in life than knowing Christ?

3. Total confidence in the plans of God (vv. 9–11)

    a. Because He did not abandon His Son at death (v. 10)
    b. Because He will not abandon me at death (vv. 9, 10)

Praise the Lord for this confidence. You and I can be assured that our God is our refuge and strength. We need not have fear when we place our faith and trust in Him.

Conclusion

This is why Jesus went to the cross. He died so that we might be set free. It is through Him that we have life, and this life is for today and forever.

Date: March 13

Suggested Title: The Way of the Cross—The Journey to the Cross

Scripture: John 1:1; Genesis 22:13–14

Contributor: Don Wilton

Full Sermon Outline

Introduction

If we have someone trying to share something very important with us, we sometimes cannot get a hold of the picture this person is presenting to us. And so we ask for the big picture—the whole story. After we get the big picture, we can then probably better understand the smaller points. The whole story with Jesus is that He loves you and me. We are all sinners, and without Christ we are doomed to a Christ-less eternity. As we consider "the way of the Cross," we must consider the big picture. What Jesus did on the cross for you and me was not an afterthought. It certainly was not a knee-jerk reaction on the part of God. The opposite, in fact, is true. This is God's plan for your life and for mine. All of us have sinned and come short of God's glory. The psalmist reminds us that we were born "dead" in our trespasses and sins, and Paul tells us that we are all destined to die and go to an eternity without Christ because we are all "in Adam" (1 Cor. 15:22). Adam sinned and became separated from God. He was thrown out of the garden of Eden. He was banished from God's presence.

Let us consider the big picture as we journey to the Cross.

The Journey to the Cross
1. Was started before the world began (John 1:1)

This is an amazing fact. Way back in the beginning, God always was because He always is! This is hard to comprehend because we are so limited by time and space, but John tells us that before time began, God always was. Some people may use the old-fashioned expression "way back yonder," but that can't even come close to describing our eternal God. The incredible truth is that way back then, we find the Word. He is Jesus. And Jesus was not only *with* God way back then, but Jesus *is* God. What this means is that we can now understand how it is that "God was in Christ reconciling the world to Himself." And Jesus frequently reminded His disciples that He was, in fact, God. The cross was not an afterthought.

2. Was illustrated in the sacrifice of Isaac (Gen. 22:13–14)

Most people love this great story. It really is an epic account of two aging parents who yearn for a child of their own. There are so many lessons to be learned from their struggles and especially their efforts in taking matters into their own hands. Sin has such dire consequences—only God's way is perfect and right. Nonetheless, God had made a promise to Abraham, and God always keeps His promises. Isaac was born even at their lofty old and impossible age. How well his father loved him and doted on him. So when Abraham was told to go and sacrifice his only son … just look at this picture. Moments before Abraham would have killed his only son, God intervened and provided the perfect sacrifice of the ram. There He is. Jesus Christ. God's perfect sacrifice for you and for me on the cross.

3. Was spoken of by the prophets (Isa. 55:6–7)

The prophets were men of God who foretold many great and wonderful things from the heart of God. In many instances they spoke God's truth to those in their time who needed to hear what God had to say to them. They became spokesmen who prophesied concerning things to come and often told of all that a holy and righteous God had in store for mankind. Back in the Old Testament, the Israelites had God in a "box." They had to go to the temple and approach God through the high priest. Isaiah let them know that God was not only able to be found, but also He was able to be called upon. And all of this was made possible through the Lord Jesus Christ on the cross.

4. Was witnessed in the manger (Luke 2:17)

What an incredible event. Jesus Christ, born in Bethlehem of the Virgin Mary and announced as the Savior of the world. Everything that took place around that manger pointed to everything that everyone and anyone ever needs for life. It was in this place that we see Him. The one who came because God "so loved the world." Even the angels could not but help praise God by saying, "Glory to God in the highest, and on earth peace, goodwill toward men!" (Luke 2:14). This is Jesus. Born so that He might die for the sins of the world.

5. Was blessed by the Father (Mark 1:11)

Many may have wondered why the Lord Jesus took part Himself in baptism. There are many reasons. Perhaps the fact that everything He did was designed to show believers what they must do. But one very important thing happened here. God spoke from heaven and affirmed His beloved Son.

Conclusion

God's blessings only come through His Son. This is why Jesus came to this earth to die on that cross. He is the only way because He is truth. And through Him alone, we have life. Trust Him today!

Date: March 13

Suggested Title: The Way of the Cross—Preparing for the Cross

Scripture: Matthew 17:1–9

Contributor: Don Wilton

Sermon Starter

Introduction

One of the greatest preachers of all time, Charles Haddon Spurgeon, once said in the late 1800s, "Every time I open the Book I make a beeline for the cross." This is so true when one considers all that God has done for us in and through the Lord Jesus Christ. This means that everything in the Scriptures points to the sacrifice of Jesus on the cross. Paul, the great apostle, added, "For I determined not to know anything among you except Jesus Christ and Him crucified" (1 Cor. 2:2). As we prepare for Easter (March 27), we find the Lord Jesus engaging His disciples in one encounter after another. It all pointed to the cross. He was preparing them for this greatest event ever. The transfiguration of the Lord Jesus was no exception. A closer look at exactly what happened between Jesus and His disciples on that mountain will help to enhance our understanding of the eternal significance of all that Jesus was about to do for sinful man when He gave His life for our sin on the cross. Jesus initiated this event because He wanted us to know His divine purpose for our redemption.

We Are Prepared for the Cross

1. Jesus had a purpose in what He did (v. 1).

This was a deliberate act with a deliberate design. Jesus took the disciples, led them, and demonstrated to them.

2. Jesus displayed His power in what He became (v. 2).

The power of His leading, transforming, and His resurrecting is shown.

3. Jesus demonstrated truth in whom He raised (v. 3).

The truth of life after death, which is our living hope, is made clear (1 Cor. 15:20).

4. Jesus proved truth by allowing them to see what they saw (v. 4).

He allowed them to cross over the line of faith and gain a glimpse of sight (1 Cor. 13).

5. Jesus appeased their fear by what He said (v. 7).

The fear of death and hell was removed.

6. Jesus pointed them to the future by what He commanded (v. 9).

He, once again, pointed to the power of His glorious resurrection from the dead.

On the Mount of Transfiguration Jesus not only pointed to His death, burial, and resurrection, but He also prepared the hearts of the disciples to know, see, and believe that salvation belongs to our God. He, alone, has been raised from the dead.

Conclusion

All roads lead to the cross! Are you on the road that alone brings life eternal?

Date: March 20

Suggested Title: The Way of the Cross—When God Prayed

Scripture: John 17:1–5

Contributor: Don Wilton

Full Sermon Outline

Introduction

Here was the Lord Jesus in the Garden of His betrayal. He had come to this earth in total obedience to the Father. He had lived and taught and walked and demonstrated His unfailing love. Now the time had come. The Son of God would be delivered up to die at the hands of sinful man in order that sinful man might be forgiven and be reconciled to a holy and righteous God.

As the dark shadows of man's hatred slowly spread their deadly tentacles around the spotless Lamb of God, we get to listen in on what sounds like one of Shakespeare's soliloquies. We hear only the voice of the Son. But upon further reflection, we realize that the restoration of the glory Jesus once had with the Father from the time before the world existed served to unite them in one common sound that came forth from the heart of God. Yes, indeed, God is at prayer! Jesus' work was about to run its course, although His ministry would never run out.

When God Prayed We Are Reminded
1. God's timing is always perfect (v. 1).

Perhaps Jesus Himself emphasized the matter of God's perfect timing when He taught the disciples to say when they prayed, "Your will be done on earth as it is in heaven" (Matt. 6:10). Like little children, one of our greatest dilemmas is trying to figure out why things happen when they do and for what purpose. Why did God wait so long to send

Jesus? Why did Jesus only begin His ministry at the age of about thirty? Why did He have to die so young? God's timing is always perfect. Jesus repeatedly spoke about God's time and now begins this conversation by presenting to us the perfectness of God's order. He knows.

2. God's glory is ultimate (v. 2).

This is the climax of the incarnation. Indeed of life itself. Could it be that death is, in fact, cause for the greatest celebration ever? By giving all glory to the Father, Jesus demonstrated:

> a. The sovereignty of God over evil
> b. The compassion of God for all people
> c. The finality of redemption in Jesus for all people

In other words, Jesus was saying, "Father, through My death and resurrection may You be glorified because My death will be the ultimate demonstration of Your love to a lost and dying world."

3. God's authority is granted (v. 2).

Everything Jesus had done, was doing, and would do was with the full and complete authority of God the Father. The giving of God's authority to the Son was seen in three ways:

> a. The giving of it. God handed it to the Son by virtue of His sovereign position as Lord and King over all, in all, and through all.
> b. The extent of it. The sovereign authority of God, given exclusively to the Son, was extended to whosoever believes (John 3:16). All who would hear His voice, repent of their sin, confess Jesus as Lord, and believe in their hearts that God raised Jesus from the dead would be saved.
> c. The scope of it. The amazing thing about the death, burial, and resurrection of the Lord Jesus is that "God was in Christ reconciling the world to Himself" (2 Cor. 5:19). When God granted Jesus the authority to lay down His life, He was, one and at the same time, granting His authority to all who would

believe the right of eternal life with Him. The scope of this authority reaches far beyond the act of the cross and embraces all who would accept Christ's sacrifice on the cross.

4. God's position is absolute (v. 3).

Sadly, one of the most hotly debated issues of our time relates to the matter of salvation. Who can be saved? By what means? Do good works count? Can my goodness be good enough for God? How about my church? And what if I genuinely believe in some other god in addition to Jesus? And then, is Jesus the only way to God? When Jesus fell on His face before the Father just days before the cross, God's position was settled. He settled this as Creator, Sustainer, Provider, and Redeemer. He is the only true God. There are no other gods that can take His place. And He has made the way possible for all to have life in Christ. Jesus' death and resurrection validates all of these.

5. God's work is complete (v. 4).

After Jesus died on the cross for our sins and was raised by the power of God on the third day, His work was over. It was complete. Everything necessary for the forgiveness of our sins and the assurance of our heavenly home with Christ was done. What work was complete?

    a. His work of obedience to the Father

    b. His work of glorifying the Father

    c. His work of redemption for all who would believe in His name

6. The Son's return home was guaranteed (v. 5).

The mission given to the Son by the Father was now complete. In full obedience Jesus had laid down His right to be seated at the very throne of God in heaven to come down to this earth and be born in a lowly manger. He had grown up and had carried out His mission to the fullest extent of His obedience. Now He was about to be crucified for the transgressions of man, who had become separated from a holy and righteous God: "God demonstrates His own love toward us, in that while we were still sinners, Christ died for us" (Rom. 5:8). Now the Father guaranteed the return of His beloved Son to His rightful place, as God, and at His right hand. To God be the glory, great things He has done![1]

Conclusion

God's timing is perfect, His redemptive work is complete, and His position and authority as Redeemer is absolute. Have you responded to His love? Today is the perfect time for you to respond to Him.

Note

1. Fanny Crosby, "To God Be the Glory," 1875.

Date: March 20

Suggested Title: The Way of the Cross—Because Jesus Died

Scripture: Matthew 27:45–56

Contributor: Don Wilton

Sermon Starter

Introduction

Most people are intrigued by the question of purpose. It seems that man has an insatiable appetite to write books that endeavor to answer this question, and even more is said and debated on talk shows by gurus of every description. People want to know where they came from, what they are supposed to be doing on earth, and where they might end up after they die.

When Jesus went to the cross to die for our sins, He settled these questions. Rick Warren's book asks the question, "What on Earth Am I Here For?" and starts with God. As Paul told the believers, "For by Him all things were created that are in heaven and that are on earth, visible and invisible, whether thrones or dominions or principalities or powers. All things were created through Him and for Him" (Col. 1:16). This epic story of the cross is what this is all about. Jesus, in full obedience to the Father, gave His life—a ransom for many.

This passage in Matthew 27 tells the story of the cross. It is not easy to read and certainly not easy to understand. But when Jesus went to the cruel Roman cross, He accomplished the only means by which all people can find true purpose and meaning in life. The bottom line lies in the fact that Jesus is life. He is "the way, the truth, and the life" (John 14:6). Without Him there will be no purpose. And whatever there is will not last. Jesus' death on the cross and His glorious resurrection essentially answer the five most critical questions related to life's purpose and significance.

Because Jesus Died

1. My sin can be forgiven (Acts 3:19).

As the Son of God, Jesus was the only one who could take our place. He acted on our behalf, taking on Himself the sin of the world.

2. My prayers can be heard (Matt. 6:9–13).

As the Son of God, Jesus was the only one who could make it possible for us to have communion with the Father.

3. My name can be written (Rev. 13:8, 20:12).

As the Son of God, Jesus was the only one who could carry God's full authority to write the names of those who are called His children in the Book of Life.

4. My mansion can be prepared (John 14:1–6).

As the Son of God, Jesus was the only one who could guarantee our reservations in heaven, where we will be seated at the throne of God forever and forever.

5. My tears can be removed (Rev. 21:4).

As the Son of God, Jesus is the only one who can comfort our hearts and lives when we hurt on this earth, and His Spirit is the only one who can wipe away all tears for all time and eternity.

Conclusion

God's divine purpose for my life is to set me free from sin and deliver me to the joy of salvation in Him.

Date: March 27—Easter Sunday

Suggested Title: The Way of the Cross—One Glorious Day

Scripture: Luke 24:1–8

Contributor: Don Wilton

Full Sermon Outline

Introduction

As a believer the most wonderful thing about Easter must be the resurrection of our Savior and Lord. Yes, He has risen! He is alive! God has raised Him from the dead. It seems like fresh is in the air. The horror of the cross is laid to rest. The beating of the whip on His back is silenced. The jeering crowds are nowhere to be found. The skeptics have taken a seat. Surely the devil must be choking as he realizes that the shaking of the earth is God's way of announcing His triumph over sin and death and the grave. Not even a stone could have contained Him. Not even the wrap of the grave's garment could have held Him down. Jesus had come forth in glorious triumph. This was no ordinary day indeed.

As we study Luke's account of all that transpired on that first day of the week, we will be inspired to see our Savior as He really is. We will look upon Him and see ourselves as we will be—for we will all be "made alive" in Him. This is Christ who by His Spirit dwells in us. He is the one who has changed us forever. Through His death on the cross we have the forgiveness of our sins and through His resurrection we have eternal life.

That Glorious Day
1. That day was just beginning (v. 1).

    a. There was something fresh about it—it represented a fresh beginning and a fresh start.

    b. There was something hopeful about it—it represented a new
       hope and a fresh reason to get up and stand up.
    c. There was something promising about it—it represented a
       stark contrast to the ugliness of the days before.
    d. There was something new about it—it represented a new
       beginning.

2. The women were preparing for it (v. 1).

    a. They were in the right place.
    b. They had the right attitude.

On a glorious day like this it is important to be reminded of the importance of positioning ourselves in the right places in order to see what God has in store for us. For so many people, church attendance has become an unnecessary interruption to a day's outing at the park. That's unfortunate because you just may miss a blessing by not being in God's house. How sad it would have been if these women had not been there on resurrection morning.

3. The stone was rolled away (v. 2).

    a. The stone of unbelief had been shattered.
    b. The stone of fear had been removed.

As God's Word presents us with great facts concerning the miraculous raising up of our Savior by the power of God, so are we presented with a picture of the significance of the stone that was rolled away. The unbelievers who crucified our Savior really believed this stone could hold the King of the Jews down. But not so! The devil must have trembled in his boots when that stone was rolled away. The watchful soldiers were cast aside, and Jesus came up and out of the grave—alive and well and completely whole. And with that stone went the fear of the human heart. Man's proverbial fear of life and the future and of dying and death. What rolled away with the stone? All our inhibitions and skepticism. All our doubts and fears.

All our arguments and debates. All our false doctrines and religions. All our false gods and idols. They all rolled away with that stone on that glorious day.

4. The body was gone (v. 3).

    a. Death had lost its sting.
    b. The grave had lost its hold.

In one glorious moment God stamped His authority over death and the grave. This vast unknown lost its sting. This vague and dark shape of meaningless nothingness dissolved when Jesus came out of that tomb. All of a sudden everything He had taught His disciples was true. There was life after death. The story about the rich man and Lazarus (Luke 16) was not only accurate, but actually true. No wonder Jesus Himself had told the story. He did not make it up after all. Not one person who has died is dead. And, "As in Adam all die, even so in Christ all shall be made alive" (1 Cor. 15:22).

5. The angels were present (vv. 4–7).

    a. They spoke.
    b. They had something to say.
    c. They made an announcement.
    d. They preached the gospel.
    e. They kept the focus.

It would seem that this message spoken by the angels was "steadfast" and true (Heb. 2:2). It is worth listening to because they were explaining what had just happened on that glorious day. Just like they had done so many times before, these special representatives of God appeared with one purpose in mind. They knew that on the third day Jesus would be raised by the power of Almighty God.

Conclusion

Jesus is risen! He is risen indeed! But does His resurrection impact your life? Have you responded to His sacrifice on your behalf? If so, are you living in the power of His resurrection? Have you surrendered to Him all your doubts and fears?

Date: March 27

Suggested Title: The Way of the Cross—Living the New Life

Scripture: Romans 6:1–11

Contributor: Don Wilton

Sermon Starter

Introduction

Part of the joy in being a pastor is the privilege of holding the hands of hurting people. You and I do not even need to watch *Cops* to prove that men and women are in desperate need of wholeness and significance. The good news is Jesus Christ died on a cross for our sins, was buried in a grave, and was raised up by the power of God Himself. Look at the empty tomb. He is not there. He has risen. All of us can live a new life in and through the Lord Jesus Christ. Consider this passage in Romans. God will tell you how you can have a new life. You can begin again.

1. Where does this new life begin? (Rom. 10:9–10)

    a. By confessing that Jesus Christ is Lord
    b. By believing that God raised Jesus from the dead

2. What does this new life mean? (Rom. 6:5–11)

    a. We are united with Christ in His death (v. 5).
- Our old self is crucified with Him (v. 6). Old = *palaios* = useless.
- Our body of sin is done away with (v. 6). Sin is rendered powerless by the death of Christ and His resurrection.
- Our slavery to sin has ended (v. 7; cf. Rom. 6:17–18, 22).

b. We are alive with Christ in His resurrection (vv. 8–11).
  • Because we have a new heart (Ezek. 36:26)
  • Because we have a new spirit (Ezek. 36:27; 18:31)
  • Because we have a new song (Ps. 40:3)
  • Because we have a new name (Rev. 2:17)
  • Because we have a new beginning (2 Cor. 5:17)

Conclusion

This is the gospel of the good news about our Lord and Savior, Jesus Christ. This is why Jesus said, "I am the way, the truth, and the life. No one comes to the Father except through Me" (John 14:6). He was pointing to His death on the cross. It was through His death that He defeated sin and death and the grave. And it was by the power of God that He was raised to walk in newness of life. This is our life. This is new life. It is in Christ who has risen from the dead. This is why we do not grieve without hope when loved ones are called "home." Otherwise this testimony about Jesus is just not true. I believe it by faith. Do you?

APRIL

The Implications of the
Cross and Resurrection

Date: April 3

Suggested Title: In My Place Condemned He Stood

Scripture: 1 John 2:1–2

Contributor: Gary L. Shultz Jr.

Full Sermon Outline

Introduction

A man was walking out of the library followed by his daughter, who wasn't more than four years old. Apparently he had been trying to study while watching his daughter because he was struggling to juggle all of her toys and his papers, all while toting a heavy backpack full of books. He stopped after they went out the door and asked his daughter if she could help him carry some of their things to the car. He then took his backpack off his shoulder and handed it to the little girl, but right when he let go, she began to drop it and cried, "Daddy, I can't, help me." The burden was too heavy for her to bear. So the father picked the bag back up, put it back on himself along with all the rest that he was already carrying, and somehow managed to walk off without dropping anything. This father required something of his child, but she was unable to meet his requirements, so he took the burden upon himself when she couldn't handle it.

Jesus Bears Our Sins

This is how our Heavenly Father deals with us. Our Father requires that we live a holy, righteous, and perfect life before Him, but this is a requirement we cannot meet because of our sin. So our Father took our burden, our sin, upon Himself, through the death of Jesus Christ on the cross so that we could meet His requirements and experience a relationship with Him. We understand this from what 1 John 2:1–2 teaches us about Jesus and His saving work. Jesus is our Advocate, our Righteous One, and our Propitiation.

John begins chapter 2 by pointing out an important truth: as Christians we're not supposed to sin. This is a summary of everything he has already said in 1:5–10. God is light and in Him there is no darkness at all (1:5). If we as Christians say we have fellowship with God because we have accepted Jesus Christ as our Savior, but we keep on walking in darkness, in sin, we make ourselves out to be liars (1:6). Only when we walk in the light as God Himself is in the light can we have fellowship with each other and be sure that the blood of Jesus Christ has cleansed us from all sin. However, we as Christians still do sin; in fact, if we say we don't sin, we deceive ourselves and make God a liar (1:8, 10). The only way to keep walking in the light and fellowshipping with God is to confess our sins to Him, knowing that when we do He is faithful and just to forgive us our sins and cleanse us from all unrighteousness (1:9).

As Christians we're not supposed to sin, but when we do, our response cannot be to ignore our sin or despair of ever overcoming it. The answer to committing sin is not to delude ourselves or to give up, but to accept the forgiveness of God available through Jesus Christ. Sin is a burden that we cannot bear, but Jesus has borne it for us.

1. Jesus is our Advocate (2:1).

The first way John describes this is by telling us that Jesus is our Advocate with the Father. The word *advocate* is a legal one. It refers to someone who speaks in defense of someone else, like a defense attorney. Jesus, as our Advocate, continually pleads our case before the Father by interceding and praying on our behalf (cf. Rom. 8:34). Jesus prays on our behalf because we have two things that repeatedly speak against us and against our salvation: our own sin and the accuser of the brethren who constantly brings up our sin before God (cf. Rev. 12:10). Jesus as our Advocate prays for our forgiveness, standing in our place before the Father.

2. Jesus is our Righteous One (2:1).

The second way that John describes how Jesus bears our sins is by referring to Him as "the righteous." Jesus is able to stand in our place before the Father as our Advocate because He is the Righteous One, the one who lived a perfect life without sin. When we are united to Christ through faith, His righteousness becomes our righteousness, because we are declared righteous in Him (Rom. 3:21–24). Therefore when Jesus intercedes for us, He bases His intercession on His own perfect righteousness, not ours. This is why we can be completely confident that when Jesus advocates for us, our forgiveness and salvation is assured (Heb. 7:25). The Father sees us as forgiven because He sees us clothed with the righteousness of Christ.

3. Jesus is our Propitiation (2:2).

Jesus is able to be our Righteous One, and therefore our Advocate, because He is the propitiation for our sins. The word *propitiation* refers to the atonement of Jesus Christ, or what He did for us in dying on the cross. Jesus died on the cross in our place. He took the punishment that we deserve as sinful human beings and bore it as our substitute. Jesus was able to do this for two reasons. First, because He is God; therefore, He could suffer the infinite punishment that our sin deserved. Second, because He was a righteous man without sin, He could be our legitimate substitute. The idea of propitiation teaches us that in dying on the cross, Jesus satisfied the wrath of the Father against sin and turned it away from us. Everyone who is covered by Christ's atonement is freed from the burden of God's just and holy wrath against sin, because Jesus has borne that burden in our place.

Conclusion

Christ's atonement covers our sin and cleanses us from its effects, allowing us to be forgiven and to have a relationship with God. When

Jesus acts as our Advocate on our behalf, He does so as the Righteous One who is the propitiation for our sins and for the sins of the whole world. People's sins can be forgiven on the basis of Christ's atonement, if they would only believe.

Date: April 3

Suggested Title: His Wounds Have Paid My Ransom

Scripture: Mark 10:45

Contributor: Gary L. Shultz Jr.

Sermon Starter

Introduction

Jesus never leaves us any doubt about why He came to this earth. He came to die so that we might live. Jesus' suffering and death were no mistake or unforeseen misfortune. They were not surprising to Jesus, and He purposely prepared Himself and His disciples for His suffering and His death. Mark 10:45 comes at the end of the third passage where Mark records Jesus telling His disciples exactly what was going to happen to Him. Jesus came to this earth not only to live a perfect life but also to be our perfect sacrifice on the cross, dying in our place for our sins. He came to pay our ransom so that we might be freed from our sin and live.

1. Jesus gave His life as a ransom.

Jesus tells His disciples that He didn't come into this world to be served by others, but to serve others. The way Jesus serves is by giving up His life for others as a ransom. When we use the word *ransom* we usually think of kidnapping, but a ransom in Jesus' day was the price paid to release a prisoner from jail or a slave from bondage. The person who paid the ransom would make an enormous, sacrificial payment that matched the value or paid the debt of the slave or the prisoner in order to procure his freedom. The ransom payment covered or atoned for the debt that the slave owed. Jesus means for us to understand that we are the prisoners and slaves, locked up in bondage to our sin and that we must be freed by His sacrificial death.

2. Jesus paid the ransom for all.

The ransom Jesus paid was a ransom for many, but the word *many* doesn't mean a select group or only some. Jesus uses the word *many* as an allusion to Isaiah 53, where the *many* refers to the sinners and transgressors for whom the Suffering Servant pours out his life. The *many* are the many nations: all people, Jews and Gentiles. Jesus pays a cosmic ransom, a ransom for the sins of every person who has ever lived and ever will live. Jesus does this for us because we can't pay our own ransom. He freely, willingly, and lovingly gives His life so that we can have life, because as the Son of God He is the only one who can pay the ransom. His ransom is His death on the cross in our place, or on our behalf, as the word *for* indicates.

Conclusion

The only way Jesus could redeem us from our sin was to give His life as a ransom. To prove that His ransom can change our lives and that it actually paid for our sins, Jesus rose from the dead. Jesus is God, the grave couldn't hold Him, and He offers his salvation to us through faith. When we believe in Jesus, His death in our place, and His resurrection, we experience Jesus' ransom for our sins and the eternal freedom it brings.

Date: April 10

Suggested Title: Victory in Jesus

Scripture: Revelation 5:1–14

Contributor: Gary L. Shultz Jr.

Full Sermon Outline

Introduction

God's purpose has always been to have perfect people in a perfect place, perfectly enjoying him. Unfortunately our sin keeps us from experiencing that purpose. Left to ourselves we will never gain victory over our sin or experience God's purpose for us. Thankfully, God has a plan to conquer our sin through His Son Jesus Christ. According to Revelation 5:1–14, Jesus is the center of God's plan for us, and He accomplishes God's purpose for us by dying for our sins on the cross. When we put our faith in Jesus Christ and follow Him in worship, we share in His victory.

1. There is no victory on our own (vv. 1–5).

John the disciple was worshipping God when he received a series of visions that became the book of Revelation. In this passage John is caught up to see the throne room of heaven and invited into a splendid scene of worship. In the midst of this worship, John sees God holding a scroll. While we don't know exactly what is on the scroll, its appearance here likely indicates that it contains the entire purpose of God's redemption, His entire plan of salvation. An angel asks if anyone can open the scroll, but no one in heaven or earth can open it. John is crushed, weeping at the realization that no one in God's creation is able to accomplish God's salvation plan. None are capable of gaining victory over sin ourselves, of accomplishing our own salvation.

2. There is victory through the Lamb (vv. 5–7).

One of the twenty-four elders surrounding God's throne tells John to stop crying, because there is a solution: the Lion from the tribe of Judah, the Root of David, has overcome and is worthy to open the scroll. John looks and sees a Lamb, standing as if slain, who comes and takes the scroll. These images help us to understand that John sees Jesus Christ. Genesis 49:8–10 speaks of a coming worldwide King from the line of Judah, a lion who would conquer His enemies. Isaiah 11:1 refers to the Root of David, a coming Messiah who would also conquer His enemies. However, Jesus was worthy to open the scroll not because of His might, but because of the cross. The lion has become the slain Lamb, the Lamb who takes away the sins of the world (John 1:29). Jesus conquers sin by dying, like a lamb, and delivering His people through His blood (cf. Ex. 11–12; Isa. 53:7). Jesus accomplishes God's saving plan and gains victory over our enemy—sin—by dying for our sins as our sacrifice.

3. The victorious Jesus is worthy of worship (vv. 8–14).

In light of who Jesus is and what He has done, the only correct response to Him is faith expressed in worship. When Jesus takes the scroll, the four living creatures and the twenty-four elders worship Him, singing a song of how worthy He is for saving people from all over the world. Then the angels and even all of creation give Jesus the same worship.

Conclusion

If we are in Christ through faith, we have been given victory over sin and we can experience God's plan for us. Therefore Jesus is worthy of our highest worship.

Date: April 10

Suggested Title: Redeemed by the Blood of the Lamb

Scripture: Ephesians 1:3–14

Contributor: Gary L. Shultz Jr.

Sermon Starter

Introduction

All of us carry weight in this life, and not just the physical kind of weight. We carry stress, our concerns and worries, the burdens of others, and most importantly, our sin. Even with all this weight, it's easy for us to fall into the trap of thinking that we have everything figured out or that we can take care of our problems on our own. Sometimes there are things we can fix, but most of the time we don't do much to improve our situations. Oftentimes, before we even know it, we're doing all we can just to stay afloat, overcome with the things we're carrying and not able to figure out what we're going to do about it.

This is why God our Father sent God the Son, Jesus Christ, to us, because we can't fix our lives on our own. This is why God tells us to cast our cares upon Him, because He cares for us, and this is why Jesus invites each one of us to come to Him, telling us that even when we are weary and heavy-laden He will give us rest for our souls (Matt. 11:28–29). As Ephesians 1:3–14 teaches us, the Father has sent Jesus to do what we can't do: to fix, heal, and redeem our broken, weighed-down lives. In Christ we find everything we'll ever need, and we experience it because of His redeeming blood.

1. Jesus gives us all our spiritual blessings in Him (vv. 3–6).

Our Father God has an amazing plan to save and bless us, but we only become part of that plan when we are in Christ, because everything the Father does for us, He does through His Son, Jesus Christ. As verse 3 tells us, every spiritual blessing we experience comes to us because of Christ. We are chosen in Christ so that we could be holy and blameless before Him, or rescued from our sins (v. 4). In love we are predestined to be part of the family of God through Jesus Christ, to be adopted as sons and daughters through faith (v. 5). God has freely bestowed all of His glorious grace upon us when we are in Christ, in the Beloved (v. 6). That Jesus Christ is the Beloved means His is the supreme object of the Father's love (cf. Col. 1:13). At Jesus' baptism and transfiguration, the Father names Jesus as His beloved Son, and when we are in Christ we are also beloved, caught up in the love that goes back and forth between the Father and the Son (cf. John 17:22–23). We can't make any of these things happen for ourselves; we can only experience them by coming to God in Christ.

2. Jesus redeems us by His blood (vv. 7–8).

How are all of our spiritual blessings possible? Because in Christ we have redemption through His blood, the forgiveness of our trespasses, according to the riches of His grace that He has lavished upon us. We often speak of God's love as free, and it is in the sense that it is freely offered; but in the sense that God's love costs God nothing, that is not true. The love that God offers us in salvation costs us nothing but cost Him everything, the death of His Son on an executioner's cross. The price Jesus paid was His blood. Jesus' violent, bloody death on the cross as the sacrifice for our sins is how our deliverance has been won.

Jesus accomplished redemption for us through His blood. When we are in Christ we experience redemption; we are liberated from imprisonment and bondage. The background of this term is the Exodus of God's people from slavery in Egypt (Ex. 12–14). We must understand that we are slaves, captive to sin, self, and the devil, and unable to free ourselves. Christ pays the price to free us, to redeem us, by dying as our sacrifice, taking the punishment our sins deserve upon Himself. When we accept Jesus as our substitute by turning from our sin and trusting Him, His payment is applied to us because we are now in Christ, and our sins are forgiven. We could never do this on our own because we could never lift the heavy weight of our sin, no matter how hard we try or how much we might think we can. God has to do it for us, and He does it for us through Christ's redemption. In Christ, God has lavished His grace upon us, giving up everything (Himself) so that we could have everything (every spiritual blessing).

3. Jesus brings together all things in Himself (vv. 9–14).

The spiritual blessings that we experience through Christ's redeeming work on the cross also include our eternal life with Him. A time is coming when all things will be reconciled to God through the blood of Christ's cross (Col. 1:20), when all things will be summed up in Christ (v. 10). God's redeemed people will dwell forever with Him because all sin has been paid for by Christ's atonement, resulting in a universe that one day will be centered and united in Christ. All of this is according to the kind intention of God's will, as He is the one who works all things out according to His will (v. 11), for the praise of His glory (v. 12). In order to help us know what is coming, God seals all who believe in Him through the gospel of Jesus Christ with the Holy Spirit of promise (vv. 13–14). The presence of the Holy Spirit in our lives is a sign that we belong to God and we are His people in Christ. The Holy Spirit is the pledge of our inheritance, the down payment of our salvation. Our future life with God, our salvation when we die, our being caught up together with Christ when He returns, is guaranteed by our present possession of the Holy Spirit.

Conclusion

Blessed be the God and Father of our Lord Jesus Christ who saves our lives for eternity through the redemption of Christ's atonement, doing what we cannot do so that we can experience everything in Him.

Date: April 17

Suggested Title: Following Jesus with Great Expectations

Scripture: John 14:12–14

Contributor: H. B. Charles Jr.

Full Sermon Outline

Introduction

John 14:12–14 is a part of the Upper Room Discourse (John 13–16). The disciples assembled to celebrate the Passover, not attend the Last Supper. It was a festive occasion, until Jesus broke the bad news. One of the twelve would betray Him (John 13:21). He was going away. And Peter would deny Him (John 13:38).

It seemed the mission of Jesus was doomed to fail. But in John 14:12–14, Jesus declares that this new phase of His mission will not only continue the work He performed on earth; it will exceed it. In a real sense, the Acts of the Apostles is a commentary on John 14:12–14. But it is not the end of the story. The mission of Jesus continues through you and me. This scripture gives three reasons why we should follow Jesus with great expectations.

1. We have a sovereign promise that enables us to do great things for God (v. 12).

In order to embrace this promise, you must first recognize that Jesus is talking to and about born-again Christians. Jesus identified the beneficiaries of this promise as "he who believes in Me." This promise is not limited to the original disciples, the apostolic age, or the early church. It applies to any and every believer. It also gives us an objective way to identify those who have true saving-faith.

a. True believers share the work of Christ.

- The importance of Christian service. Jesus assumes believers work. We are justified by faith alone. But it is not a faith that is alone. True faith is accompanied by holy desires, loving obedience, and good works (Eph. 2:8–10). Faith works!
- The nature of Christian service. Faith works. But the good works of true believers are more than random acts of kindness. We are to continue the work of the Lord Jesus. We are to fulfill the Great Commission (Matt. 28:18-20).

b. True believers surpass the work of Christ.

What does it mean for believers to do "greater works" than Jesus did? It is "greater" in nature. It makes sense that the Father would use Jesus to represent Him, save the lost, and advance the kingdom. Jesus is the unique, divine, and sinless Son of God. But it is a greater work for God to use sinful people like you and me. It is also "greater" in scope. The ministry of Jesus was limited by time and space. But His disciples were commissioned to reach "the end of the earth" (Acts 1:8). We have means of reaching the ends of the earth today that the early church could not imagine.

Furthermore, it is "greater" in effect. Jesus ministered to multitudes during His early ministry. But when the Lord ascended to the Father, His movement only consisted of 120 people (Acts 1:15). But on the day of Pentecost, more than 3,000 people were baptized as followers of Christ (Acts 2:41). Since then, untold millions have trusted Jesus as Savior and Lord. And there is no limit to what the Lord can do in and through us if we follow Him with great expectations.

2. We have a special partner that enables us to do great things for God (v. 12).

Jesus said, "Most assuredly, I say to you, he who believes in Me, the works that I do he will do also; and greater works than these he will do, because I go to My Father." This is the reason why the followers of Jesus will do greater works. The mission of Jesus is to continue through His disciples. This required the Lord's departure. But the Lord's departure would result in the Holy Spirit's arrival. After the Lord Jesus was glorified through His crucifixion, resurrection, and ascension, He would send the Holy Spirit to abide in every believer (John 7:37–39). This is the reason we can live and minister with great expectations. We have a special partner who lives in us to help us to know the truth, live obediently, resist temptation, endure hardship, and do great things to the glory of God.

3. We have a special privilege that enables us to do great things for God (v. 13).

a. Pray in the name of Jesus.

What does it mean to pray in the name of Jesus? First, to pray in the name of Jesus is to pray with dependence upon Him. The privilege that enables us to pray to the Father is not based on our worthiness. We go to God in prayer with confidence in the name of the only One who is worthy of an answered prayer. Likewise, to pray in the name of Jesus is to pray with devotion to Him (Col. 3:17). It is to pray for things that are pleasing to Him. It is to pray for things that line up with His character. It is to pray for things that advance His cause.

b. Pray to the glory of God.

Verse 13 says, "And whatever you ask in My name, that I will do, that the Father may be glorified in the Son." The purpose of prayer is not that you may have your desires granted, needs met, goals reached, dreams fulfilled, or problems solved. It is that the Father may be glorified. God is glorified in the Son (14:31). In the name of Jesus, we are to live and labor to reach lost men, women, boys, and girls with the gospel of salvation.

c. Pray with great expectations.

Note the scope of this promise of answered prayer. Verse 13 says, "Whatever you ask in My name." Verse 14 says, "If you ask anything in My name." Nothing is excluded from the word *whatever*. Everything is included in the term *anything*. This is a claim of deity. Only God can answer prayer. Yet Jesus claims to be the means of answered prayer. Do you believe this? If you do, pray with great expectations to the glory of God.

Conclusion

Are you sharing in the work of Christ? Are you part of His community so that together with others in His body you can do greater things? Are you praying in such a way that your answered prayers would advance His cause and glorify His name?

Date: April 17

Suggested Title: Jesus Gives Living Water

Scripture: John 7:37–39

Contributor: H. B. Charles Jr.

Sermon Starter

Introduction

It was the Feast of Tabernacles (John 7:2) that remembered God's faithfulness during Israel's wilderness wanderings. Each day of the feast was marked by a ceremonial libation to remember how Moses drew water from a rock, to confess their spiritual thirst, and to pray for divine refreshment. On the final day of the feast, the priest would perform this libation seven times. On this last day of the feast, the great day, Jesus offered living water. Jesus satisfies needs that religion can never meet. And Jesus still offers living water for the thirsty, to those who believe, and by the Holy Spirit.

1. Jesus gives living water for the thirsty (v. 37).

On the last and great day of the feast, Jesus cried out, "If anyone thirsts, let him come to Me and drink." This is a call to salvation. Jesus issues the invitation in simple terms: "Come and drink." This is a personal call. Each must come. It is also a call to receive. No one needs to find or dig a well. Just come to Jesus and drink. It's that simple. Yet it is that difficult. To receive, one must admit thirsts. Jesus does not give living water to self-satisfied people. Only the thirsty may come. Only sinners can receive living water. Only needy people receive divine satisfaction.

2. Jesus gives living water to those who believe (v. 38).

How can thirsty people receive the living water Jesus offers? Jesus says, "He who believes in Me, as the Scripture has said, out of his heart will flow rivers of living water." To receive the living water, you must believe in Jesus. Salvation is a gift you receive, not a reward you earn. And this gift is received by faith. You do not work for living water. You must trust the One who promises to give living water to the thirsty. What must you believe about Jesus? You must believe what the Scriptures say about the divine person and redemptive work of Jesus.

3. Jesus gives living water by the Holy Spirit (v. 39).

What is this living water Jesus provides? John explains: "But this He spoke concerning the Spirit, whom those believing in Him would receive; for the Holy Spirit was not yet *given,* because Jesus was not yet glorified." Jesus gives something better than water that quenches physical thirst. Jesus gives living water that satisfies spiritual thirst. This living water is God the Holy Spirit. When Jesus made this promise, the Holy Spirit had not been given. But we who live on this side of the crucifixion and resurrection of Jesus are beneficiaries of this wonderful promise of the Holy Spirit. When one places faith in Christ, the Holy Spirit immediately, completely, and permanently takes up residence in his or her heart (Rom. 8:9). And the indwelling presence of the Life-Giver King is living water that satisfies every spiritual thirst!

Conclusion

Are you thirsty for living water that will satisfy the deep thirsting of your soul? Come believe! Come receive!

Date: April 24

Suggested Title: The Work of the Holy Spirit

Scripture: John 16:5–15

Contributor: H. B. Charles Jr.

Full Sermon Outline

Introduction

Who is the Holy Spirit? There are two answers to that question. First, the Holy Spirit is a person. The Holy Spirit is not an "it" or force or power. The Holy Spirit is a living being. Second, the Holy Spirit is God. That is, the Holy Spirit is a Person—the third member of the Godhead.

Remembering these two truths about the Person of the Holy Spirit answers a lot of questions. The remaining questions are about the Holy Spirit's work. What is the ministry of the Holy Spirit to believers? What did the Holy Spirit come into the world to do? What is the work of the Holy Spirit?

Jesus answers these questions for the disciples in John 16:5–15. It is a part of the Upper Room Discourse, the discussion at the final meal Jesus shared with His disciples before Judas betrayed Him. In this discourse, Jesus braces His disciples for life and ministry without the benefit of His physical presence with them. One comfort Jesus gives His disciples is the ongoing presence of the Holy Spirit. Here are three ways the Holy Spirit works in the world today.

1. The Holy Spirit helps (vv. 5–7).

Jesus rocked the disciples with bad news in the Upper Room. One of them would betray Him. He was going away. Peter would deny Him. Their hearts were understandably filled with sorrow. These men had given up everything to follow Jesus. Now He was going away. What could Jesus say to comfort them? In verse 7 Jesus said, "Nevertheless I tell you the truth. It is to your advantage that I go away; for if I do not go away, the Helper will not come to you; but if I depart, I will send Him to you."

How in the world could Jesus going away be an advantage? Remember that when Jesus was on earth He lived in a human body that could only be in one place at one time, but when Jesus departed and sent the Holy Spirit, He could be with every believer at every place and at every time. That's exactly what He did on the day of Pentecost. Now, every believer has the presence, power, and partnership of the Holy Spirit dwelling on the inside, and we can expect Him to do great things in us, through us, and among us.

2. The Holy Spirit convicts (vv. 8–11).

The Holy Spirit comforts believers. At the same time, the Holy Spirit convicts unbelievers. He confronts the world with its sin and error and seeks to lead the world to repentance, faith, and obedience. In verses 8–11, Jesus teaches three ways the Holy Spirit convicts the world.

    a. The Holy Spirit convicts the world of sin. It is the Holy Spirit who convicts unbelievers of their guilt before God, their need for salvation, and of the total sufficiency of the Lord Jesus Christ. The good news of Jesus is preceded by the bad news of sin. No one can receive the message of salvation without first being convicted of sin. The Holy Spirit confronts the world with its sin to lead lost people to the Lord Jesus Christ, who is the only hope of salvation.

    b. The Holy Spirit convicts the world of righteousness. It is the Holy Spirit who convicts the world of righteousness, because Jesus has gone to the Father, and we do not see Him. Jesus came to the world to establish the kingdom of God. The requirement for citizenship in the kingdom of heaven is righteousness. Jesus fulfilled and proclaimed the righteousness of God. But how will the world know what the kingdom of

God is about in Jesus' absence? The Holy Spirit carries on the righteous ministry of Jesus until He returns.

c. The Holy Spirit convicts the world of judgment. It is the Holy Spirit who convicts the world of the judgment to come, because the ruler of this world has been judged by the finished work of Jesus at the cross (Col. 2:13–14). Jesus has won the victory over sin, death, and Satan. The Holy Spirit convicts the world of the judgment to come and bids the lost to defect and run to the cross of Jesus. It is with Jesus that the righteous judgment of God is fully satisfied.

3. The Holy Spirit guides (vv. 12–15).

a. The Holy Spirit guides us to the truth (vv. 12–13). The Lord had many things to say to the disciples during the Upper Room Discourse, but the disciples were not able to bear them. However, the Holy Spirit would fill in the unaddressed matters. Jesus called Him "the Spirit of truth." God the Father and God the Son are characterized by truth. And so is God the Holy Spirit. And it is the ministry of the Holy Spirit to guide the disciples of Jesus in all truth. He does not speak on His own authority. But He speaks the things He has heard and declares them to us.

b. The Holy Spirit guides us to the Lord Jesus. The Spirit of truth points believers to the one who is the Truth (v. 6). Jesus says He will "glorify Me" (v. 14). Likewise, Jesus said the Spirit of truth will witness about Him (John 15:26). The Holy Spirit is the "shy" member of the Trinity. He does not show up to glorify Himself; He always points to the Lord Jesus Christ. And when believers are led by the Holy Spirit, they will not show off how spiritual they are. The believer will speak and behave in a way that brings glory to Jesus. True believers join the Holy Spirit in glorifying the Lord Jesus Christ.

Conclusion

What is the Holy Spirit saying to you today? If He is convicting you of sin, agree with Him by turning from your sin and to Christ. Are you a believer in need of guidance? Ask Him for He only speaks truth.

Date: April 24

Suggested Title: Who Is the Holy Spirit?

Scripture: John 14:26

Contributor: H. B. Charles Jr.

Sermon Starter

Introduction

It is the Last Supper, and Jesus and the disciples are in the Upper Room. Within hours Jesus will be betrayed, arrested, convicted, beaten, and crucified. The disciples had given up everything to follow Jesus. They would now have to face life without Him. Or would they? Throughout the Upper Room discourse, Jesus assured the disciples that He was leaving them, but He was not leaving them alone. Another person—just like Jesus—would be with them to help them resist temptation, live obediently, and serve faithfully.

Jesus declares to the disciples, "But the Helper, the Holy Spirit, whom the Father will send in My name, He will teach you all things, and bring to your remembrance all things that I said to you" (v. 26). The Lord Jesus promised the disciples that the Holy Spirit would be with them when He went away. But who is the Holy Spirit? What is the ministry of the Holy Spirit? How can we benefit from the Spirit's presence today? John 14:26 teaches three facts about the Person and Work of the Holy Spirit.

1. The Holy Spirit is a helper.

In the Upper Room Discourse (John 13–16), Jesus referred to the Holy Spirit as "the Helper." The Holy Spirit is a Comforter. He comes alongside of us in times of need to give help, comfort, and support.

The role of the Holy Spirit as Helper brought immediate comfort to the troubled disciples. But this truth also provides ongoing comfort to us today. We are not orphans in this work, struggling along to find our way home. We travel with sovereign company. God the Holy Spirit is our Helper, who comes alongside us every step of the way in this adventure of faith.

2. The Holy Spirit is a gift.

How do you receive the Holy Spirit? Jesus makes it clear that the disciples would not have to work to receive the Holy Spirit. The Holy Spirit is a gift to all believers.

The Holy Spirit is a gift from the Father. The Father took the Lord Jesus Christ from this world and seated Him at His right hand in heaven, but He has not left us alone. God the Father sends the Holy Spirit to believers in Jesus Christ. The Spirit's presence is a divine gift to the church. The very Spirit that lived in Jesus and raised Him from the dead is given to all believers that we may live and serve to His glory.

3. The Holy Spirit is a teacher.

The Holy Spirit would teach the disciples, continuing the ministry of Jesus to them. The Holy Spirit would also remind the disciples of the things the Lord Jesus taught them. These teachings and reminders would produce the God-breathed New Testament. We do not need the Holy Spirit to teach us in the same way He taught the first disciples since we have been given the completed revelation in the Bible (2 Tim. 3:16–17). But we do need illumination that only the Holy Spirit provides. The Holy Spirit teaches us the truth of the Word of God and testimony of Jesus Christ.

Conclusion

Have you thanked God for the gift of the Holy Spirit? Do you regularly turn to the Spirit for help and guidance as He speaks to you through God's Word?

MAY

God's Family Plan

Date: May 1

Suggested Title: Men and Women Are Different!

Scripture: Ephesians 5:33

Contributor: Steve Scoggins

Full Sermon Outline

Introduction

God must have had a sense of humor when He came up with marriage because men and women are so different. Even the way we use the word *different* is different. Suppose a wife were to cook up a new recipe for her husband and then ask him what he thought. If he said, "It was different," he would be saying that it is something that he had never tried before. But she would hear instead that he doesn't like it! In marriage counseling, a counselor may feel like an interpreter: "What he just said was..." "What she just heard was..."

Ephesians 5:33 is a summary verse for this lengthy section on husband and wife relationships. Did you notice that God gave the husband and wife different commands? God acknowledges the differences He put into us by giving the husband a command that matches the wife's need and the wife a command that matches the husband's need.

1. Husbands are to love their wives because a wife's greatest need is expressed love from her husband.

This command is even stronger in Ephesians 5:25: "Husbands, love your wives, just as Christ also loved the church and gave Himself for her." If you think you love your wife too much, and you don't love her as much as Jesus loves her, then you don't love her too much.

Women are inherently romantic while most men tend to be romantic only when they are engaged to be married. Many men have been known to say something like this: "I told her I loved her when I married her. She ought to know it." Biblically that won't do. Women need to be told and shown that they are loved.

Then there's the story of a barber in a two-chair shop. His partner bragged one day, "I have been married ten years, and I have never sent flowers to my wife!" During lunch, the second partner snuck out to the flower shop, ordered a dozen roses for the man's wife, wrote a mushy note, and sent it in his partner's name without telling him. The next day the partner reported, "Well I came home last night and the kids were at the grandparents' house, a candlelit dinner was on our table, and my wife had a glow in her eyes. I didn't know what was going on, but I went along with it!"

Many women commit adultery not because of a sexual need but because they have unmet emotional needs in their marriage. They have been taken for granted but suddenly are met with attention and affection from a man who is not their husband.

An article that appeared on twoofus.org stated that a website designed to "help" married people have affairs reported that the most popular day for female sign-ups was the day after Valentine's Day. The second most popular day was the day after Mother's Day.[1] We men ignore special occasions at our own risk.

We should pray, "Lord, don't let there ever come a day when my wife would have to look to someone else for the expressed love she should be receiving from me."

2. Wives are to respect their husbands because men need to be built up and believed in.

The greatest gift a wife can give to her husband is to believe in him. We men tend to run from those who criticize or doubt us and run toward those who believe in us and praise us. A wife fulfills her command from God when she praises her husband, when she lets him feel that she is honored to be his wife.

Jeremiah the prophet, during a hard time in his ministry cried out, "Oh, that I had in the wilderness a lodging place for travelers; that I might leave my people, and go from them!" (9:2). The wife should be that haven for her husband.

3. We need to obey these commands even though they are not what we need ourselves.

The key to marriage is when we decide to act "supernaturally" instead of naturally. Naturally a man would think, "I don't need flowers, so why should she?" Supernaturally we need to think, "I may not need these romantic elements but she does, so I will gladly give them to her."

Couples often find themselves caught up in a vicious circle. The man neglects his wife and she gets hurt. Because she is hurt, she unloads on him about how he is failing her. Since men run from criticism, he neglects her even more. So she is more hurt and more critical.

The only way to break a vicious circle is to make a commitment to obey the command God has given you, regardless of whether or not your spouse is living up to God's command. Husbands, begin expressing your love toward your wife even if she has become cold to you. Wives, praise every step the man makes in the right direction in your marriage even if he has made many steps in the wrong direction. Determine that the vicious circle stops with you!

Conclusion

Paul points to the way Jesus loves us in this chapter as the model for a husband-wife relationship. We will never be able to be the spouse we should be on our own. We need the example of Christ before our eyes. We also need the presence of Christ in our heart through His Holy Spirit reminding us to be the spouse that He has called us to be.

Note

1. http://www.twoofus.org/educational-content/articles /female-infidelity/index.aspx.

Date: May 1

Suggested Title: Jesus' Teaching Makes Sense for the Home

Scripture: Matthew 7:24–27

Contributor: Steve Scoggins

Sermon Starter

Introduction

Jesus compared someone who obeys His teaching to someone who built his home on the rock rather than the sand. This metaphor was meant to represent all of a person's life, but it can also be literally used in building a Christian home. A Christian home should be by nature a home that is built on the rock of Jesus' teaching.

You will find the teachings of Jesus very practical in building a home. The following are some examples of how the teachings of Jesus can apply to a marriage:

1. Give and it shall be given unto you (Luke 6:38).

Jesus points out that what we receive will be determined by what we give. We see that is true in life. Friendly people tend to have more friends. Loving people receive more love. Whatever we hope to receive from our spouse, we ought to first be committed to giving it to him or her. Do you want to be respected? Then give respect. Do you want to be loved? Then shower your spouse with love. If a man is cold to his wife, she will be cold to him. Why not start giving warmth to her and see what happens?

2. Don't just forgive seven times. Forgive seventy times seven (Matt. 18:21–22).

In spite of all of our romantic ideals for marriage, we should never get past the fact that we are putting two sinners under the same roof for a long time. Couples will often hurt each other and disappoint each other. No marriage will survive if we do not learn how to forgive. The essence of the word *forgive* is "to let go." If you are still bringing up things from the past, you haven't forgiven your spouse.

3. Seek first the kingdom of God ... and all these things shall be added to you (Matt. 6:33).

The strongest marriages come when both husband and wife both put Jesus first in their lives.

When Baptist preacher R. G. Lee proposed to his wife, he said, "Lady, I would like for you to be second place in my life." She said, "You better explain." He replied, "I have given Jesus first place but I would be honored to have you as second place in my life." She accepted, saying, "If Jesus is first place, then I know you will be the husband you ought to be and the father to our children you ought to be."

Conclusion

Conflict often happens in a marriage because the husband and wife are on "two separate pages." They constantly fight over whose opinion is right, the husband's or the wife's. Why not get on the same page by allowing Jesus' Word to be the last word in your home? "Because Jesus says so" is a much better argument than "Because I say so."

Date: May 8

Suggested Title: How to Effectively Teach Your Children About God

Scripture: Deuteronomy 6:4–9

Contributor: Steve Scoggins

Full Sermon Outline

Introduction

Today's passage is considered to be the central passage in Judaism: "Hear, O Israel: The LORD our God, the LORD is one! You shall love the LORD your God with all your heart, with all your soul, and with all your strength." It is quoted more often than any other Bible passage in Jewish services and in Jewish homes. This key passage puts great importance on our duty to teach our children.

All of our churches are concerned with offering great ministries to help children in their faith. Good parents want their children involved in Sunday school and children's programs. But the main responsibility for passing our faith on to our children rests with us parents. How can we effectively teach our children about God?

1. Model what you teach your children about faith in God (vv. 5–7).

We are first to love God with all of our hearts ourselves. We are to put these commands in our own hearts before we put them into our children. We can't teach our children to love the Lord if we don't love the Lord. It has been said that more of the Christian life is caught rather than taught. We want our children to catch the love of the Lord that is seen daily in our lives.

Teaching by example is the best way to teach children. If you want them to see the importance of reading the Bible, let them see you reading the Bible. If you want them to see the importance of serving the Lord and helping others, let them see you do it first. If you want them to love their wife or husband one day, love your spouse the way the Bible says.

In a recent marriage study couples were asked, "What do you want to imitate in your parents' marriage?" One young man from a tragically broken home replied, "Nothing!" He will have to overcome the lack of good modeling by his parents.

An informal "raise your hand" survey in church services with the question, "How many of you who are here today were raised in a Christian home?" would show inevitably the majority raising their hands. The best way to "make disciples" is to raise them in Christian homes.

2. Teach your children often (v. 7).

This passage calls for teaching your children many times every day. Once a week does not meet this command! We are to be constantly reacting to what we are seeing in life with our children and showing them how the Bible applies to what they are seeing.

One modern application is that many young parents fear most the day when they will have to have "the sex talk" with their children. If you think one talk means you have done your duty, you are fooling yourself. It's possible that some children see thousands of sexual images on TV alone by the time they graduate from high school. One talk will not counter that.

We need to develop an open relationship with our children where we can discuss any subject with them. They ought to feel free in coming to us with their questions. One parent was shocked when his eight-year-old son asked him about a specific sex act. But his instant reaction was wonderful. He said, "Thank you, son, for asking me instead of asking your friends."

Jesus said He has come to give us an abundant life. We believe that the Bible's way of life is far better than what the world is trying to communicate to our children. We need to constantly teach God's good ways and respond to the wrong information from the world, but do it in such a way that our children see that God's ways are best.

3. Teach your children in planned and unplanned ways and times (v. 7).

Families that have planned family devotions are obeying this passage. Your kids ought to have memories of your times studying God's Word and praying together. But there are priceless times when we seize the "teachable moments" as we walk along the way as well (picking them up from school, for instance). Listen to what your children are saying. React to what they are watching and hearing. React to news on the radio and TV that they become aware of as teaching moments.

4. Our goal in teaching our children is to bring them to where they love God with all of their hearts.

There are important spiritual truths that we need to teach our children. We need to teach our children the plan of salvation. We need to make sure our children know the great stories of the Bible. But if they can quote John 3:16 by heart and can tell all about David and Goliath and Noah and the ark but do not love the Lord, then we have not done what this passage calls for us to do.

We parents have a duty to teach God's biblical moral standards to our children. This task is heightened by the fact that our culture no longer agrees with the teaching of the Bible. Part of teaching children basic morality is keeping in mind that we are preparing them for life. God has made it so that our actions bring consequences. When we punish them when they do wrong and reward them when they do right, they are learning that in life they will live in a world where there are consequences for their actions. Moral teaching alone never lasts unless a child is brought into a life-changing, life-empowering relationship with Christ.

If we lead them to know Jesus and love Jesus, they will obey Him. Jesus said, "He who has My commandments and keeps them, it is he who loves Me" (John 14:21). The love relationship with the Lord becomes the source of the strength to live out all that we teach them as parents.

Conclusion

Parent, you are the most powerful teacher your children will ever have. You are teaching them by your own actions whether or not you know it. You should be proactively teaching them in planned devotions and then being their constant coach and teacher as you walk through life with them.

Date: May 8

Suggested Title: Marriage Is a Good Thing!

Scripture: Ecclesiastes 4:9–12

Contributor: Steve Scoggins

Sermon Starter

Introduction

The Bible is positive about marriage. Proverbs 18:22 says: "He who finds a wife finds a good thing, and obtains favor from the LORD."

It's a good thing when two Christians get married.

God pronounced all of His creation to be good in Genesis until He came to the point where He saw that Adam had no companion. Then we hear these words: "It is not good that man should be alone" (Gen. 2:18).

The writer of Ecclesiastes could be describing the benefits of marriage when he says, "Two are better than one." He then gives the benefits when you are not alone, when you have someone you are committed to.

1. Marriage is a good thing because one lifts the other up when one falls (v. 10).

This can be seen practically and physically in marriage. Married people have someone to take care of them while they recover from illness or an injury. But the "lifting up" that we experience is oftentimes an emotional lifting up. It is good to have someone to encourage you when you are discouraged. It is good to be around someone who is up when you are down.

2. Marriage is a good thing because it is a source of warmth in a cold world (v. 11).

We need a warm haven from a cold world. It is easy to be cut down by someone we know, to receive a devastating blow in our workplace, or to be rejected in our society. Our marriage should be a magnet that draws us home when we are torn down in the world. We should be able to say, "Back home I have someone who believes in me. I can count on my spouse to be in my corner."

3. Marriage is a good thing because it brings protection from danger (v. 12).

Anyone who lives long enough will one day face a huge problem. When we face a great enemy—a great struggle—we face it better with someone than if we are all alone.

Conclusion

While advice in Ecclesiastes could apply to a strong marriage, also to be recognized is the fact that a good marriage needs more than a husband and a wife. It also needs the presence of the Lord inside of both of them. "A threefold cord is not quickly broken" (v. 12). When Jesus is present in a home, He will help both the husband and wife to be everything the other needs.

Date: May 15

Suggested Title: Making Time for Family

Scripture: Ephesians 5:15–17

Contributor: Ryan Rush

Full Sermon Outline

Introduction

With all of the technology at our disposal today, one might imagine that we would have more free time than ever—but that hardly seems to be the case in most households. Between work, school, children's activities, and everything else demanding attention, it seems our schedules have no margin at all. According to a US Bureau of Labor and Statistics study in 2013, the average American adult spends each weekday working 8.7 hours, sleeping 7.7 hours, and filling another 3.3 with household chores and life necessities.[1] That leaves only around four hours to really live life: worship, pray, connect with loved ones, exercise, and simply relax. That's not much margin!

The apostle Paul addresses this very challenge in Ephesians 5:15–17, and offers us tremendous insight into how our families might get the most out of every day.

The passage challenges each of us to ask three questions about our calendars:

1. Where does my time go?

Verse 15 challenges us to "walk circumspectly, not as fools but as wise." *Young's Literal Translation* helps us better understand the significance of the idea of being very careful: "See then **exactly how** you walk."[2] The Greek word he uses (*akribos*, from which we get acrobatic) is calling us, in essence, to aim our lives in a very specific direction. To pay close attention to how we're spending our time.

When you take the time to conduct an inventory of your own schedule, you might be surprised where your time is going. You might also find that you have more time than you think!

When you're cleaning out a closet, what do you do? You take everything out, evaluate each item, and then begin returning things to the closet. But not everything makes the cut. Invariably, you come upon things that are wasting space and can be discarded. Then, even the things you replace can be returned in a more orderly fashion. By the time you're done, it's often shocking how much space you really have. The same goes for our calendars.

It shouldn't be a surprise that God would challenge us to pay attention to our time. Time management is God's idea. In Genesis 1, during the creation account, God made the day and night on day one. He separated the light from the darkness. But God didn't make the sun, moon, and stars until day four. Why did He make them? Verse 14 tells us they were to be "for signs and seasons, and for days and years." God created a predictable cycle of days, months, seasons, and years so that we could monitor and manage our schedules.

A second question is a bit more surprising:

2. What is wasting my time?

If you look closely at the passage, you'll find this to be a key time management question that many people miss. Ephesians 5:15 includes the word *then*—pointing back to verses one to fourteen. Any time there is a "then" or "therefore" in a passage, it reveals that the words are a concluding thought from the previous one. What is Paul speaking of in the previous verses? He is calling on God's people to step out of darkness and into the light. Paul had concluded the passage in verse 14 with what is likely an ancient hymn: "Awake, you who sleep, arise from the dead, and Christ will give you light." He's offering the illustration of missing out on life because of the empty pursuit of things that are not of God.

Once you are saved, you experience the security of God's grace. The enemy cannot rob you of your salvation, but he can rob you of your effectiveness in the time you have on earth.

As an example, think about pickpockets. Pickpockets seem very skilled at grabbing something without drawing notice from the victim. But how can a person not feel his wallet being removed, for example? It's not necessarily their skill at sleight of hand, but the pickpockets' skill at distraction that allows the theft. Pickpockets show you postcards, pretend to help, bump into you from the side, or even ask for help. They don't have to be perfect; they only have to distract you. That's how the enemy works: distractions!

Sin is destructive in many ways, but one of its losses is simply robbing the sinner of all the time that could be invested in God's work. Sin's distraction results in long-term destruction.

One of the most important steps to good time management is to repent of any known sin and ask the Lord to show you any subtle ways you might be disobeying God. And then, you're ready for the third question:

3. What choices need to be made?

Look back at verse 16, and the call to "redeeming the time," or as it says in the NIV, "make the most of every opportunity." Given the call to discernment in the previous verse, Paul then makes the case for choosing the best over the second-best. To make the most of any opportunity means to set aside the lesser opportunities that arise.

The very first computers operated on a simple system in which they were able to read only two things: ones and zeroes. Every decision these supercomputers made was nothing more than a series of ones and zeroes. Computers today use the exact same system. Even the fastest, most modern PCs on the market today read only two things: ones and zeroes. They just read more of them and read them faster. Our lives are very much the same. No matter what your background or place of employment or family status or hopes and dreams, your life can be explained by a continual string of two decisions: yeses and nos. Every day when you wake up, you begin making yes and no decisions—choices that will determine both your outcome for the day, your destiny in life, and the legacy you leave behind.

And in reality, those yeses and nos determine our priorities in life. Our true priorities are the things we say yes to at the expense of all other commitments and distractions. They get the first yes on our calendar, and the unimportant things get a no answer until the priorities have been fulfilled. That's how priorities are lived out in real life.

Conclusion

Considering the high calling of the Christian life and the high priority of home life, we cannot afford to let our days pass by wasted and unfruitful.

What will you say yes to? The most important place to begin is saying yes to Jesus. Allow Him to be the master of your life—and your family—and the rest will begin to be more fruitful than you ever imagined.

Notes

1. Bureau of Labor Statistics, "Charts of Time Use Survey," http://www.bls.gov/tus/charts/, accessed February 28, 2015.
2. Robert Young, *Young's Literal Translation* (Bellingham, WA: Logos Bible Software, 1997), Eph. 5:15–16.

Date: May 15

Suggested Title: The Power of a Generation

Scripture: Judges 2:8–11

Contributor: Ryan Rush

Sermon Starter

Introduction

Every member of the body of Christ must recognize the significant responsibility we hold to pass along a godly heritage to the next generation. Such a high calling is the role of not only parents, but every one of us. The implications are profound. Judges 2:8–12 reveals what happens when Joshua and his contemporaries passed away. Even with all of the progress the Israelites had made, the very next generation walked away from the Lord. The passage reminds us of three important principles of generational legacy:

1. Generational legacy can break down swiftly without attention.

Few would question the faith of Joshua and his leaders. Imagine the great works they had seen God carry out! And yet they had neglected a critical element in their victory campaign: they hadn't adequately passed their faith along to their children. The Scriptures tell us in verse 10 that they not only didn't know the Lord; they didn't even know what the Lord had done. It is imperative that the church give attention to the instruction of future generations.

2. Generational legacy begins at home.

As family life has broken down in recent years, many churches have sought to fill in the gaps in educating children and youth. Such efforts are profoundly important—and a part of the solution to which God has called us. Yet, we know from Scripture that the primary way the faith was to be passed along was not through festivals or rituals, but in everyday interactions with parents at home. Deuteronomy 6:6–9 had been a clear mandate to all Israelites to teach the things of God diligently to their children at home and throughout daily life. Without the everyday examples of the things of God, the intermittent rituals become empty and meaningless. Such seems to be the case in the closing days of Joshua's leadership.

3. Generational legacy can be turned around.

Judges 2:16 tells us that, as history unfolded, the Lord raised up judges "who delivered them," and at times it worked. More importantly, the Lord eventually sent our Savior Jesus Christ to provide real salvation from the ways of rebellion and destruction for every generation. Deuteronomy 5, in the midst of the revealing of the Ten Commandments, provides us a wonderful promise of how God can restore a generation. After commanding the Israelites not to worship any image, God gave a warning of harm that would impact three to four generations. But gloriously, in verse 10, God promises to show "mercy to thousands, to those who love Me and keep My commandments." It seems to reveal that the blessing of God is far greater than the curse of a rebellious generation.

Conclusion

The prospect of a coming future generation who walks away from God—even after being raised in our churches—is an ominous one indeed. However, by God's grace, and through the careful attention of each of us to passing along a godly heritage, we can reverse the current trends. It begins with each of us dedicating our home lives to His glory and taking ownership of the future of our children.

Date: May 22

Suggested Title: The Spirit-Led Family

Scripture: Ephesians 5:17–6:5

Contributor: Ryan Rush

Full Sermon Outline

Introduction

Ephesians 5 and 6 contain some of the most profound instructions in Scripture on how we are to maintain a healthy family life. Verses offer us insight on everything from submission and parenting to love and marriage. However, it's important to understand that Ephesians is one whole letter—all of the parts fitting together as a whole. Therefore, we need to recognize that the verses preceding these practical instructions have tremendous implications for home life as well. The apostle Paul addresses something critical to home life in Ephesians 5:17–21. He speaks about the source of power through which our relationships are to be cultivated: the Holy Spirit who indwells every Christian.

As a current example, if you have a video game that stops working, the power surge protector may be the first place to look. If the surge protector is in the off position, the video game and anything else plugged into the power strip won't work. The problem isn't with the unit not working. The problem is the lack of a power source.

The same is true for many families. Some would argue that healthy home life in America is at an all-time low. And while we recognize that the church is a place of healing for those who have been through family challenges and we want to welcome and not condemn those who are hurting, we must also recognize that healthy families are essential to both the church and society. There is no doubt that God's most basic plan for family life is a long way from our current reality. What can be done?

Prior to his more practical advice on home life further down in the passage, Paul gives us some powerful insight into God's solution: three points to unleashing God's power in your own family.

1. Establish a family mission statement (v. 17).

Paul compels Christ followers to live wisely and to specifically "understand what the will of the Lord is." After a strong exhortation to make the most of our time in prior verses, it stands to reason that we should know exactly what God wants us to do with that time. What is the point of being efficient time managers if we don't use our time effectively anyway?

To tie this into home life, a great first step would be to adopt a clear mission statement to live by on a day-to-day basis—one that every member of your family can embrace. This doesn't have to include every detail of your goals and dreams, but it should provide a reminder to which we can consistently return to remember what matters most. And it needs not be mysterious or profound. On the contrary, most of God's will in Scripture is clearly spelled out. Passages such as 1 Thessalonians 4:1–3 state clear instructions and include the phrase, "For this is the will of God." Yet even if such a mission is obvious, it's imperative to a healthy home that these decisions be clearly spelled out and regularly remembered. One family, for example, laid out the following mission statement: "It is our desire to honor our Lord Jesus in every endeavor, to reflect His grace and truth in everyday life, and to put one another before ourselves."

Remember that before you can know any mysteries of God's will, you must begin with the basics of God's will. God's will is like driving a car at night. You steer toward what you can see with the headlights, then you move forward. When you do what you're supposed to and move forward in obedience, God reveals a bit more. The more you use the revelation you have, the more you're given. If you ignore the light you've been given and don't move, don't expect to be able to see around the next corner.

Make a list of what you know you're supposed to do. Set some goals. Put them on the calendar—not just on a checklist.

2. Let Christ be the head of the home (vv. 5:22–6:5).

Many who study the "family section" of this passage have focused on the flow of yielding and care mentioned there: wives submitting to husbands in verse 22, husbands loving wives in verse 25, and children obeying parents in chapter 6:1. But the most common "chain of authority" mentioned in the passage by far is much more important. Look back at how many times the lordship of Christ is mentioned in the passage: verses 22–27 and 29 all speak of the Lord's role in the midst of these other relationships. Our home life isn't lived in a vacuum, but done so as an act of worship—meaning every action we make toward one another should be "in the fear of God" (v. 21) or stated another way, "out of reverence for Christ" (NIV).

As you live out your family mission daily, never forget the ultimate reason: you're doing so to bring honor and glory to Jesus.

And finally, Paul gives more insight into how to transform your home life:

3. Let the Spirit guide your conversation (vv. 18–21).

Believers are called upon to avoid drunkenness—to avoid being under the complete control of alcohol, and instead to be "filled with the Spirit"—to be under the complete control of the Spirit of God. And note the evidence of such total control: being filled with the Spirit leads to "speaking to one another with psalms and hymns and spiritual songs" in verse 19. It leads to giving thanks to the Father for everything in verse 20. And it leads to a willing mutual submission to the needs of one another in verse 21.

Imagine the household that Paul pictures here: one that is full of praise, thanksgiving, and love. Does that reflect your own home? How might your words reflect the Spirit's control as you interact with your family this week?

Conclusion

When Christ takes over home life, He introduces a brand-new atmosphere of humility, joy, and gratitude. It doesn't mean that every moment will be perfect or that family life will be conflict-free, but it does mean that you'll have a new sense of purpose for every decision and an eternal perspective for everyday life that makes life richer and more meaningful.

Would you take the bold step of inviting the Lord to lead your household from this day forward?

Date: May 22

Suggested Title: Beauty Secrets

Scripture: Song of Solomon 1:5–27

Contributor: Ryan Rush

Sermon Starter

Introduction

At first glance, the topic of beauty doesn't seem like one that is particularly spiritual or important. On the contrary, the way in which we are attracted to others—and our perception of what is attractive—influences our potential relationships, affects every marriage, and impacts the way we perceive ourselves. It's no wonder that God set aside an entire book of the Bible to speak about the topics of beauty, love, and attraction. In it, He begins with the picture of the king and his lover describing their attractions to one another—and in so doing, provides us with some important "beauty secrets" from God's Word.

The first secret is revealed in the woman's thoughts about her own appearance in verses 5–6. She hopes that her lover will look away because she doesn't see herself as meeting the standard she should.

1. Beauty is a moving target.

Beauty is a wonderful blessing from God that draws people together, but it is a dangerous standard on which to build a relationship. Why? No one is perfect. In fact, if we're seeking to base beauty on perfection, we're all in trouble! And even if an individual somehow measured up to the modern standards of beauty, it would be impossible to maintain that standard with age. That's why Proverbs 31:30 says "beauty is passing."

2. Attraction should come from a deeper place than appearance alone.

Song of Solomon reveals the woman asking how she might spend time with her beloved out in the open with others. She then asks, "Why should I be as one who veils herself by the flocks of your companions?" (v. 7). In Old Testament times, veils were used by prostitutes. She is unwilling to compromise or chase after him; she is choosing no short-cuts to attractiveness. And in so doing, she is calling the king to a deeper attraction.

And that leads to the most profound secret of beauty revealed in the passage:

3. You have the power to make someone beautiful.

Verse 15 is one of many that demonstrates this profound principle. The king says to his bride, "Behold, you are fair, my love! Behold, you are fair! You have dove's eyes." Notice he doesn't focus on her perceived imperfections, but points out other ways she is beautiful. In other words, he highlights her high points. In fact, the king tells her she's beautiful ten times in the passage! Beauty can be ascribed. This works in two ways:

- When a person realizes the beauty she has, she will fulfill the attributes of beauty. Confidence is beautiful. And beauty is self-fulfilling.
- When a person focuses on honest attributes (more than flattery) and highlights beauty, it draws that beauty out.

Conclusion

In our human relationships, it is essential that we flee from the lie that attraction is based on physical beauty alone. Such a shallow existence is robbing far too many people of meaningful relationships and drawing many into the temptation to walk away from existing ones.

Even more importantly, these principles remind us of how God sees us. People spend their whole lives trying to airbrush their lives to manufacture goodness and acceptance by God. But when we receive the grace of Jesus, He sees us as spotless and beautiful.

Date: May 29

Suggested Title: The Image of God at Home

Scripture: Psalm 128; Ephesians 5:1

Contributor: Ryan Rush

Full Sermon Outline

Introduction

This is Memorial Day weekend in America. Sadly, it has been reduced to simply another day off for many, but it represents far more. Memorial Day is set aside for us to remember the sacrifice that has been paid for our freedom by those who fought for—and defended—our freedoms.

There were similar "Memorial Days" in ancient Israel as well. If you were an Israelite during the time of King David, one thousand years before Jesus' appearance, you and your family would have made your way to Jerusalem at least three times a year for the pilgrim festivals to worship the One True God. Maybe worshippers sang the Songs of Ascent, Psalms 120–134. In the midst of these beautiful songs are written some of the most profound words in the Bible related to family life—giving us a wonderful glimpse of what God intended for our homes. Perhaps the best example is our text for today.

Psalm 128 is the picture of a bountiful nation. The people's blessing is directly related to the health of their families. And what is it that brings such health? The secret to their health is really an insight into the heart of why home life and its restoration is so vital to the well-being of our own nation.

As you read the passage, notice that three times the psalmist speaks of blessing. You see words such as *happy*, *peace*, and *prosperity*. What's the key to this happiness? It's found up front in the first verse: blessings come to "every one who fears the LORD, who walks in His ways."

The word *ways* is translated elsewhere in the Hebrew Scriptures simply as "road." The idea is that a person is blessed when he walks along the same road as God—or put simply, when he does what God does.

So the source of blessing comes in walking in obedience, but that obedience is far more than saying we should understand and then do what God says. The source of blessing is found in doing what God does. Similarly, Ephesians 5, one of the most profound passages on the family, begins with the command to "be imitators of God, as dear children." These and other passages are speaking of how we have been created in the image of God.

We find the most basic definition of this image in the description itself; for Genesis 1:26 states that mankind is made "in Our image, according to Our likeness." To be made in the image of God is to be given the privilege of demonstrating His likeness in our own attributes: God is faithful, and we can likewise demonstrate faithfulness. He is loving, holy, good, and wise. We can reflect all of those things.

Even more, as we look through Psalm 128, we will see a direct link between that image and the family. Notice three important implications of that image:

1. The image grows at home.

In the simple flow of this passage, the writer goes from the blessing of living out the image to the blessing of the family. Now that we understand the image, we see how practical this becomes. While Genesis 1:26–27 speaks of man being made in the image, the very next verse speaks of man's commission to "be fruitful and multiply."

God designed the home to be the primary location for us to bear His image. In fact, throughout the remainder of Scripture, God reveals Himself to people in family terms: we know Him in part as God the Father and God the Son; our salvation is seen as an adoption; and we are spoken of as "children of God." Even Ephesians compares the church to a marriage.

2. When the image is broken, everything is broken.

Notice the progression of blessing in Psalm 128: you … your wife … your children … your nation … your children's children. When we reflect God's image, the impact is felt throughout our homes and beyond. So the opposite must also be true: when the home is unhealthy, the nation will soon follow.

Do you remember how old copiers used to work? When you made copies of copies, each generation got worse. That is how an image breaks down: Genesis 3 speaks of the fall of mankind, and then in the lineage of Adam in Genesis 5:3, it speaks of Seth being made in the likeness of Adam. With each generation that moves away from the ways of the Lord, the image grows more faint. Perhaps that is why, in Deuteronomy 5:8–10, God warns that making an image to worship would result in generational curse—it is a practical reminder that when the image of God is obstructed, the family will miss out on God's attributes, and future generations will be robbed of His goodness. This is serious. And that's why our world is so messed up—the image of God is incomplete. Many of us never experience a true picture of God. Many families aren't sharing a true picture of the image.

Finally, let's go back to Psalm 128. Notice the natural picture of home: the description of a fruitful vine and olive plants. What we experience at home, as we reflect God's image, is supposed to be natural. We demonstrate God's faithfulness, His holiness, and His grace, and our children see it and respond.

3. When you fix the image, you fix the home.

How do we get the image of God back? How can we restore our homes to what they were supposed to be? We must get intentional about restoring the image of God at home. And in Scripture, God gives us a wonderful way to start: Colossians 1:15 reminds us that Jesus is the "image of the invisible God."

When we look to Jesus, we see the perfect image—nature—of God. By the power of the Holy Spirit, He can restore us to a reflection of His image. If you want to fix what's broken, look to Jesus.

Conclusion

Death Valley in California is one of the hottest, driest places on Earth. The stark desert landscape appears to be almost devoid of life. But every few decades, on very rare occasions, Death Valley will get a rainstorm. When it does, the water quickly washes away and is absorbed by the dry ground. What happens a few months later, however, is spectacular. Locals call it a "super-bloom," and it is breathtaking.[1] Such an event took place in the spring of 2005, when all of Death Valley was covered with every color and shade of wildflower seemingly overnight. How could this be in such a desolate place? It turns out that Death Valley isn't dead after all. Its soil is filled with seeds just waiting to be watered. And such is the home without Christ. Could your home be the story of transformation because you come to Jesus today?

Note

1. Minnesota Public Radio, "Death Valley super-bloom ahead?", http://blogs.mprnews.org/updraft/2015/02/death-valley-wildflower-super-bloom-ahead/, February 26, 2015.

Date: May 29

Suggested Title: The Submissive Household

Scripture: Ephesians 5:21–6:1

Contributor: Ryan Rush

Sermon Starter

Introduction

The topic of submission is hardly a popular one in modern culture. Sadly, the topic often elicits a picture that has nothing to do with Scripture. In its biblical form, submission is both a blessing and command for any healthy household.

Ephesians provides one of the most compelling cases for submission in God's Word. And in this writing, Paul gives us some important insights into the topic. As it turns out, everyone benefits from submission when they understand God's definition.

1. Everyone is under submission (v. 21).

We are mistaken if we believe only women are under submission. On the contrary, the passage begins by calling everyone to be in submission to one another in verse 21. Scripture is full of examples of those to whom we should submit: governing authorities, bosses, elders, and even Christian leaders. No one is *not* under submission.

2. Mutual submission is both loving and practical (vv. 22–29).

This and other passages make it clear that the call to submission gives no one the right to lord over or exploit another person. On the contrary, according to the passage the husband is to be ready to sacrifice for his wife in every way. Therefore, her yielding to his leadership is one of trust and expectation—recognizing that he will always put her needs before his own.

In 1 Peter 3:7, when husbands are instructed to be considerate with their wives, a powerful warning is provided: "that your prayers may not be hindered." You can't expect to be callous in your earthly responsibility and assume your spiritual relationship with God won't suffer.

When submission happens the right way, everybody wins. God calls everyone in the family to lean on one another in healthy ways and to trust the line of communication and authority He has ordained.

3. Submission to one another reflects our relationship to God (v. 32).

When we are called to submit to one another, it's more than a practical way to establish order at home. As Paul closes out this passage—specifically the portion exhorting husbands to love sacrificially, he reveals something profound about the entire process of order in the home. When we lovingly accept our roles at home of mutual submission and sacrifice, we provide a beautiful reflection of the relationship God has with us. In verse 32, Paul shows that the entire conversation reveals that the godly household will show our own standing with God, demonstrating how much He loves us and how in following Him we reveal our love in turn to Him. God's relationship to us is not one of fear or abuse.

Conclusion

As the words of the old hymn so beautifully state, "He leadeth me, O blessed thought! O words with heav'nly comfort fraught!"[1] When we submit to the Lord, our lives are both fulfilled and joyful regardless of circumstances. And likewise, when we submit to one another out of reverence for Christ, we gain insight into that love in new and exciting ways.

Note

1. Joseph Filmore, "He Leadeth Me," 1864.

JUNE

To the Ends of the Earth

Date: June 5

Suggested Title: Join the Movement—Expect Great Things

Scripture: Acts 4:1–22

Contributor: Rob Wilton

Full Sermon Outline

Introduction

After the life, death, and resurrection of Jesus, He told His followers that the Holy Spirit would empower them to witness all over the world. In Acts 2, the Holy Spirit pours out upon the church and the movement starts. In the beginning of Acts 3, Peter and John are used by the Spirit to heal a man who was lame from birth. In Acts 4 we get a little taste of what happens to those who are faithful to this movement. This command of being witnesses around the world continues from Acts into today. Every person who has been saved by the gospel has been empowered by the Holy Spirit to continue this movement.

Will you join this movement? For those who commit to proclaiming the gospel, you can expect great things. The greatest work in all the world is the work of Christ. As followers of Christ we anticipate an amazing eternity with Christ. This world is ultimately not our home and this life is not our own. However, in Christ we know that Jesus does offer to us an abundant life today where we get to expect great things.

Acts 4 gives a preview of what we can expect.

1. Persecution (vv. 1–3)

If you commit to join the movement, you will be persecuted. According to the world this doesn't sound that great. However, to suffer for Jesus is the greatest privilege in the world. He sacrificed it all for us, and we should be willing to do the same for Him. Jesus was ultimately rejected by the world, and His church will receive the same rejection. There is a false gospel being preached that claims a life in Christ is free of pain, suffering, and persecution. Throughout Acts you will find men and women who are committed to Christ suffering for the cause of Christ. There is a spiritual battle in this world, and Satan wants to stop this movement. Not to experience any resistance from the enemy might mean that you are not doing anything of significance for Jesus. College sports teams don't study film on the water boys. They study film of the opposing team's best players. In the same way, Satan is going to go after those who impose the greatest threat to him.

2. Salvation (v. 4)

There is only one thing that Jesus has promised to prosper on this earth. Jesus has promised to bless the advancement of His kingdom. Although Peter and John had been thrown in jail for the gospel, Jesus still used this for His glory. A revival broke out and thousands came to faith in Jesus. If you are committed to this movement of Jesus, you are guaranteed victory for Jesus and His movement regardless of the resistance.

3. Defense (vv. 5–7)

Jesus is enough! We believe that at the name of Jesus every knee will bow, and we also believe that Jesus has entrusted us with the mission of sharing the gospel. With so many false gospels being preached, sometimes the church has to rise and defend the gospel. Peter and John are brought before leaders and are asked about Jesus. In the following passage we find three elements of their defense.

> a. Exaltation (vv. 8–10). How was he healed? Jesus Christ. Enough said. Unfortunately there are lots of people and churches who are on mission for Jesus without proclaiming Jesus. They fall back to their gifts, their methods, their ministries, and their properties as the reason for their impact. When Peter and John are asked about the miracle, they

unapologetically exalt Christ. In our defense of Jesus we must always start with Jesus.

b. Explanation (v. 11). Peter shares with them about the truth of Jesus through an illustration that connects with their world. Jesus is the capstone of the building that can bring either destruction or salvation. To embrace Jesus means that your life will be secure. To reject Jesus means that your life will be destroyed.

c. Exclusivity (v. 12). Religion will tell you that you need to do a bunch of things in order to receive salvation. The gospel proclaims Christ alone. The true message is not the "we can." The true message is that "we can't, but *Jesus* did." Because Jesus did, we can. There is salvation in no one else.

In the last point of our message in Acts 4, we find that if you join the movement you will experience movement. The church was created to be on the move. People need Jesus and Jesus has empowered us to preach His gospel all over the world.

4. Movement (vv. 13–22)

Is your legacy a movement or a monument? So many funerals are celebrations about the things of the world. A favorite sports team, the amount of money or business that was created, the fame or popularity in the world. Nothing in this world matters except what has been done for Jesus. What will people talk about at your funeral?

Because Peter and John were committed to the gospel and the movement of Jesus, an uncontrollable movement launched throughout Jerusalem that continues today. The people of Jesus that received Jesus were now proclaiming Jesus everywhere. The movement was no longer limited to a jail cell; it was unleashed all over the streets of the world. Filled with the Holy Spirit, all people are called to proclaim the gospel of Jesus and make disciples who make disciples who make disciples.

Conclusion

Commit your life to Jesus and His movement that will victoriously advance till Jesus returns.

Date: June 5

Suggested Title: Join the Movement—Be a Witness

Scripture: Acts 1:8; 8:26–40

Contributor: Rob Wilton

Sermon Starter

Introduction

The church has been commissioned by Jesus in the power of the Holy Spirit to be a witness for Jesus all over the world: "But you will receive power when the Holy Spirit comes on you; and you will be my witnesseses in Jerusalem, and in all Judea and Samaria, and to the ends of the earth" (v. 8 NIV).

The book of Acts is the story of the church obeying this command. Every story in Acts presents some important truths for the church in regards to being a witness. Acts 8:26–40 presents one of those powerful stories. Philip is used by the Holy Spirit to lead someone to Jesus. This story presents five principles of witnessing. These principles should not be followed as a numerical formula but rather as a biblical foundation of how we are called to be a witness for Jesus.

Five Principles of Witnessing

1. Listen (v. 26)

Witnessing for Jesus begins with Jesus. The church gets in trouble when we begin to do what we want to do. The church gets in trouble when we declare to God what He should bless. Witnessing is first about listening to the plans of God. Philip listened to an angel from the Lord.

2. Go (v. 27)

The greatest responsibility for the church is to listen to Jesus and then do what He says. Philip heard a word from the Lord and then immediately obeyed. No waiting, no strategizing, no learning, no preparing. Immediate action.

3. Observe (vv. 27–34)

After Philip listened and obeyed God, he observed all that God had prepared. Jesus wants to bless the advancement of His kingdom. Even though Philip was led away from the city and into the desert, he immediately connected with a divine appointment. Philip found an Ethiopian who was searching for Jesus. The Ethiopian was reading the Word and was even looking for someone to teach him the Word. What an amazing provision from God! Jesus wants to give us divine witnessing appointments.

4. Proclaim (v. 35)

After the Ethiopian asked for Philip to explain the Scriptures, Philip proclaimed Jesus from the Scriptures. This proclamation had two vital focuses. It was from the Scriptures and it was all about the good news of Jesus. Witnessing is about sharing Jesus; we can definitely share Jesus through our actions, but Jesus commands us to speak the gospel. Open your mouth and preach the gospel.

5. Trust (vv. 36–40)

After Philip proclaims Jesus, the Ethiopian believes in Jesus and is baptized. Remember that only Jesus saves. Jesus provides this divine appointment and even the water in the desert for this baptism. After the baptism the Holy Spirit immediately carried Philip to another place. Some would look at this story and say that Philip shouldn't share the gospel with someone that he couldn't disciple. In response to this, we must trust Jesus. The same Jesus that called and connected Philip to the Ethiopian is the same Jesus who saved the Ethiopian, is the same Jesus who would provide someone to disciple the Ethiopian. Because of this, the gospel was now advancing to Africa, and Acts 1:8 was coming alive!

Conclusion

Who in your life needs Jesus? Listen. Go. Observe. Proclaim. Trust.

Date: June 12

Suggested Title: Join the Movement—For the World

Scripture: Romans 15; Acts 28

Contributor: Rob Wilton

Full Sermon Outline

Introduction

Let's take a journey through the last days of Paul's life. In Romans 15, the apostle Paul is writing to the church in Rome. He hopes to get to Rome to encourage the church in Rome. However, in this passage we are going to find out that Paul did not write the book of Romans only for Rome. This was written with the hope of continuing the movement of Jesus to Spain and to the ends of the earth. From the moment that Jesus saved Paul, Paul relentlessly proclaimed and advanced the gospel around the world. This world is our mission field, and we together are a part of an amazing movement of God.

Three Challenges for Continuing the Movement
1. Stay broken for the world (Rom. 15:25–29).

As one who had been saved by the amazing grace of Jesus, Paul couldn't bear the thought of people around the world missing this grace. He was broken for the world, and that brokenness compelled him forward.

When was the last time that you wept for your friend who doesn't know Jesus? When was the last time you sacrificed for your friend who doesn't know Jesus? When was the last time you took an entire day to pray for the unreached people of the world who don't know Jesus?

We need to stay broken for the world.

In Acts 26–28, Paul is under arrest but makes an appeal to get to Rome. His appeal is granted and he begins his journey. Unfortunately,

Paul is shipwrecked on his way to Rome because of a major storm. When they crash on the island of Malta, God begins to use Paul in powerful ways.

This leads us to the second challenge in the movement.

2. Be relentless for the world (Acts 28:7–9).

This part of Acts and Paul's journey is a reminder that we are called to be relentless for the world. Paul had a passion to get the gospel of Jesus to Spain through Rome, but he also had a passion for everyone to know Jesus. He understood that not even a shipwreck on the island of Malta was a mistake. Our God is completely sovereign, and nothing is by chance. Paul understood that his life was not his own and that the entire world needed Jesus. No matter where Paul went, he was relentless for the world.

When do you serve Jesus? When the church puts on a mission opportunity? When the pastor tells you to serve? When your family tells you to serve? When you are on a mission trip around the world? When you are preaching onstage?

A true movement of God happens when God's church is relentless for the world. A true movement of God happens when we recognize that the Holy Spirit has called all who have Jesus to share Him with this world.

3. Finish well for the world (Acts 28:30–31).

Paul eventually gets to Rome. In Rome, Paul is allowed to live by himself with a soldier to guard him under house arrest. He sets up two meetings with strategic religious leaders. In the first meeting Paul shares his story and the gospel. These leaders are intrigued and want to hear more. Paul encourages them to bring more people for another meeting. Although Paul is under house arrest, he sets up a revival in his home. From morning till evening Paul shares about Jesus and people believe. The movement continues!

We should be so thankful for those who are finishing well for the kingdom of God. We should be thankful for the pastors who have spent their lives preaching Jesus—people like Dr. Billy Graham, who has spent a lifetime sharing with people about Jesus.

Jesus honored Paul's desires that were shared in Galatians, "I have been crucified with Christ," and in Philippians, "for to me, to live is Christ, and to die is gain." No one can confirm how or when Paul died, but historically we understand that he was beheaded in Rome.

Although Paul's life ended on this earth, there are two things to know: First, today Paul is not alone—today he is alive and surrounded by the church in heaven. Many people in heaven are thanking Paul for his faithfulness in staying broken for the world, being relentless for the world, and finishing well for the world. Second, the message that Paul proclaimed is alive today. The reason why we are proclaiming the gospel of Jesus is because of the faithfulness of God through Paul.

Conclusion

Let's pray that you and I would be known for nothing but the gospel of Jesus. Let's stay broken for the world, be relentless for the world, and finish well for the world.

Date: June 12

Suggested Title: Join the Movement—Give It All

Scripture: Acts 26:1–32

Contributor: Rob Wilton

Sermon Starter

Introduction

Are you willing to give it all for the mission of Jesus? From the moment that Jesus saved the apostle Paul, Paul gave it all to Jesus. We should be totally inspired by the missionary journeys of Paul, for everywhere that he went he had extreme focus upon the Great Commission.

In Acts 21, Paul has been arrested in Jerusalem, and in chapter 23, he is sent from Jerusalem to Caesarea. In Caesarea, Paul is under house arrest but still sharing the gospel and developing relationships with leaders. Eventually Paul gets an opportunity to speak to King Agrippa and make an appeal to Caesar in Rome. Paul did not just make an appeal for his life; more importantly, he made an appeal for the gospel.

In Acts 26:1–32, we can recognize that Paul was willing to give it all for the mission of Jesus.

Consider the testimony of Paul as he made an appeal to get to Rome, and also some of Paul's writings.

1. Paul died to live.

In Acts 9 the great persecutor of the church has an encounter with Jesus. Up to this point Saul had been a God-fearer that believed he was truly pleasing God with his life. When he met Jesus he was absolutely horrified that He had not been following the true God. This brokenness led to repentance. This repentance led to surrender. This surrender led to a true and meaningful life. Will you die to live? "Then He said to them all, 'If anyone desires to come after Me, let him deny himself, and take up his cross daily, and follow Me'" (Luke 9:23).

2. Paul lived to die.

We know that Paul was eventually killed for the gospel, but in this instance King Agrippa sends him to Rome from this spot. King Agrippa was more concerned that he might be converted than with Paul being harmful. Paul lived to die and wanted to get the gospel at any cost to Rome and then ultimately to Spain.

From the moment Paul died to live, he lived to die. In our world we have created a subculture of Christianity that is more about us than Jesus. There are only two options when it comes to Jesus. You are either for Him or against Him. Those who follow Jesus have been saved to proclaim Jesus. Period.

Paul understood that his life was not his own and this world was not his home. Will you live to die? "I have been crucified with Christ; it is no longer I who live, but Christ lives in me; and the life which I now live in the flesh I live by faith in the Son of God, who loved me and gave Himself for me" (Gal. 2:20).

The movement of Jesus is proclaimed by Jesus in Matthew 28:18–20. In verse 20 Jesus speaks of the end of the age. When is this end? The answer to this is found in Matthew 24:14: "And this gospel of the kingdom will be preached in all the world as a witness to all the nations, and then the end will come."

Conclusion

The gospel is being proclaimed all over the world, but there are still so many people in this world who have not heard about Jesus. What are we willing to do so that the world will know? We should follow the example of Paul. Paul died to live and Paul lived to die. He gave it all!

Date: June 19

Suggested Title: Jonah: A Most Reluctant Missionary

Scripture: Jonah 1–4

Contributor: D. Allen McWhite Sr.

Full Sermon Outline

Introduction

The book of Jonah is likely the clearest example of missionary sending that we find in the Old Testament. While there are many Old Testament references to the nations coming to Israel and to Israel's God, the story of Jonah powerfully illustrates the fact that God gives His people a clear and unmistakable mandate to carry His message of salvation to the nations, no matter the fear and no matter the cost.

1. The greatest hindrance to reaching the nations with the gospel may be the actions and the attitudes of God's people.

When God spoke to Jonah and told him to go to Nineveh, Jonah did more than politely decline. He pushed back—hard! He did not want to do what God had so clearly told him to do, so he literally ran in the opposite direction. Jonah actually attempted to flee from the presence of the Lord (3:1). This does not mean that he thought he could somehow hide himself from the omnipresent God; rather, it indicates that Jonah simply wanted to find some way of escape from this missionary call of God.[1] The motivation for this disobedience seems to be that Jonah took issue with God's desire to withhold judgment from the pagan, godless nation of Assyria that, in Jonah's view, did not deserve the mercy of God (4:1–2).

While this attitude of harsh ethnocentrism may not be as prevalent among evangelical believers today, we would do well to closely examine our own reasons for disobeying the missionary call of God, for our rationales are no less sinful. The painful reality is often this: it is not the lack of receptivity among pagan peoples, but instead the lack of obedience among God's missionary people that can most seriously hinder the spread of God's fame and glory among the nations.

2. There is no escaping the missionary call of God.

In spite of Jonah's attempt to evade the clear missionary call of God, he found that he was unable to do so. Through a dramatic series of events, including an involuntary submarine voyage in the belly of a great fish, Jonah discovered that no amount of human discourse, debate, or disobedience can change the fact that God desires for all nations and all peoples to worship Him. Jonah's lack of cooperation did not in any way impede or invalidate what God wanted to accomplish in the great city of Nineveh. It is significant that the words God first spoke to Jonah in verse 2 of chapter 1 are the same words that He spoke again in verse 2 of chapter 3—"Arise, go to Nineveh, that great city." The missionary call of God is unalterable. God's heart has always been—and it always will be—directed toward all peoples and all nations. We can argue against, rationalize, make excuses for, and try to explain away our failure to obey God's missionary mandate in hopes that we might in some way be granted an "exception" by God, but this is a fruitless cause. If we cannot escape from the missionary God, we certainly cannot escape from His missionary call.

3. Even the most "resistant" people are not beyond the reach of God and the power of the gospel.

Although Jonah was the most reluctant of missionaries, God was in no way reluctant to extend His mercy and salvation to the people of Nineveh. Chapter 3 tells us that the reaction of the people to Jonah's preaching was nothing less than miraculous. Jonah's sermon was terse, and considering his still simmering reluctance, it was likely not delivered with much compassion: "Yet forty days, and Nineveh shall be overthrown" (v. 4). But in spite of the reluctance of the messenger (or, perhaps, because of it), God showed Himself to be strong in the city of Nineveh. Verse 5 tells us that the people believed God and that from the greatest to the least, the people acknowledged their sinfulness. Even the king responded to Jonah's call for radical repentance.

While we may sometimes wonder whether the simple message of repentance and faith can penetrate hard hearts and lead to salvation, the book of Jonah reminds us that nothing is too hard for God. It is God's desire that all nations worship Him; therefore, we should not be surprised when even the most resistant of peoples turn to God in repentance and faith. If the book of Jonah teaches us anything, it teaches us that success in the missionary task is not dependent upon the persuasiveness of the preacher, and it is not even dependent upon the perceptiveness of the people. What happened in Nineveh happened because of one thing— the power of God. It is this truth that keeps us going in pursuit of the missionary task and that gives us assurance of its ultimate triumph.

Conclusion

The great missionary impetus of God is clearly seen in the final verse of the book of Jonah (4:11), where God Himself asks the question: "Should I not pity Nineveh, that great city?" Jonah, the most reluctant of all missionaries, is still struggling with his missionary call. Yet God, the most determined of all missionaries, is revealing His own heart—a heart of love and compassion that would ultimately send His own Son into the world to die on a cross for the redemption of mankind. Surely, this merciful and gracious heart of God should be reflected in the attitudes and actions of His redeemed people. The command, "Arise, go to Nineveh, that great city," was not a one-time call. It is echoed again in Jesus' words: "Go therefore and make disciples of all the nations" (Matt. 28:19), and this time, it is our call.

Note

1. C. F. Keil and F. Delitzsch, *Commentary on the Old Testament in Ten Volumes* (Grand Rapids: Eerdmans, 1984), 10:391.

Date: June 19

Suggested Title: Blessed to Be a Blessing

Scripture: Genesis 12:1–3

Contributor: D. Allen McWhite Sr.

Sermon Starter

Introduction

When Christians hear someone refer to "The Great Commission," Jesus' words in Matthew 28:18–20 most often come to mind. However, some 2,100 years before Jesus ever spoke those famous words, God had already given the same message to a man called Abraham. In many ways, Genesis 12:1–3, which we know as the call of Abraham, is the story of the Bible because it sets the stage for everything that is to follow in both the Old and New Testaments, and it reveals the missionary heart of God in a clear and powerful way.

1. The God of the Bible is a sending God.

Abraham was called to leave the place where he was living in Ur of the Chaldees and journey to a place that God would show him. The reason God gave to Abraham for uprooting him from all that was comfortable and familiar was both shocking and exciting. God wanted to bless "all the families of the earth" through Abraham and his descendants (v. 3). The unmistakable conclusion is that God could not bless the nations through Abraham as long as Abraham stayed where he was. He had to make the journey from where he was to another place where God needed him to be. This divine sending is God's plan for the salvation of the nations: "As the Father has sent Me, I also send you" (John 20:21).

2. The blessings of God upon His people are inextricably linked to His heart for the nations.

Even though Abraham was told to leave his country, his family, and his security, God made a powerful promise to Abraham: "I will bless you and make your name great; and you shall be a blessing" (v. 2). God wanted to bless Abraham, but that blessing was never intended to be something that Abraham held jealously to himself. When God blesses His people, it is always for the greater purpose of blessing the nations. God desires His people to be conduits through which His blessings flow to draw the nations to Himself. Tragically, and far too often, God's people attempt to dam up the flow of God's blessings in order to create their own private lakes. This is sin, pure and simple. It is a selfish and hedonistic understanding of the blessing of God that was never God's desire or design.

3. God's sending of His people to bless the nations is the very essence of the gospel.

Galatians 3:8 tells us that the gospel was preached to Abraham in advance with the words, "In you all the nations shall be blessed." Before the fullness of God in Jesus Christ ever appeared to the shepherds in Bethlehem, the good news had already been proclaimed to Abraham in Ur of the Chaldees. God desires to bless His people so that we, in turn, will be a blessing to the nations.

Conclusion

As North American Christians, we are most blessed by God. We must begin to view God's blessings in the way that God views them. Once we have been blessed, it is our responsibility, under God, to bless the nations by going and sharing the great truth of God's redeeming love. "For everyone to whom much is given, from him much will be required" (Luke 12:48).

Date: June 26

Suggested Title: Lights in the World

Scripture: Philippians 2:14–30

Contributor: D. Allen McWhite Sr.

Full Sermon Outline

Introduction

Nothing is more beautiful and compelling than the glittering light of a bright star in a moonless, velvet-black sky. In the country in a pasture at night, we can see this display of God's handiwork in the heavens without it being dimmed and diffused by the harsh lights of the city. In such a setting, the sharp contrast between darkness and light is impressive. Scripture often speaks of the witness of His people by using this imagery of light shining in the darkness. Philippians 2:15 reminds us that "in the midst of a crooked and perverse generation," we have been called to "shine as lights in the world." This verse stresses the critical importance of our gospel witness in the world—especially in those places where the spiritual darkness is greatest.

So, how do we shine as lights in the world? What is it that will make our witness striking and compelling in a world that is so enveloped by and enamored with the darkness? In Philippians 2:17–30, the apostle Paul gives us the examples of three men, each of whom presents a different facet of what it takes to radiate the light of the gospel in the midst of overwhelming spiritual darkness.

1. True light is self-emptying (vv. 17–18).

Paul describes his own life as one that was "being poured out as a drink offering." In making this analogy, Paul is looking back to the Old Testament sacrificial system. In most instances, a drink offering was not an independent offering; it was offered along with a burnt offering (Ex.

29:40; Num. 15:4–5, 6, 10).[1] On such occasions, when the wine of the drink offering was poured out upon the already scorching-hot altar, it would be consumed in a hissing puff of smoke and cloud of steam. It would be vaporized—leaving nothing behind. Paul wanted his life to be like that drink offering. He was not looking for ways to hold on to his life; rather, he wanted his life to be poured out and used up for the sake of Christ.

One of the reasons why more Christians are not going to the ends of the earth is because many of us do not want to be "poured out." Instead, we want to "hold on." We want to hold on to our comfort, hold on to our security, hold on to our "stuff." The spiritual darkness of the world will never be pierced by the light of the gospel unless and until God's people determine that the lives God has given us are to be presented back to Him as living sacrifices (Rom. 12:1), poured out and used up in pursuit of His glory among the nations.

2. True light is self-denying (vv. 19–24).

In these verses Paul gives testimony to the life of his young protégé, Timothy. What he has to say about Timothy is both affirming and tragic. Paul first states that he has no one with him who is like Timothy because Timothy "sincerely cares" for the welfare of others. This is a great affirmation of Timothy, but what does it say about the other believers that were surrounding Paul? Then, in a statement of even greater contrast, the apostle declares, "For all [others] seek their own [interests], not the things which are of Christ Jesus." This is surely an indictment of many Christians in Paul's day—and in our own—whose primary focus was and is on themselves.

When you begin to realize that (1) over two billion people in this world have never heard the good news of the gospel; (2) that there are almost two billion more who have heard the gospel but have rejected it; and (3) that there are nearly an additional two billion people who may call themselves "Christians," but who still do not know the Christ of the New Testament, then you begin to realize we can no longer be content to live and let live. We can no longer afford to be preoccupied with the pursuit of our own interests, to the neglect of the billions of people who are racing headlong toward a Christ-less eternity.

3. True light is self-sacrificing (vv. 25–30).

Epaphroditus is one of those individuals in Scripture that we know very little about. He is only mentioned in these few verses of Scripture. We know that he was probably a member of the church at Philippi and that he had likely brought a gift from the Philippian Church to Paul during his imprisonment (v. 25). We also know that Epaphroditus had become very ill and had almost died (v. 27), perhaps as a result of his long journey from Philippi. But what really sets Epaphroditus apart is what Paul has to say about him in the final verse of this chapter, where he writes that Epaphroditus was "not regarding his [own] life" (v. 30). Some translations state that Epaphroditus was "risking his life" (NASB, ESV). The word Paul uses here literally means to do something that is rash or reckless.[2] This was actually a gambler's term which meant "to throw down a stake" or, in modern parlance, "to roll the dice."[3] Epaphroditus was willing to gamble his very life for the sake of Christ; he was willing to throw himself out on the game-board of life and risk losing everything to do what Christ had called him to do.

Conclusion

Many North American Christians become queasy and draw back from Christ's call to go to the ends of the earth when they realize that being light in a crooked and perverse generation calls for self-emptying, self-denial, and even "rolling the dice" with their very lives. As North American Christians, we need to be reminded again that there is risk in following Christ into places of great spiritual darkness. Yet, as John Piper states, "this very risk is the means by which the value of Christ shines more brightly."[4]

Notes

1. John D. Davis, *Davis Dictionary of the Bible,* 4th ed. (Grand Rapids: Baker, 1972), 573.

2. W. Robertson Nicoll, *The Expositor's Greek Testament* (Grand Rapids: William B. Eerdmans, 1980), 3:447.

3. Marvin R. Vincent, *Vincent's Word Studies of the New Testament* (New York: Scribner's, 1887; McLean, VA: MacDonald Publishing, n.d.), 3:441–42. Citations refer to the MacDonald edition.

4. John Piper, *Don't Waste Your Life* (Wheaton, IL: Crossway Books, 2003), 88.

Date: June 26

Suggested Title: Why Do We Go?

Scripture: Mark 10:28–31

Contributor: D. Allen McWhite Sr.

Sermon Starter

Introduction

Whenever we have visiting missionaries, evangelists, and church planters from far-flung places who tell us about serving people largely devoid of any awareness of God and any sense of a need for Him in their lives, we can be reminded of Peter's brutally honest words to Jesus. Peter said to Jesus, "See, we have left all and followed You" (v. 28).

Why do we go?

1. We go because this is an integral and inescapable part of what it means to follow Jesus.

It is significant that Jesus did not argue with Peter when Peter said, "Jesus, we have left all to follow You." Jesus did not tell Peter that he had misunderstood what it meant to follow Him or that he did not need to make this kind of sacrifice. Instead, Jesus accepted Peter's statement as one of fact, without questioning it. The truth is, Peter *had* left everything to follow Jesus (Luke 5:11). This is not a higher call, and this is not a deeper call. This is, in Jesus' eyes, normal Christianity. It is, in fact, the most basic essence of what it means to follow Him.

2. We go because there are greater and more significant riches that Jesus wants us to discover (vv. 29–30).

While Jesus did not argue with Peter's statement about leaving everything, He did point Peter toward an even greater reality. Jesus speaks of a hundredfold return in houses and lands and family. As David Garland states so well, "Those who become homeless will have a home among those who receive them. Those who surrender families will become part of a greater family not based on biological kinship. Those who leave fields will be given greater fields of missionary opportunity."[1]

3. We go for the sake of Christ and the gospel (v. 29).

Don't miss what Jesus says in the last part of verse 10:29. Ultimately, it is not our understanding of discipleship that thrusts us out to the nations. Neither is it our quest for greater spiritual blessings. We go because of (1) our love for Christ and (2) our burden for a lost world.

Conclusion

When we are unwilling to go for Jesus—or when we are unwilling to send out our own children and grandchildren—it says more about those two things than it does about anything else.

Note

1. David E. Garland, *Mark*; *The NIV Application Commentary*, ed. Terry C. Muck (Grand Rapids: Zondervan, 1996), 400.

JULY

Let Freedom Ring

Date: July 3

Suggested Title: Duty to God, in One's Duty to Country

Scripture: 1 Peter 2:13–17 ESV

Contributor: Alex McFarland

Full Sermon Outline

Introduction

In this sermon, we will conclude with some points of how this passage applies to a Christian understanding of God and country.

Peter wrote his first letter to "the exiles in the Dispersion" (1 Pet. 1:1) from Rome toward the end of the reign of the Roman emperor Nero (around AD 62–63). The overarching theme and purpose of his letter was to encourage his audience to endure the persecution they were facing, or were about to face, all for the sake of Christ and in the hope of His coming kingdom.

It is important to understand the nature of Nero's reign—he was famous for persecuting Christians. For example, when a massive fire broke out in Rome, which destroyed a large part of the city, Nero cunningly passed the blame for the fire off onto this new "sect" called Christianity. As a result, many Christians were arrested, tortured, and even crucified. Nero even used the burning corpses of Christians who had been crucified as "street lamps" during the night.

The persecution that these Christians in Asia Minor, to whom Peter wrote, were facing was no less severe. When we understand this horrendous background, our passage becomes all the more astonishing.

Peter exhorted his readers to think of themselves as exiles in this fallen world. Christians, therefore, should view themselves primarily as citizens of God's kingdom and should spend all their efforts in living for that kingdom, setting their hopes fully on "the grace that will be brought to you at the revelation of Jesus Christ" (1 Pet. 1:13).

1. Fulfillment of responsibility to our country is really fulfillment of an obligation to God (v. 13).

Peter instructs his readers to be subject to the emperor. What? Yes, "for the Lord's sake" they were to be subject to every human institution. Remember, possibly at the very moment Peter wrote this, Nero was crucifying some of his brothers and sisters in Christ. Nevertheless, Peter exhorted his readers to live a life worthy of the Lord in the face of such persecution.

Peter was not ignoring the terrible situation that his audience was facing. In fact, he immediately went on to describe what a good government was supposed to do, namely, "to punish those who do evil and to praise those who do good" (v. 14). But just the opposite was happening in Rome. Nero was perpetrating all sorts of evil, and those who were leading moral lifestyles were being put to death as evildoers.

2. Fulfillment of duty to authority is a testimony to the watching world (vv. 14–15).

Peter surely understood the difficulty of obeying what he wrote. So he went on to point out the basis upon which he could make such a command: "For this is the will of God, that by doing good you should put to silence the ignorance of foolish people" (v. 15). Christians, who are first and foremost citizens of God's kingdom, are to live according to the will of their heavenly King. Christians living in the face of persecution will receive an inconceivably great (and eternal) reward in the future.

The lifestyle that Peter was calling his audience to live is summed up in his command to live "as servants of God" (v. 16). Such a servant mindset resonates well with what the psalmist wrote: "For a day in your courts is better than a thousand elsewhere. I would rather be a doorkeeper in the house of my God than dwell in the tents of wickedness" (Ps. 84:10). This section is concluded with the literary technique of chiasm:

"Honor everyone.
    Love the brotherhood.
    Fear God.
Honor the emperor." (v. 17)

The two clauses at the center of the chiasm indicate the priority that the church and God take in the life of a Christian. (Notice that only God is to be feared, not the emperor.) The two outer clauses demonstrate that the emperor is not God, but the emperor is rather to be honored just like everyone else. Do not miss, however, that Peter still called for his readers to show honor, not hatred or disrespect, to the emperor.

3. Fulfillment of one's duties as a citizen is appropriate, since we are ultimately God's subjects (vv. 16–17).

So how does this passage relate to our theme of God and country? Well, the point is mainly one of contrast between situations. On the one hand, we see that Peter could call his audience to show respect to an evil emperor and to be subject to the authority residing over them, even if that authority was involved in their persecution. On the other hand, we see our situation today. Christians in America enjoy some freedoms that are available nowhere else in the world. We can assemble for worship on Sundays without fear. While we do struggle against our own modern forms of idolatry, there is no one trying to force us to bow down to the emperor and confess him as lord.

Conclusion

Christians are to be exemplary citizens. So if Peter, in the situation he was writing to, could exhort his readers to honor the government and the emperor, then surely Christians should do the same today. And Peter is not the only biblical writer to teach along these lines. For Paul wrote, "I urge that supplications, prayers, intercessions, and thanksgivings be made for all people, for kings and all who are in high positions, that we may lead a peaceful and quiet life, godly and dignified in every way"

(1 Tim. 2:1–2). He also wrote in Romans 13 that human governments exercise a divinely appointed authority and so should be respected.

Remember that we are first citizens of God's kingdom, but we are also citizens of America. So a patriotism that is expressed through honor and respect for our country is in line with the biblical mandate to godly citizenship.

Date: July 3

Suggested Title: Why Jesus' Resurrection Should Bury Our Fears About Death

Scripture: 2 Timothy 1:10

Contributor: Alex McFarland

Sermon Starter

Introduction

Death, especially our own death, is a topic that we regularly attempt to banish to the outskirts of our minds. Thinking about death makes us uncomfortable. We would much rather think about last week's basketball game or who's running for office or what we are going to eat for dinner tonight. Anything but death!

1. Death is a defeated enemy.

Why do people have such an innate uneasiness when it comes to death? Death, according to the Bible, is our (as well as God's) enemy. Indeed, but death is a defeated enemy. Jesus Christ took death's best shot on the cross and prevailed over death through His resurrection on the third day.

2. The resurrection dispels the fear of death.

Imagine a man who had been serving for six months as a missionary to a small indigenous tribe situated along the bank of a narrow river in Ecuador. Since he arrived he'd had little success in reaching this tribe. The people feared a god that supposedly lived in a nearby river. They believed that coming into contact with the river would lead to their death.

One day the missionary gathered the entire tribe to the bank of the river and began to preach the gospel to them, as he had done before. This time, however, when he reached the point in his message about how Jesus has conquered death through His resurrection, the missionary paused to give a demonstration, hoping somehow to get through to them. This missionary, knowing the people's belief that any contact with the water of the river would result in death, jumped into the river, swam around in the water for a while, and got back out onto the bank in front of his audience. As time passed, it became clear to the people that he was not going to die.

Even the chief eventually got into the water, and one by one the people began to accept that the river could not harm them. The chief explained, "I know a man (the missionary) who has been to the other side and come back again." Jesus, through His death and resurrection, has prepared the way before us. Regarding death and the grave, we Christians know a man who has "gone to the other side and come back again"!

Conclusion

Second Timothy 1:10 promised that Jesus has "abolished death and brought life and immortality to light through the gospel." From this, we have three reasons not to fear death: First, Jesus has (literally) "destroyed" death. The word actually means "unemployed." Think of it: Jesus put death out of a job! Second, Jesus has revealed life and light, and He gives to the world "immortality." Third, this gospel—good news—is for all people. Death has been conquered, immortality is possible, and all people may experience this. This is truly good news, and in this our fear of death may be overcome!

Date: July 10

Suggested Title: Jesus' Victory over Death

Scripture: 1 Corinthians 15:50–58 ESV

Contributor: Alex McFarland

Full Sermon Outline

Introduction

We will examine the concluding nine verses of chapter 15 of Paul's first letter to the Corinthians. Paul's purpose in 1 Corinthians 15 is to discuss the resurrection, its validity and verification via eyewitness testimony, and all that we have in light of Christ's victory over the grave. Paul planted the church at Corinth and wrote this letter to deal with the church's arrogant boasting about their spiritual gifts, as well as to further instruct them on some points of his gospel message, such as the resurrection.

There were some in the church at Corinth who did not believe in the resurrection. Paul insisted that if there were no physical resurrection, then of course Jesus would not have been raised from the dead. If Jesus had not been raised from the dead, then humans would still be enslaved to sin. Further, our departed loved ones, who we thought were in heaven, would be lost. But Paul reminds us that Jesus has been raised, and this has profound implications for how Christians are to think and to live.

How does Christ's resurrection assuage our fear of death? Let's consider three realities:

1. Christ's resurrection accomplishes what physical effort could never do.

We come to 1 Corinthians 15:50–58. Paul began with a negative assertion: "Flesh and blood cannot inherit the kingdom of God, nor does the perishable inherit the imperishable" (v. 50). God's kingdom is His sovereign rule over His people who have been redeemed by His grace. Paul taught that the kingdom, which in Jewish thought was supposed come at the end of the age, had broken into the present age through the resurrection of Jesus from the dead. Citizens of the kingdom of God can enjoy even now the benefits of salvation that are described all throughout the New Testament. By "flesh and blood" Paul did not have in mind the unbiblical concept of a separation between the physical and spiritual realms, which was the belief of some of the Corinthians. Rather, by this phrase Paul was referring to the sinful nature that all humans possess as a result of the fall. In order to inherit (note that an inheritance is not something earned, but is a gift) the kingdom of God, one must be given spiritual life, thus fulfilling Old Testament prophesies such as the famous passage found in Jeremiah 31.

2. Christ's resurrection is life-changing in ways that human effort could never be.

Paul then went on to say that we, that is, Christians, will be transformed when Christ returns to consummate His kingdom. The perishable bodies that believers now possess in this fallen world will be transformed to be like Jesus' glorious resurrected body. That is why Paul was so insistent in rejecting the Corinthians' false belief that there would be no bodily resurrection. Christ has gone ahead of us by experiencing death and rising from the grave. He serves as the model for what will happen for all who are found in Him.

Almost as if he were mocking death, Paul quoted from Isaiah 25:8 and Hosea 13:14 and wrote, "Death is swallowed up in victory. O death, where is your victory? O death, where is your sting?" (vv. 54–55). But someone might say, "How can Christians have such confidence in the face of death since people still die?" True, people die every day, and this makes it seem as though death has not been defeated. That is where, once again, Jesus' death and resurrection come into play.

3. Christ's resurrection has a permanence that no prize of this world can possibly equal.

Jesus really did defeat death by dying on the cross and rising again, but His victory has not yet fully been consummated. The full consummation of Christ's victory over death will be realized when He comes again. So how does Christ's victory impact Christians living in the present? Death is depicted as some sort of poisonous creature, perhaps a scorpion. In one sense, death still does have a sting; it stings every time those closest to us die. But in a much greater sense, death no longer has a sting. When death "stung" Jesus, He emptied the stinger of its poison, so to speak. Death is not the end for the one who has placed faith in Jesus as Savior and Lord. On the other side of that brief moment of death there is a life in which we will worship for eternity in the presence of God in the renewed heaven and earth.

Conclusion

Christ's resurrection is a multifaceted (and precious) reality that this generation needs to know. How are we to live in light of this amazing truth? Paul tells us: "Therefore, my beloved brothers, be steadfast, immovable, always abounding in the work of the Lord, knowing that in the Lord your labor is not in vain" (v. 58).

First, in contrast to living our lives in fear, we are to be *steadfast* in our faith, which is placed in the power of God and His faithfulness.

Second, the word *immovable* connects back to the beginning of the chapter when Paul wrote that the Corinthians had taken their stand on the firm foundation of the gospel. Every aspect of our lives is to be centered on the truths of the gospel. The gospel is not just what offers salvation, it is what continues the process of salvation until Christ's return (the technical term is *sanctification*). We are to abound in the work of the Lord. This means that we are to imitate the things we read that Jesus did and said, as recorded in the Gospels. The reason why we know that such kingdom work is not in vain is connected to the main theme of chapter 15: we serve a living Savior who will be faithful to His promise to give us resurrection bodies and the life of the age to come!

Date: July 10

Suggested Title: Loving God, Loving Country

Scripture: 1 Timothy 2:2–4

Contributor: Alex McFarland

Sermon Starter

Introduction

First Timothy 2:2–4 says to pray "for kings and all who are in authority, that we may lead a quiet and peaceable life in all godliness and reverence." Some today maintain that Christians shouldn't speak about social and political issues, but this verse seems to indicate otherwise. More than one commentator has noted that this scripture is basically a call to pray for, work toward, and desire a culture most conducive for the spread of the gospel. For the Christian, love of one's country naturally breeds a desire that God be present in the culture, and that His blessings be present.

In our parades we can see American military veterans afforded respect. First may be older gentlemen dressed in faded uniforms making their way along the main route of the parade. These men served in wars such as World War II, the Korean War, and Vietnam. Following these veterans may be younger men whose military service has been more recent. We can feel privileged to live in America, the land of the free and home of the brave.

First Timothy 2 tells us three things about an appropriate type of patriotism:

1. God cares about the leaders of a nation, and so should we.

2. Prayer can make a difference in the direction a nation takes.

3. God's desire is for the people of a nation to be saved through the gospel, which should be the desire of each Christian as well.

Some today seem more concerned with talking about all the faults of this country rather than expressing their thankfulness to live in it. But loving our country—and praying for the nation and its leaders—is "good and acceptable in the sight of God our Savior" (v. 3).

Conclusion

How may we best love our nation? A great start is to help more and more people in the nation come to know the True God, and "come to the knowledge of the truth" (v. 4).

Date: July 17

Suggested Title: Freedom from Sin and Suffering

Scripture: Genesis 6:5; Genesis 1:31; James 1:14-15;
Revelation 21:4; Romans 8:18

Contributor: Stephen Cutchins

Full Sermon Outline

Introduction

"Why," we ask, "must everyone experience pain?" It is the common ground on which all humanity stands. The real question is, "Why must it be this way?" The problem of pain is considered "the most serious intellectual obstacle that stands between many people and religious faith," according to Christian apologist Francis Beckwith.[1] There are three attributes of God that when looked at in combination seem to be in direct contradiction with the presence of pain and evil in creation. God is described as infinitely powerful, good, and knowledgeable.

Did God Create Evil?

In Genesis 6, "the LORD saw that the wickedness of man was great in the earth, and that every intent of the thoughts of his heart was only evil continually" (v. 5). However, all throughout the creation account, God affirmed that His creation was good. "Then God saw everything He had made, and indeed it was very good" (Gen. 1:31). What happened between chapter 1 and chapter 6 of Genesis? Did God make a mistake?

God created a world in which evil was possible, but it was creatures that made evil actual by choosing things that were not good. "He created the fact of freedom; we perform the acts of freedom. He made evil possible; men made evil actual," said theologians Norman Geisler and Ronald M. Brooks.[2] God did not create evil—because evil is not a thing. It is the absence of good. Further, evil is more than just the absence of good; it is the privation of good. Absence only implies that something is not there. Privation implies that something ought to be present and it is not. An example of the difference between an absence and a privation would be a blind man versus a blind rock. In the rock, sight is not expected; therefore, blindness would be an absence of sight. However, for the man, sight is expected; therefore, the blindness is a privation of sight. "Evil exists in a good thing as a lack or imperfection in it, like a hole in a piece of wood," Geisler said.[3] To say that evil is a "thing" is not true. While God is the creator of all things, He did not create evil because evil is not a "thing."

Why Does God Allow Evil to Continue?

Why could God not have blown a great wind that made it impossible for Eve to get to the fruit she was tempted to eat? It seems that God could also miraculously turn a gun into a banana just before a murder happens. Could God have stopped the events of 9/11 by causing each of the terrorists to have a spontaneous heart attack before they killed thousands of people? God can't stop all evil acts without destroying all freedom to choose between good and evil, which would remove free will. Could God have not given man free will? At first, this option makes sense. However, the only way for God to allow love to be shared between a creature and a Creator is for both to choose to participate in the relationship.

Why does God allow evil? If He didn't, there would be no freedom to choose good. In God's sovereignty, He gave us free will. Evil exists in our world as a direct result of man's abuse of free will. Since the time of Adam and Eve, humanity has chosen to use freedom for selfish motivations. "But each one is tempted when he is drawn away by his own desires and enticed. Then, when desire has conceived, it gives birth to sin; and sin, when it is full-grown, brings forth death" (James 1:14–15).

Why Does God Not Destroy Evil?

> If God is all-good, He would destroy evil.
> If God is all-powerful, He could destroy evil.
> But evil is not destroyed.
> Hence, there is no such God.

"The classic form of this argument has been rattling through the halls of college campuses for hundreds of years," said Geisler in 1978.[4] This argument is still valid. However, it is not true because it leaves out one crucial word: *yet*. Just because God has not yet defeated evil does not mean that evil will not be defeated or destroyed by God in the future. In fact, the argument seems to boomerang on itself and point to the absolute necessity of God one day dealing with evil. And Geisler's thoughts? "Since we have not yet finished with history, it is possible that all evil in history will one day cease."[5] Because God has not yet removed evil, we live in an evil world that results in pain and suffering. The tired old argument that was stated before should be altered to the following:

> If God is all-good, He will defeat evil.
> If God is all-powerful, He can defeat evil.
> Evil is not *yet* defeated.
> Therefore, God can and *will one day* defeat evil.

We can depend on Revelation: "And God will wipe away every tear from their eyes; there shall be no more death, nor sorrow, nor crying. There shall be no more pain, for the former things have passed away" (21:4). God is yet to destroy evil. However, Christians can have assurance that God will remove evil and pain from the presence of His people in the new heaven and new earth. And while we live in the fallen world we must realize it is not, as Geisler said, the best possible world, but "it is the best way to obtain the best possible world."[6] And perhaps this is what Paul meant when he said in Romans: "For I consider that the sufferings of this present time are not worthy to be compared with the glory which shall be revealed in us" (8:18).

Conclusion

God not only acknowledges our pain but also wants to help in times of pain and trouble. Despite the fact that He is not the cause of evil, He is active in our lives to use painful situations for good. God never wastes a hurt. An individual's response is what determines whether that person becomes better or bitter when pain comes their way. God is much more concerned with our character than He is with our comfort.

Notes

1. Francis J. Beckwith, *To Everyone an Answer: A Case for the Christian Worldview: Essays in Honor of Norman L. Geisler* (Downers Grove, IL: InterVarsity, 2004), 203.
2. Norman L. Geisler and Ronald M. Brooks, *When Skeptics Ask* (Wheaton, IL: Victor Books, 1990), 62.
3. Norman L. Geisler, *The Roots of Evil* (Grand Rapids: Zondervan, 1978), 20.
4. Geisler and Brooks, *When Skeptics Ask,* 63.
5. Geisler, *The Roots of Evil,* 35.
6. Ibid., 59.

Date: July 17

Suggested Title: The Promise of Freedom

Scripture: Ephesians 2:8–9; Philippians 3:20–21; Psalm 18:2

Contributor: Stephen Cutchins

Sermon Starter

Introduction

Although we are already children of God, we have not yet experienced the fullness of our freedom from sin through salvation. As we keep His promise of transformation in view and fix our desire on the goal of perfection, we will grow in purity here and now. There are three aspects to the process of our salvation.

1. Freedom from the penalty of sin

When we believe in Jesus Christ for eternal life we experience justification. Justification-salvation is freedom from the penalty of sin and is a movement from death to life. It is not the strength of our faith but the object of our faith that gives us victory. Paul makes it clear in Ephesians 2:8–9 that justification is experienced by the grace of God through faith in Christ: "For by grace you have been saved through faith, and that not of yourselves; it is the gift of God, not of works, lest anyone should boast."

2. Freedom from the power of sin

Once we are alive in Christ, we begin the ongoing process of sanctification. Sanctification-salvation is being freed from the power of sin in our lives. This ongoing transformation causes us to be more like Christ. Those who believe in Jesus Christ for eternal life have already won but have not yet finished fighting. God allows us to go through our Christian walk, not to win the victory but to show to the world that He that is in us is greater than he that is in the world. We don't fight *for* victory—we fight *from* victory.

3. Freedom from the presence of sin

Christians also look forward to glorification. Glorification-salvation is freedom from the very presence of sin and is the ultimate state of every believer. Think about how wonderful it will be to see Jesus and to be free of all the sinful and fallen aspects of this world and our flesh. As Christians, we have an amazing future ahead of us. Experiencing new life through faith in Christ is truly overwhelming, but the best is yet to come. Paul wrote about this to the church in Philippi: "For our citizenship is in heaven, from which we also eagerly wait for the Savior, the Lord Jesus Christ, who will transform our lowly body that it may be conformed to His glorious body, according to the working by which He is able even to subdue all things to Himself" (Phil. 3:20–21).

Conclusion

Remember that God is at work and never wastes a hurt. Realize you are not alone and the journey is important. Sometimes waiting is important, so be prepared to be still and have hope. Our freedom from pain is delayed but not denied. When tough times come, Jesus is enough. Ask yourself: What is God doing here? Ask yourself: Will I trust Him? Refer to Psalm 18:2: "The LORD is my rock and my fortress and my deliverer; my God, my strength, in whom I will trust; my shield and the horn of my salvation, my stronghold."

Date: July 24

Suggested Title: Free from Your Past

Scripture: John 4:1–42

Contributor: Rick Ezell

Full Sermon Outline

Introduction

A thirty-nine-year-old mother of four adolescents suddenly suffered a splitting headache. Before she knew what had happened, she was undergoing surgery for a brain aneurysm. The operation was successful but had an unusual side effect. Partial amnesia caused her to forget sixteen years of her life. In her mind, she was twenty-three, the mother of four small children. Sixteen years of happiness and achievement, pain and regret erased. Would it be a blessing to erase your past?

The Story of a Troubled Past

A woman with a troubled past lived in Sychar, Samaria. John recorded her story. She was not given a name, just referred to as the Samaritan woman. Samaritans were Jews who had intermarried with the Assyrians. Putting it mildly, they were hated by the Jews. Yet Jesus traveled through Samaria, rather than taking the more customary route east of the Jordan River through Perea. Jesus did not bypass Samaria. And this woman was the reason. It was high noon—the sun at its peak. A scorcher. Through the waves of heat on the rock-solid path to the well known as Jacob's Well she strolled, carrying an empty jar. While the other women came at dawn to avoid the heat, she went at midday, avoiding their scorn, ridicule, and stares. She arrived alone.

Her heart was as heavy as the water jar she toted. Her soul was as empty as its contents. Her spirit was as dry as the dust that stirred from her sandals. She pondered the futile road she had wandered. She reminisced about the roads she might have taken and the happiness she might have found. But her mind echoed the words, *What's done is done. You can't go back. You can't relive the past.* The failed relationships. The empty promises. The wrong choices. The wayward walks. She had ventured down one path after another, seeking fulfillment, and each time she had lowered her bucket, hoping to quench her thirst for love and meaningfulness and satisfaction, she had come up empty and disappointed. Again and again. The empty water jar was a fit reminder of her life.

The Savior Who Knows Our Past

Jesus, a Jewish man, was sitting by the well. He saw her. He gazed beyond her appearance and her pretension to see the hurt of her heart, the hollowness of her soul, and the aridity of her spirit. He spoke to her. He offered her water—His water, the living water to soothe the hurt, fill the soul, and quench the spirit.

Jesus knew her past. He revealed her past and current marital status. But He did not call her a sinner. He offered no evangelistic appeal. He presented no structured plan of salvation. He didn't lecture her. He didn't even pray with her.

The Reflection of a Haunted Past

Jesus allowed her to see her reflection in the water—a face and a life that she did not like. She was haunted by it. Embarrassed. She wished it could be relived and redone. But it couldn't. It was her past—always before her, always staring back at her.

Here was the Savior of the world conversing with a Samaritan adulteress, giving her the opportunity to move beyond her checkered past, offering her the gift of all gifts—a gift that would allow her to overcome the pain her past brought into her present. All these years she had given of herself—her virginity, her morality, her self-respect, her value, and her significance in a hope to find what this man was offering her.

The Testimony of a Forgiven Past

In a moment, she was cleansed and freed. The guilt of her sin removed. The chains of her past broken. The barrenness of her soul sprung to life like a parched desert after a downpour. She bubbled like a babbling brook.

Her newfound life couldn't be contained. She had to tell someone. To the women that had shunned her and the men that had used her, she told about the man who told her everything she ever did. Jesus sent her on her way with her past behind her and a new future before her. He didn't just give her a new smile; He provided her a new purpose. She wasn't to become merely a container for the living water, but a conduit so that living water would flow to others. And flow it did. She couldn't stop talking about the Savior who knew everything about her. He had transformed her life. Her future looked bright for the first time in a long time. She could face the new day and the old acquaintances. Her water jar lay empty in the sand, but her soul was full to overflowing.

Conclusion

Our lives are empty too. Her jar was a symbol of her life. We have our symbols as well. We scrape and crawl and climb to the top of this hill called life. Some of us achieve success and status, and others languish in the trenches of failure and defeat, but regardless of where we are, our souls are dreadfully empty. Outside we may appear to have everything in perfect order, or we may appear to be in complete chaos. Inside we are dying.

We peer into the reflection of ourselves. All we can see is the hurt and pain of decisions made and the lost opportunity of happiness forfeited. We can never go back. We would love to go back to retrieve a verbalized thought, to correct a sordid mistake, to take a different road, to undo an event that led us down the path we are now on. But we can't enter a time machine and redo what we have already done.

What we need is a new start, a fresh beginning. We desperately desire a cleansing, something or someone who will take away the sting of the past memories. We want to leave our empty jars behind, our souls filled with the cleansing and purifying water of God's love so we can run down a new path, toward a new life.

What the Savior did for the Samaritan woman, He can do for us. When we allow the love of Jesus to intersect with our lives, He can turn us around, chart us a new course, give us hope for tomorrow, and fill the emptiness of our soul.

Date: July 24

Suggested Title: Free to Face the Future

Scripture: Philippians 3:12–14

Contributor: Rick Ezell

Sermon Starter

Introduction

In the classic movie *The Lion King*, Rafiki is a wise ape that teaches the young lion Simba about the past—a past the young lion is trying to forget. In a poignant scene, Rafiki sneaks up on Simba and uses his staff to hit the lion on the head. Simba rubs his head and complains, to which Rafiki wryly responds that the hurt doesn't matter because it's in the past. Simba, still rubbing his head, responds, "Yeah, but it still hurts."

Rafiki then explains that while the past can hurt, the lion can either run from it or face it and learn from it. As he says these words, he swings his staff at Simba again. Only this time, Simba sees it coming and ducks out of the way. Rafiki, knowing the cub has learned, says, "Ah! You see? So what are you going to do now?" The scene ends with the lion king bounding off to face the past.[1] That is something we must do too.

1. Assess the past (v. 12).

Before an architect begins a blueprint, he inspects the property site, assessing environmental factors that could either enhance or restrict his final design. Before Paul could move forward he had to see where he had been to determine where he was. His was a life in process, not completion. He knew he had more to do.

2. Forget the past (v. 13).

Biblically speaking, *to forget* means "no longer to be influenced or affected by." This does not suggest that our sins and past mistakes will somehow be erased from the memory bank. Rather, it simply means that the power of the past is broken by living for the future. The past cannot be changed, but the meaning of the past can change. If there was anyone who had a past that would prevent him from living for God it was Paul. Even though he had ordered the massacre of believers and opposed God's work, he did not allow that past to stop him.

3. Learn from the past (v. 14).

Paul wrote, "One thing I do"—not "These forty things I dabble at." Paul would not allow for distractions. His past informed his future. He was single-minded in his pursuit that came from learning from the past. The key to learning from your past is discovering your "one thing." And, once discovered, pursue it with single-minded devotion.

4. Move past the past (vv. 12, 14).

The verbs Paul employed depict a runner from the arena, bent forward, his hand outstretched, his body straining to win. Paul was moving past his past. He allowed his past to inform his present, but not to control his future. A life controlled by the past sucks the life out of the present. How safe would you be trying to drive a car by only looking in the rearview mirror? But while every car has a rearview mirror, it also has a windshield. The windshield is larger than the rearview mirror—a fit reminder to spend more time looking forward rather than looking backward.

Conclusion

We are the sum total of our past experiences. We know the past can't be changed. But letting go of painful and debilitating events so they no longer control the present will free us in the future.

Note

1. *The Lion King*, directed by Roger Allers and Rob Minkoff (1994; Walt Disney Pictures).

Date: July 31

Suggested Title: Free from Guilt

Scripture: Psalm 32:1–5

Contributor: Rick Ezell

Full Sermon Outline

Introduction

Noël Coward, the famous playwright, is said to have sent an identical note to twenty of the most famous men in London. The anonymous note read simply: "Everybody has found out what you are doing. If I were you I would get out of town." Supposedly, all twenty men actually left town. Guilt has a powerful effect.

Guilt is the dread of the past; a pain that wells up within the heart because we committed an offense or failed to do something right. It is a phantom pain, like amputees experience after a limb has been removed. Often people experience this same kind of dread obsessed by the memory of some sin committed years ago. It never leaves them, crippling their enjoyment of life, their devotional life, their relationship with others. They live in fear that someone will discover their past. They work overtime trying to prove to God they're truly repentant. They erect barriers against the enveloping, loving grace of God.

Before we beat guilt up too much, let me remind you that guilt is like an electric fence that gives a jolt when boundaries are crossed. It sends an alarm to awaken us that something needs our attention. Like pain, guilt tells us when something is wrong. When you feel it, you don't just sit there; you do something about it.

Of all people, David had good reason for feeling guilty. Scholars believe that David wrote Psalm 32 after he cried to God for forgiveness for his double sin of adultery and murder. David's guilt was immense. He wrote, "My guilt has overwhelmed me like a burden too heavy to bear"

(Ps. 38:4 NIV). David's release from guilt was sweet. This psalm offers practical steps to free one from guilt.

1. Admit your guilt (v. 5).

Our society has witnessed the downfall of politicians, ministers, businesspeople, and other leaders. Isn't it interesting, that when caught, many sidestep the issue of admitting guilt? Instead they blame others or are blinded by their own self-righteousness. Several years ago one TV preacher, however, stood before his congregation, both in person and on television, with tears streaming down his face, and cried out, "I have sinned against You, my Lord." Another time, David acknowledged his sin in a psalm: "Against thee, thee only, have I sinned" (51:4 KJV). David knew the importance: "I acknowledged my sin to you" (Ps. 32:5 ESV). The first step on the road to recovery and relief is admitting that something is wrong in our lives.

2. Confront your guilt (v. 5).

Guilt must be confronted and dealt with. To overcome it, we can't continue to hide its reality. We must deal with it. If guilt is not dealt with, then guilt will deal with us. It may affect you:

- Psychologically (v. 3). David's conscience "groaned all day long." David could not get the wrong out of his mind. It awoke with him. It followed him throughout his daily activities. It gnawed at him as he tried to sleep.
- Spiritually (v. 4). Sin separates us from God. It drives a wedge in our relationship with our Maker. That barrier will remain until we deal with it.
- Physically (v. 4). Like water that evaporates on a sunny day so did David's physical condition. I've heard of people who have lost their appetite, unable to sleep, experience a shortness of breath, or become sick all because of guilty feelings.

3. Confess your guilt (v. 5).

The next step to recovery is to tell it like it is to God. Confession is not telling God something He doesn't already know. In fact, the word *confession* means "to agree with." When we confess our sins to God, we agree that we have rebelled against His authority. We agree that we have missed the mark or standard set for our lives. We agree that something twisted in us needs straightening out. Guilt is dispelled only when the truth is told. Only when confession is made will guilt melt like a block of ice.

When we confess our guilt to the Lord, He promises to:

- Forgive it (v. 1). He takes it away, like a burden lifted.
- Cover it (v. 1). He hides it from His sight.
- Not count it (v. 2). He does clear our record. The debt is paid or cancelled.

4. Forget your guilt (vv. 1, 5).

God forgets our confessed sin, and so should we. God doesn't just put a record of our past mistakes in a closest, He obliterates them. They are gone forever. It's the same as when we are working on a computer and we don't save our work. If we try to find it after we've restarted the computer, it can't be found. There isn't a way of getting it back. It's gone.

That's exactly what God did for David. When David confessed his sin to God, suddenly his sin and guilt were gone forever. And that's exactly how it is for us. When we confess our sin God erases the sin and the guilt. We need to forget it and get on with life. God doesn't remember any confessed sin, so why should we?

Conclusion

If we ever feel spiritually paralyzed and feel like David when guilt is overwhelming us, we must remember that there is no need to ask for repeated forgiveness. It is given the first time we ask. Every time we cry anew for release from guilt, we are denying the effectiveness of Christ's death and the freedom that comes from forgiveness.

Date: July 31

Suggested Title: Forgiveness and Freedom

Scripture: Psalm 51:1–19

Contributor: Rick Ezell

Sermon Starter

Introduction

Robert Garth, a fifteen-year-old boy from a very poor family, robbed and killed a man. For fifteen years he lived with that guilt, doing everything possible to escape the pain. At age thirty, he turned himself into the police, was eventually sentenced, and sent to prison. He later wrote: "My time in prison was easy compared to the fifteen years I lived with my crime in my mind. My incarceration in the mind of my guilt was the worst thing I have ever known in my life. Nothing they could ever do to me by incarcerating me for the rest of my life even, could measure up to the awful sense of being in the prison of my own guilt through the fifteen years that I hid my sin."[1]

King David went through a situation with guilt as well. During a midlife crisis, he saw Bathsheba, a very beautiful woman, bathing herself in the twilight. He was aroused. He summoned her to the palace. When she became pregnant he sought to cover up his sin. Eventually he had her husband killed, and she moved into the palace. Then the prophet Nathan confronted David with his crime. At last, the crime David had hidden was public. Now, he was forced to deal with it. Psalm 51 reveals how David dealt with his sin, freeing him from guilt.

1. Acknowledge your sin (vv. 3–4).

David accepted full responsibility for his sin. He never tried to push it off on anyone else. Notice how often he uttered the personal pronouns *me*, *my*, and *I*. He didn't blame heredity, society, or his fallen nature.

He just looked himself in the mirror and said, "I'm the one. It's my responsibility."

2. Admit the sinfulness of sin (vv. 1–2, 4).

David didn't soft-pedal with his sin. He used four different words to describe what he had done.

> a. *Transgressions* means a revolt against the law (v. 1).
> b. *Iniquity* reveals the perverseness of man's nature (v. 2).
> c. *Sin* describes missing the mark (v. 2).
> d. *Evil* is vile things that deserve condemnation (v. 4).

3. Address confession to God (v. 4).

David realized that what he had done was fundamentally a violation of God's holy standard. Ultimately his sin was an insult and an injury to God, the God who had blessed him. He confessed his sin to God, the only Being who can forgive sin. Breaking free from guilt requires confessing our sin.

4. Receive the answer to guilt (vv. 7–12).

David asked God for grace as an answer to his guilt.

- Remove the sin (vv. 2, 7, 9)
- Restore the joy (vv. 8, 12)
- Renew the fellowship (v. 11)
- Refocus on the future (v. 12)

Conclusion

Once we turn from our sin, we are in a position to receive God's forgiveness. Living free of guilt may be difficult for some people—not because Christ won't forgive us or because others won't forgive us, but because we won't forgive ourselves. David's story reminds us that a voice within wants to replay the past to remind us of our hurt, our failures, our pain. But we must listen to a stronger voice—the voice of God—that says: you are forgiven; now live free of guilt.

Note

1. Lynnell Mickelsen, "Robert's Deadly Secret," HIS (April/May 1986): 24–27, cited in David Jeremiah, *Slaying the Giants in Your Life* (Nashville: Thomas Nelson, 2009), n2.

AUGUST

Growing in Christ

Date: August 7

Suggested Title: God's Hand and the Word of God

Scripture: Ezra 7

Contributor: Larry Steven McDonald

Full Sermon Outline

Introduction

Living in a world that elevates tolerance as the ultimate aspiration, many find themselves living in the "muddy middle," trying to accept and affirm all views as legitimate. The consequence of such living is that with tolerance as our primary commitment, we become intolerant of anyone who is not tolerant. Clear thinking sees the contradictory nature of this way of life.[1] Instead of seeking the way of tolerance, our culture desperately needs individuals who are committed to seeking the truth. In the Bible, Ezra was such a man. His ancient and time-proven example is one worthy of our following. Let's consider the context of Ezra's life before looking at the hand of God upon his life.

Following the desolation of Jerusalem and Solomon's temple by the Babylonians, the rebuilding of the temple had been completed with the return of Zerubbabel and fifty thousand of his countrymen (Ezra 1–6). Between chapters 6 and 7 of Ezra, there was a gap of about six decades in which the events of the book of Esther took place. After this, Ezra returned to Jerusalem with about two thousand priests and Levites to rebuild the spiritual and moral lives of the people (Ezra 7–10). Ezra was described as a teacher of the law of Moses who had the "gracious hand of God" upon his life (Ezra 7:6, 9, 28; 8:18, 22, 31; Neh. 2:8, 18). What a striking declaration of God's favor upon a man!

Ezra's Commitment

Why was God's hand upon Ezra in this way? The answer is found in the commitment Ezra had made in his life (v. 10). Ezra was devoted to the study, observance, and teaching of God's Word. The word *devotion* meant "to be firm, to be established, to be fixed." Ezra was not a man who wandered aimlessly. He had firmly established in his heart the direction of his life. Stephen Covey in *Seven Habits of Highly Effective People* stated it this way: "Begin with the end in mind."[2] God's hand was upon Ezra because Ezra had made a commitment to be a man of God, and this commitment centered upon God's Word. Ezra's focus was threefold:

1. Study God's Word.

First, Ezra was devoted to the study of God's Word (v. 10). The word *study* has shades of meanings such as "consult, inquire, investigate, search, and seek." In other Near Eastern languages, the word for study was also used to indicate the treading of wheat, providing us with a graphic picture of its figurative use of reading and reviewing a topic repeatedly. For Ezra, studying the Bible was far more than just a casual reading of it. He knew human wisdom was finite and that he needed a perpetual and indestructible foundation upon which to base his life. Ezra sought to build the Word of God into the very core of his being so that his lifestyle and decision making would be founded upon God's eternal principles.

2. Obey God's Word.

Second, Ezra was devoted to obeying the Word of God (v. 10). In his life, the study of the Bible was not a dry, academic pursuit that had no effect upon his personal life. Ezra allowed his biblical study to move out of the intellectual realm so that it affected every area of his life. His study of Scripture was with a heart toward obedience. If God said it, Ezra was committed to obeying it.

Speaking through James, the half-brother of Jesus, God tells us that when we study the Bible without obeying it, we deceive ourselves. We become hearers of the Word and not doers (James 1:22–25).

3. Teach God's Word.

Third, Ezra was devoted to teaching the Word of God (v. 10). Different Hebrew words are used in the Old Testament that have been translated *teach*. This particular one carried with it the aspect of training as well as educating. Ezra was not satisfied to merely give out Bible knowledge to his listeners. He wanted his students to grasp both biblical content and its application to life. He wanted them to be trained in the godly living that comes from applying biblical principles to daily life. As we have already seen, Ezra knew that in order for this to happen in the lives of his listeners, it had to be taking place in his own life as well.

Teaching only comes as a natural result of studying and obeying. It is only when an individual has a good foundation in studying, understanding, and living out God's Word that he should go on to teach. As God also reminds us through James, teachers will incur a stricter judgment (James 3:1).

Conclusion

The beloved Dr. Howard Hendricks, who was on the faculty of Dallas Theological Seminary for sixty years, told of a professor who made an impact in his life. He passed this professor's home many times, early in the morning and late at night, and often saw him poring over his books. One day, Hendricks asked him, "Doctor, I'd like to know what it is that keeps you studying? You never cease to learn." His answer: "Son, I would rather have my students drink from a running stream than from a stagnant pool."[3] If we do not learn the lessons taught and lived out by Ezra, we will be a stagnant pool that pollutes and poisons. But if we follow Ezra's example of drinking deeply from the well of the Bible, we will be a running stream from which others can drink, live, and flourish in their spiritual lives.

Notes

1. For more reading on this subject see D.A. Carson, *The Intolerance of Tolerance* (Grand Rapids: Eerdmans, 2012).

2. Stephen Covey, *Seven Habits of Highly Effective People: Powerful Lessons in Personal Change*, 25th anniversary ed. (New York: Simon & Schuster, 2013), 102.

3. Howard Hendricks, *Teaching to Change Lives: Seven Proven Ways to Make Your Teaching Come Alive*, repr. ed. (Colorado Springs: Multnomah, 2003), 18.

Date: August 7

Suggested Title: The Word of God

Scripture: 1 Peter 1:23–2:3

Contributor: Larry Steven McDonald

Sermon Starter

Introduction

John Bunyan, author of the classic *The Pilgrim's Progress*, wrote in the cover of his Bible, "Either this book will keep you from sin, or sin will keep you from this book." Bunyan understood what many in the war against sin don't—the Word of God is *the* weapon you simply cannot neglect.[1] One of the key ways to "be strong in the Lord and in the strength of his might" is by "the sword of the Spirit, which is the word of God" (Eph. 6:10, 17 ESV). The Bible is central and foundational in a person's spiritual growth, beginning with salvation and continuing in sanctification. First Peter was written to encourage believers with hope as they go through persecution, a time when strength is needed most.

The Word of God in Salvation (vv. 1:23–25)

Reminiscent of Jesus' conversation with Nicodemus (John 3), Peter speaks of being born again. This new birth takes place from an imperishable seed, which is the Word of God. Paul indicates that "faith comes from hearing, and hearing through the word of Christ" (Rom. 10:17 ESV). The Word of God is intricately linked to salvation as it is the means of how God's Spirit works in drawing a person to Christ for salvation. In this context Peter describes the Bible as:

- Living—v. 23 (see also Heb. 4:12)
- Eternal—vv. 24–25 (see also Isa. 40:6–8)
- Good News—v. 25

The Word of God in Sanctification (vv. 2:1–3)

Salvation brings about a change in a person's life. Paul describes this transformation by stating, "If anyone is in Christ, he is a new creation" (2 Cor. 5:17). What begins initially in salvation continues in sanctification, i.e., our growth in Christ. This growth is a natural part of one's life as a Christian and is not optional. Christ sets us apart to Himself and for His service. For this progressive sanctification the Bible instructs us to:

- Put away sin—v. 1
- Long for God's Word—v. 2
- Grow up in our Christian life—v. 2
- Taste and see that the Lord is good—vs 2:3 (see also Ps. 34:8)

Conclusion

Vance Havner, a twentieth-century revivalist, stated, "If you see a Bible that is falling apart, it probably belongs to someone who isn't."[2] Christians do encounter challenges in life, but the Bible gives us a sure message to sustain us with God's grace, peace, and strength through these valleys. The message of the Bible nourishes our hearts and minds for our growth in Christ.

Notes

1. John F. MacArthur Jr., "How to Slay Sin—Part 3," Grace to You, http://www.gty.org/blog/B110224/how-to-slay-sin-part-3, accessed 3/12/15.
2. Vance Havner, "Bible Scholar Quotes," http://www.verseclub .org/bible-scholar-quotes.html, accessed 3/12/15. For more information on Vance Havner, see http://www.vancehavner .com/.

Date: August 14

Suggested Title: Prayer of Repentance

Scripture: Jonah 2:1–10 ESV

Contributor: Larry Steven McDonald

Full Sermon Outline

Introduction

Many people today claim to be Christians but dishonor the name of Christ. When this takes place, God deals with us. He will not let us continue in rebellion as His children, for He wants us to share in His righteousness and holiness (Heb. 12:7–11).

Jonah was a prophet of God, and he carried all the rights and responsibilities that went with that position. God gave him the task of proclaiming God's message to the people of Nineveh, yet Jonah ran in the opposite direction. Jonah brought dishonor to his office, and God dealt with him. Not many things would inspire humility more than being in the belly of a fish. God will get our attention, but He will also give us a second chance just as He did with Jonah. Jonah is the story of a reluctant prophet and the God of second chances.

Throughout the Bible we see famous and well-known prayers, such as the Lord's Prayer (Matt. 6:9–13), Solomon's prayer dedicating the temple (2 Chron. 6:12–42), as well as Jesus' high priestly prayer (John 17). In Jonah 2 we see that Jonah prays and God responds. This prayer is often overlooked but it has very descriptive elements of prayer and repentance. As we look at it, there are four things we can clearly learn through Jonah's prayer from the fish's belly.

1. Prayer must be an honest cry for God's help (vv. 1–2).

Encased within the fish's belly, Jonah finds himself in a most foul and disgusting environment. God now has Jonah's attention, and Jonah begins to pray, saying, "I called out to the LORD, out of my distress, and he answered me; out of the belly of Sheol I cried, and you heard my voice" (v. 2). In agony, Jonah feels that he is at the point of death and that death surrounds him. His prayer is not a casual one but one that erupts from the core of Jonah's being. There is no room now for pretense or pretending; Jonah gets honest with God as he cries out in anguish and desperation. And Jonah tells us that the result is that God heard him.

If Jonah can pray from the belly of a fish, then regardless of our circumstances, whether self-inflicted or unforeseen, we too can pray. Wherever we are, in whatever difficult, challenging, or even tragic circumstances, we can pray. And God is there to help us.

In times of failure, we might be tempted to reason away or rationalize our wrong actions. Or often we take the tact of thinking, *I want to get my act together, and then I will pray to God.* Jonah tells us it does not work that way! We need to honestly pray to God during our affliction because only God can cleanse and save us. We must admit our failure to God and our helplessness to save ourselves, throwing ourselves completely upon His mercy, and admitting our dependence upon His deliverance.

This is a crucial beginning point for prayer: "God, I need you. I need your help. I cannot do it by myself." Because of our human pride, even as Christians, this can be a very difficult admission to make. But all of us will face something in our lifetimes that even in our God-given abilities, we cannot handle. Whether brought about by our own failures or by the hardships of this life, in such times we must humbly and honestly ask God for help.

2. Prayer must include acceptance of God's discipline and the believer's repentance (vv. 3–4).

The first chapter of Jonah shows the prophet in rebellion and God's severe response: Jonah is on a ship; a mighty storm comes up; Jonah is thrown overboard by his shipmates; the storm immediately stops. Then a fish swallows Jonah, and Jonah is at death's door. Jonah views all of these events as coming directly from the hand of God. God wanted to get Jonah's attention, and He knew how to get it.

Jonah accepted God's discipline by repenting. He declared, "I am driven away from your sight; yet I shall again look upon your holy temple" (v. 4). Jonah strayed from the presence of the Lord. He was not just running away from circumstances; he was running away from God. God wanted Jonah to look to His Holy Temple. The Holy Temple represented the very presence and being of God. When Jonah looked to the Holy Temple, he displayed repentance. Jonah stopped running and began seeking God's presence.

Because of His deep love for us, God will be as gentle as He can be but as tough as He needs to be in order to reprove and correct us. As dangerous and intolerable as being lost at sea or being swallowed by a fish was, it would have been far worse for Jonah to continue his life in rebellion to His God. Some of us are stubborn, prideful, and arrogant. Obviously it would be better to have a soft heart that is sensitive to God's reproof and easily repents instead of a hard heart that requires stronger correction. God does not correct us out of His wrath but out of His love; being disciplined by the hand of God is a clear indication that we are His children. Because not one of us is perfect, repentance should be a part of every Christian's daily life. When we falter, let us resist the urge to cover up our wrong. Let us instead quickly respond in repentance to God's reproof and correction so that He can cleanse us.

3. Prayer must be characterized by trust and thanksgiving (vv. 5–7, 9).

Jonah's prayer is that with thanksgiving, we must trust God's promise. Dark circumstances are completely closing in on Jonah. There appears to be no way out. Death's door looks imminent. Then he remembers the Lord, and he chooses to believe the promise that God would never leave or desert him. By so doing, Jonah comes into the presence of God. Basking in God's presence, despite his circumstances, Jonah could not help but to raise his voice in thanksgiving to God. Jonah indicates,

"When my life was fainting away, I remembered the LORD ... But I with the voice of thanksgiving will sacrifice to you" (vv. 7, 9).

When encountering hardship, too many Christians choose an attitude of questioning or blaming God: "God, why did You do this? I was just bopping along in life being Your follower, then this." At other times, Christians focus in despair upon their own failures. But Jonah responded differently. He remembered the Lord. He trusted with thanksgiving in God's promise to always be there.

4. Prayer must be from a heart that is sacrificially yielded to God's will (vv. 8–9).

Jonah sacrificially yielded to God's will. In verse 9, he states, "I will sacrifice to you." In coming back to the Lord, Jonah had to be willing to follow God's will and plan for his life. Jonah had to say, "Okay, God, I am willing to sacrificially follow wherever You will lead."

Too many Christians have the attitude, "I will follow God as long as it is easy, convenient, and comfortable." Yet Christ taught us to expect anything but comfort and ease. Jesus' own life on this earth painted a far different picture. He was misunderstood and opposed by the religious people of His day. He was despised and rejected. Christ suffered and died on the cross for us. If we will follow Christ and His example, it will include sacrifice. "Where He leads I will follow," are the words of a song that we sing wholeheartedly. We must also be ready to practice these words with the same zeal in our lives.

Conclusion

When God got Jonah's attention, Jonah prayed and responded to God honestly, at gut level. God responded to Jonah by speaking to the fish, and "it vomited Jonah out upon the dry land" (v. 10). God gave Jonah a second chance.

Whatever your background or whatever has happened to you in your life, if you choose to cling to rebellion against God or to the attitude that God will never use you, then that will be true. Yet none has done anything so horrible that God will not give a second chance. If we respond to Him in honesty and repentance, He will cleanse and restore us. There are some who believe that God cannot help or use you. Such lies are spoken to you only by the deceiver and not from your God. If you will run to God, He will receive and help you, and He will use you to accomplish His will. All of us are in desperate need of God's loving and merciful touch in our lives. Like Jonah, we can repent and trust God and see our cries of despair and desperation turned to shouts of joy and thanksgiving!

Date: August 14

Suggested Title: Prayer Deserves Priority

Scripture: 1 Kings 8:22–43

Contributor: Larry Steven McDonald

Sermon Starter

Introduction

Pollsters tell us that most Americans indicate they pray every day.[1] Yet the reality is that many do not. Quite often people attempt any and all other options to address needs or concerns, and then only pray as a last resort. Even those who do pray would admit their need to strengthen the quality of their praying—that is, the attitude with which they pray or the depth of their confessions to God. Prayer is a gift from God that He uses to build godly character in us and to deepen our relationship with Him. He desires that we make earnest, humble praying a daily discipline.

How can we strengthen our discipline of daily prayer? One of the most famous prayers in the Bible is Solomon's dedication prayer of the temple. His prayer provides wisdom for us. As we examine Solomon's prayer, we see four reasons that prayer deserves priority.

1. God is faithful (vv. 22–24).

First, prayer should be a priority because God is faithful; we can count on Him. The promise to build the temple was given to David, yet was fulfilled in his son Solomon. As Solomon voiced his prayer before God and the gathered assembly, he spoke of the faithfulness of God to keep His promises. As we consider the Lord's faithfulness, we have good reason to pray.

2. God listens (vv. 27–28).

Second, prayer deserves priority because God listens. Solomon entreats the Lord to listen to his prayer concerning the temple. Many feel that "God won't listen to me; I haven't exactly been a saint." Others might think that because God is infinite He is not concerned about their personal situations. Yet we are invited to come before the throne of grace in our time of need through Jesus Christ, submitting to Him as our perfect High Priest (Heb. 4:16). We can come confidently to the Lord knowing that He hears us.

3. God responds (vv. 38–39).

The third reason prayer deserves priority is because God responds. Solomon asked the Lord to respond graciously when His people turned to Him in prayerful confession and repentance. And God promised Solomon that He would listen and act upon the humble, repentant person's prayers (2 Chron. 7:14). We can pray to the Lord about anything that afflicts or concerns us because He responds by forgiving and acting to help us.

4. Everyone can pray (v. 43).

Finally, prayer deserves priority because everyone can pray. Solomon knew that God's promise to Abraham (Gen. 12:3) concerned all the earth's people. Therefore, he appealed for the Lord also to hear the prayers of the non-Israelites who called upon His name. The Lord desires everyone to know Him and live in right relationship with Him through Jesus' work on the cross (2 Pet. 3:9). When we do this, we also will find as Solomon did that prayer deserves priority!

Note

1. See Michael Lipka, "Five Facts on Prayer," at Pew Research Center, http://www.pewresearch.org/fact-tank/2014/05/01/5-facts-about-prayer/.

Date: August 21

Suggested Title: The Spiritual Discipline of Fellowship

Scripture: Hebrews 10:23–25; 1 John 1:3, 4; 1 Timothy 4:8
NASB

Contributor: Marcus A. Buckley

Full Sermon Outline

Introduction

When the word *fellowship* is used in a church setting, visions of pot-luck suppers and small group gatherings often come to mind. While good food and good times are certainly a component of biblical fellowship, God's view of fellowship is something far richer than a surface-deep social gathering. In his book *Life Together*, Dietrich Bonhoeffer wrote extensively about the imperative for biblical fellowship amongst believers. He noted that "the physical presence of other Christians is a source of incomparable joy and strength to the believer ... what inexhaustible riches must invariably open up for those who by God's will are privileged to live in daily community life with other Christians!"[1] Christian philosopher Dallas Willard classified fellowship as a "Discipline of Engagement."[2] This engagement is intentional, focused interaction with other believers for the purpose of edification and equipping. Such engagement is made possible by the empowering connection each believer has through and because of Christ. If we understand that the Bible teaches that disciplined fellowship among believers is critical to our health as faithful disciples of Christ, then what does the infrastructure needed for success look like?

Disciplined Fellowship Stirs Up

Derived benefits generally come as a result of focus and discipline. For example, if one wishes to improve physical health, there must be active engagement in a process that is going to provide the motivation, accountability, and hope of reaching a set goal. This is most often successful when the people have someone motivating them, such as a trainer or another individual who makes a similar commitment to improve and grow. When it becomes hard to do what is necessary, a trainer or fellow trainee can step in and provide the appropriate resource. The process of an exercise regimen is almost certainly doomed to fail if there is no end result in mind, so having a goal and the means to reach it is critical to overall success.

The writer of Hebrews declared that believers should "hold fast the confession of our hope without wavering, for He who promised is faithful; and let us consider how to stimulate one another to love and good deeds" (Heb. 10:23–24). The inspired author gave the assurance that, because of the unwavering faithfulness of God, the believer can know with absolute certainty that the salvation received through Christ's substitutionary atonement at the cross is enduring. One of the results of this individual assurance is the empowerment to incite one another to labor worthy of our Master and His calling upon our lives. The Greek word the author used is a term from which we derive our modern *paroxysm*, which connotes a recurring eruption or flare-up. Willard wrote that "personalities united can contain more of God and sustain the force of His greater presence much better than scattered individuals. The fire of God kindles higher as the brands are heaped together and each is warmed by the other's flame."[3] Each believer must spur on other believers through fellowship in the process of becoming more like Christ.

Disciplined Discipleship Supports

The writer of Hebrews continued his thought with the admonition to draw close within the fellowship framework, "not forsaking our own assembling together, as is the habit of some, but encouraging *one another*" (Heb. 10:25). The encouragement one believer derives from another when in the parameters of this intentional, disciplined fellowship brings a comfort that nothing else can replace. The Greek word here is derived from the same root as the term Jesus used to describe the role of the Holy Spirit as a helper (John 14:16). It is far too easy for believers to begin condemning one another, and many churches have closed their doors over just such behavior.

While serious doctrinal matters certainly demand steadfastness, many quarrels stem from such topics as methods, personality clashes, and even who is most important in the church. Jockeying for position has no place in the body of Christ. The spiritual body must function as the physical body—for the benefit and proper function of the whole. As Willard wrote, "the unity of the body rightly functioning is thus guaranteed by the people ... There are no 'oughts' or 'shoulds' or 'won't-you-pleases' about this. It is just a matter of how things actually work in the new life."[4]

Disciplined Fellowship Sustains

The writer of Hebrews completes his thought with the clear indication that believers are not to falter as the ultimate goal of seeing Christ face-to-face and completing our journey of discipleship approaches. Rather, we are to press on "all the more as you see the day drawing near" (Heb. 10:25). The strength derived from an intentional, disciplined model of fellowship does for the spiritual body what exercise does for the physical. The model and source of this sustenance is "our fellowship ... with the Father, and with His Son Jesus Christ. These things we write, so that our joy may be made complete" (1 John 1:3–4).

Conclusion

The apostle Paul himself used physical exercise as an illustration of the need for spiritual discipline when he wrote that "for bodily discipline is only of little profit, but godliness is profitable for all things, since it holds promise for the present life and also for the life to come" (1 Tim. 4:8). The idea here is that physical discipline is helpful for a short while, but spiritual discipline reaps eternal benefits. Believers who are in the boundaries of a disciplined fellowship will find themselves strengthened, not only for the short-term, but for the long haul of life until they are brought into the presence of God.

Notes

1. Dietrich Bonhoeffer, *Life Together and Prayerbook of the Bible*, in Vol. 5 of *Dietrich Bonhoeffer Works*, ed. Geffrey B. Kelly, trans. Daniel W. Bloesch and James H. Burtness (Minneapolis: Fortress, 1996), 29.

2. Dallas Willard, *The Spirit of the Disciplines: Understanding How God Changes Lives* (New York: HarperOne, 1999), 158.

3. Ibid., 186.

4. Ibid., 187.

Date: August 21

Suggested Title: Disciplined Fellowship

Scripture: Acts 2:42–47

Contributor: Marcus A. Buckley

Sermon Starter

Introduction

God's view of fellowship is something far richer than merely a surface-deep social gathering or cursory knowledge of others within the church. John MacArthur defined fellowship as "the spiritual duty of believers to stimulate each other to holiness and faithfulness."[1] This engagement is intentional, focused interaction with other believers for the purpose of edification and equipping. Such engagement is made possible by the empowering connection each believer has through and because of Christ. If we then understand that the Bible teaches that disciplined fellowship among believers is critical to our health as faithful disciples of Christ, then what does the infrastructure needed for success look like?

1. Disciplined fellowship supports through Scripture (v. 42).

a. Through earnest study and application of the apostle's teachings, the believers established the solid foundation upon which they built their new lives as followers of Christ.

b. All of their other types of fellowship as the body of Christ—emotional fellowship (friendship and social gatherings), physical fellowship (public worship and social gatherings), and spiritual fellowship (observance of Communion and prayer)—were predicated upon the assurance of the teachings of the apostles and Scripture.

2. Disciplined fellowship humbles through holiness (v. 43).

a. The fear felt by each believer was one of holy reverence toward God and was necessary for a right walk with Him (cf. 2 Chron. 19:7; Job 28:28; Ps. 19:9; Prov. 1:7; Isa. 11:2–3; Matt. 10:28; Acts 9:31; 2 Cor. 5:11).

b. God moves through obedient people in supernatural, miraculous ways that bless both the servant and the recipient.

3. Disciplined fellowship provides through peers (vv. 44, 45).

a. Believers assumed responsibility for taking care of the needs of fellow believers.

b. "They did not at any point sell everything and pool the proceeds into a common pot. Such a principle for Christian living would have obviated the responsibility of each believer to give in response to the Spirit's prompting."[2]

c. "Between friends all is common."—Pythagoras

4. Disciplined fellowship joins through joyfulness (vv. 46, 47).

a. As they celebrated who God was and what He had done, they overflowed with rejoicing in their state of being.

b. As they lived out lives of rejoicing, they made a positive impact on those with whom they came in contact: "In Luke's writings, 'the people' (ho laos) usually refers to Israel as the elect nation to whom the message is initially directed and for whom (together with the Gentiles) it is ultimately intended."[3]

c. Such a lifestyle resulted in others coming to know Christ as Savior.

Conclusion

Believers who are in the boundaries of a disciplined fellowship will find themselves strengthened, not only for the short term, but for the long haul of life until they are brought into the presence of God.

Notes

1. John MacArthur, *The MacArthur New Testament Commentary Acts:1–12* (Chicago: Moody Publishers, 1994), 84.
2. Ibid., 88.
3. Richard N. Longenecker, *The Expositor's Bible Commentary with the New International Version* (Grand Rapids: Zondervan, 1995), 87.

Date: August 28

Suggested Title: The Spiritual Discipline of Service

Scripture: Romans 12:1–6 NASB

Contributor: Marcus A. Buckley

Full Sermon Outline

Introduction

One of the most common mistakes we make in our churches is in the area of encouraging people to serve. Unfortunately, guilt is often one of the leading methods of recruiting. Guilt can be very effective at garnering workers in the short term. As time goes by, however, those who serve simply from obligation rather than passion will eventually grow weary and simply walk away from it. If the motives of the worker are not rightly centered upon Christ, then frustration and burnout is the inevitable outcome.

1. Disciplined service shows we are reasonable (vv. 1, 2).

From an early age most children are taught to display good manners. When someone does something gracious toward another, it is only reasonable that appreciation should be displayed. It is also reasonable to expect that one should reciprocate the act of kindness when the opportunity arises. Such acts of gratitude would rightly be understood as reasonable given the circumstances. Is it not therefore reasonable that we as recipients of the gift of salvation through Christ Jesus should look for opportunities to repay His kindness with our own obedience?

The apostle Paul called upon all believers to "present your bodies a living and holy sacrifice" (v. 1). This is a clear call to surrender all we have and all we are to the glory of the Father. Paul had highlighted the freedom from the bondage of sin believers enjoy earlier in this letter (6:11–14) and encourages them to do the "reasonable" (Gk. *logikos*) thing, which is total surrender of self to God. Some translations render the word translated "logical" or "reasonable" as "spiritual," but both of these are correct in expressing the greater truth Paul intended when the word translated "service" (Gk. *latreia*) is understood correctly. Kenneth Wuest wrote that this particular word "was used here to speak of the believer-priest's sacred service, not as the Levitical priests, offering a burnt sacrifice that was apart from themselves, but a living sacrifice that was not only part of themselves but also entailed the giving of themselves in connection with the giving of their bodies to the service of God."[1] The believer is then strengthened for further obedience by the transformative power of God's renewal of the believer's mind. This "renewing" (Gk. *anakainosis*) occurs "through the ministry of the indwelling Holy Spirit, who when definitely, and intelligently, and habitually yielded to puts sin out of the believer's life and produces His own fruit."[2]

2. Disciplined service shows we are humble (v. 3).

The Bible warns again and again of the dangers of pride, and Paul provided the safeguard here when he wrote that each believer was "not to think more highly of himself than he ought to think; but to think so as to have sound judgment, as God has allotted to each a measure of faith" (v. 3). Paul warned that the believer should not direct too much affection toward his own works and abilities (Gk. *huperphroneo*), but should rather be disposed toward thinking in a moderate way (Gk. *suphroneo*) resulting from the knowledge that everything he has is a gift from God (James 1:17). Such thinking prevents our own arrogance and leads to the "reasonable service" to the One who provided the gifts and abilities in the first place. As Paul wrote in his first letter to the church at Corinth, "as it is written, 'Let him who boasts, boast in the Lord'" (1 Cor. 1:31).

3. Disciplined service shows we are useful (vv. 4–6).

The human body is a magnificent thing, with many various parts working together as one for a purpose greater than any of the singular components. Paul uses this as an analogy of how the church, the body of Christ, is meant to operate. Believers of various backgrounds and abilities are meant to work together for the purpose of impacting the world with the gospel. Just as "all the members do not have the same function" (v. 4), so each believer has different gifts and is "to exercise them accordingly ... according to the proportion of his faith" (v. 6). God in His sovereignty has seen fit to equip each believer with skills and abilities that are to be used to fulfill the work of the kingdom. One believer's gifts are not more important than another's within the context of the body.

It is an unfortunate thing when a physical body has elements that do not function as they should. Something as relatively common as one's foot going to sleep can complicate the function of the body as a whole. The foot may at first seem more important than the eye when walking, but without the eye the foot does not know where to go. The hands are needed for picking up objects, but without the eyes the hands cannot see what to grasp, and without the feet neither eyes nor hands can approach the object. Working as a system they function properly and for the benefit of all. So it is with believers working together in service for their King. Paul reminded believers that we do not serve for ourselves, but rather "whatever you do in word or deed, do all in the name of the Lord Jesus, giving thanks through Him to God the Father" (Col. 3:17).

Conclusion

Service to the One who has paid for our sins may be logical and reasonable, but it still requires disciplined participation on our part in order to faithfully obey. While God does not need us, He certainly wants us. His desire for us is that we would faithfully execute the tasks He has called us to and equipped us for. When we fully understand the grace that has been showered upon us, the idea of giving anything less than our very best in service to God is simply not "reasonable."

Notes

1. Kenneth S. Wuest, *Wuest's Word Studies From the Greek New Testament* (Grand Rapids: Eerdmans, 1974), 206.
2. Ibid., 208.

Date: August 28

Suggested Title: Disciplined Service

Scripture: Isaiah 6:1–8

Contributor: Marcus A. Buckley

Sermon Starter

Introduction

Doing the right thing is not always easy. For many the thought of challenge or conflict is discomforting, so the path of least resistance is enticing in its level of perceived comfort. Doing what is right, as with achieving any goal, requires disciplined effort. If a person is going to participate in a 5K run (or a marathon for those overachievers out there), it isn't possible to go from zero activity to peak-level performance overnight. There are many programs designed to help people prepare for such an endeavor, but the program is useless if the individuals do not have the discipline to follow through. No one else can do it for them. They must go through the process that prepares them for the race. When they do, they will have what is necessary to perform and achieve.

1. Prepare through reverence (vv. 1–4).

    a. In a time of stress and concern (impending judgment), Isaiah is reminded of the absolute sovereignty of God.

    b. In verse 1, Isaiah uses the Hebrew *Adonai* (Lord) instead of *Jehovah* (YHWH) as in verses 3 and 5 to emphasize God's holiness.

    c. God is worthy of worship regardless of our circumstances because He is above all of them.

2. Prepare through remorse (vv. 5–7).

a. In the presence of the Holy God, Isaiah became painfully aware of his own sinfulness (v. 5).

b. "[Isaiah] was to produce the conviction of sin before God in the corrupt minds and hearts of the people ... therefore it was necessary for him to have his own soul filled with the infinite glory and holiness of God, and filled with a very humbling sense of sin ... for how can a man seem pure before His maker?"[1]

c. Isaiah also indicates that perhaps he was negatively impacted by his culture. One commentary states: "Men catch up the phraseology of their time, and use wrong forms of speech, because they hear them daily. 'Evil communications corrupt good manners' (1 Cor. 15:33 KJV)."[2]

d. God made provision for Isaiah through a means even angels could not treat carelessly (v. 6).

e. The burning coal (signifying the purifying work of God) touched the source of Isaiah's concern—his lips (v. 7).

f. Unlike physical training, it is the holiness of God that transforms us, not our own efforts.

3. Prepare through readiness (v. 8).

a. Having worshipped God and been reminded of His transforming power, Isaiah was ready to serve.

b. Isaiah was not ready to go until this point, even had he been willing.

c. Having been made ready, Isaiah is now not only able to perform the task; he is eager to do so.

Conclusion

God has a work for all believers, whether it is public or more of a behind-the-scenes task. Regardless of the specifics, the understanding that we are called and empowered by the sovereign Lord of all creation provides the impetus for disciplined preparation that enables us to faithfully serve Him.

Notes

1. *The Pulpit Commentary*, H. D. M. Spence and Joseph S. Exell, eds. (Grand Rapids: Eerdmans, 1977), 121.
2. Ibid., 108.

SEPTEMBER

The Community of the Committed

Date: September 4

Suggested Title: I Will Build My Church

Scripture: 1 Corinthians 3:5–11; Matthew 16:13–20

Contributor: Ken Hemphill

Full Sermon Outline

Introduction

Almost every child dreams of being a superhero and saving the planet, but we grow up and realize that such grandiose ideas were just childish dreams. However, our calling as Christians puts such dreams to shame. We are a royal priesthood intended and empowered to advance God's kingdom on earth until He returns. We don't often think of the church as a gathering of "kingdom agents," whose roles and ministries have a greater eternal impact than any earthly profession.

In this passage from the Gospel of Matthew, the speculation about the identity of Jesus has been escalating. Ordinary people are shouting out titles that indicate they are coming to believe that Jesus is the long-awaited Messiah. The Pharisees and Sadducees "test" Jesus, hoping to discredit Him. They request another sign from heaven to prove that He is the Messiah. He refuses to play to the crowd and tells them that the only sign they will be given is the sign of Jonah, likely a reference to His approaching crucifixion and resurrection (vv. 1–4).

This discussion provides the background for a private conversation with His disciples. Jesus first asks, "Who do men say that I, the Son of Man, am?" and the answers are varied, most believing Him to be a prophet. But Jesus is interested in knowing what the disciples believe. Peter, the spokesman for the twelve, dares to articulate the conviction— "You are the Christ, the Son of the living God." After affirming this radical declaration, Jesus announces His plan to build His church. Don't miss the significance! We cannot declare that Jesus is our King and not love His church. The church is to express His fullness (cf. Eph. 1:23) and complete His kingdom work on earth.

Jesus came to establish it, He died to redeem it, He sent His Holy Spirit to empower it, and He will come again to take His royal bride to Himself. Let's take a quick look at His description of His church.

1. Its singular foundation—"on this rock" (vv. 18–19)

All construction begins with the foundation. It determines the size and function of the building. What or who is the foundation upon which Christ is planning to build this church? Paul may have been commenting on the truth articulated in Matthew 16:18 when he wrote to the Corinthians about the relative work of himself and Apollos in the life of the church in Corinth (1 Cor. 3:5–11). He declares, "For no other foundation can anyone lay than that which is laid, which is Jesus Christ" (v. 11).

Peter is not the foundation, but Peter's confession that Jesus is God's Messiah is the foundational truth for our identity and our ministry. The church is not simply another religious organization; it is the body of Christ empowered to continue and complete His earthly ministry. Nothing is small about the church and nothing insignificant about its mission! If God laid His Son in the ditch as foundational, what must He desire to build upon that foundation?

Before we leave the passage in 1 Corinthians 3, we should note that Paul expands the imagery and issues a word of warning about the material we use to build upon the foundation God laid (v. 12). Building is not an option for the follower of Christ. The only question that remains is the quality of material we choose to use. Wood, hay, and stubble have no value and no permanence. When tested by fire, they will be "burned up." The gold, silver, and precious stones not only survive the testing of fire; they are purified by the fire. Has anyone ever told you that all your service for the King through His church will be tested so that you can be rewarded for your work (v. 14)? Paul is not talking about someone earning or losing their salvation (v. 15), but about wasting a lifetime of opportunity to lay up treasure in heaven. God has created you to have an eternal impact through His church!

2. Its supernatural empowering—"I will build"

What are you presently doing for the King through His church that requires supernatural empowering? Many Christians live in the safety zone of what they are comfortable doing. Stop! Stop now! The Holy Spirit has gifted and empowered you to participate in the supernatural invasion of the planet. In Ephesians 1:19–20 Paul prayed that believers would know the full empowering available to them, which is based on the very power that raised Jesus from the dead.

Have you been reluctant to serve in the church because you think you have nothing of value to offer? Are you sometimes guilty of serving based on your natural ability rather than on supernatural empowering?

3. Its intimate identification—"My church"

The word translated *church* is *ecclesia*. When the Old Testament was translated from Hebrew to Greek, this was the word used to speak of the "congregation" of Israel. The disciples would have understood the significance of this word. Jesus is building a new "called-out community." It is not a community made up of Jews alone, but one made up of Jew and Gentile, a community of male and female, all related to Him by the new birth. The intimacy is in the pronoun "My." We are His! We are redeemed by Him and commissioned and empowered for royal service. The church belongs to Him, and He alone can determine its mission and provide it with power.

4. Its royal responsibility—"keys of the kingdom"

Keys represent honor, authority, and responsibility. But the primary purpose of keys is to provide or prevent access. What, you may ask, are the keys of the kingdom? It is the good news that the King shed His royal authority, came to earth, took upon Himself human flesh, and died on a cross that we might become His children.

There is no message more critical and no responsibility more awesome than using the keys to open the kingdom to others. Don't be guilty of coming to church and singing about and celebrating the keys only to neglect using them to set free your family member, friend, or neighbor from the bondage of sin.

5. The King's promise—"the gates of Hades"

The "gates of Hades (or hell)" is another way of referring to death. The image here is of the church plucking lost humanity from the grasp of hell itself. There is nothing that can stop the advance of God's kingdom through the ministry of His church.

Conclusion

What we do through His church has an eternal impact. The church's mission is such that we cannot play our church games. Too much is at stake for us not to be all that God has called and empowered us to be!

Date: September 4

Suggested Title: Kingdom Accountability

Scripture: 1 Corinthians 3:10–15 NASB

Contributor: Ken Hemphill

Sermon Starter

Introduction

Students often say that school would be great if they didn't have to take tests. We don't like tests, but they seem inevitable in school and in life. Testing is really about accountability. They answer the questions, "Did you prepare and do you understand the material?" In truth the whole issue of accountability means that our work matters. God holds us accountable for the use of our gifts and abilities because we matter. Our life has purpose.

Some persons in the Corinthian church were picking sides when it came to various leaders such as Paul or Apollos. This had caused divisions in the church and had hampered its ministry (1 Cor. 1:10–17). Paul indicates that he and Apollos were merely servants through whom they had believed (1 Cor. 3:5). God had given the opportunity and empowered them for ministry and thus deserved the credit for the growth of the church. Paul seizes the moment to talk about the role of every believer in the building of the church.

1. Building is not an option (v. 10).

"Each man must be careful how he builds" includes everyone. The follower of Christ does not have the luxury of choosing whether or not they participate in the advance of the kingdom through the church. This is nonnegotiable, and therefore everyone must be careful to build with quality.

2. You do choose the materials (v. 12).

You do have a choice concerning the material you use, and that choice will both impact your life and your eternity. The contrast between "gold, silver, precious stones" and "wood, hay, straw" could not be any more graphic. The issue is quality, value, and permanency. The quality of building materials must match the foundation, which is Jesus Christ (v. 11). By the way, notice that it is the King who will supply the materials for building. Do you prioritize your service to the King through His church?

3. The day will reveal all (v. 13).

"The day" refers to the coming of the Lord: the Day of Judgment. The Bible teaches that on that day the quality of our work for the Lord will be made apparent to all—"it is to be revealed with fire." Fire will either purify as it does with metal or it can burn away the chaff. This passage does not suggest that one can earn or lose salvation by works (cf. 15). It does indicate that we can waste a life created by the King with great potential.

4. The day of reward comes (v. 14).

Don't miss this! We will receive a reward for the work that remains. Imagine what it will be like to hear the King declare—"Well done, good and faithful servant."

Conclusion

This section teaches several important truths.

- There is no insignificant member in the body of Christ.
- Everything we are and everything we have is infused with kingdom potential.
- We are responsible only for what we have been given.
- The fear of failure is the tool of the adversary.
- God loves and values us so much He holds us accountable.

Date: September 11

Suggested Title: The Gifted Community Working Together

Scripture: Ephesians 4:1–16 NASB

Contributor: Ken Hemphill

Full Sermon Outline

Introduction

Rowing is one of the most grueling sports for participants, yet when everyone is rowing in sync, rowing seems almost effortless, and the boat seems to glide across the water. Wouldn't it be wonderful if the church functioned like a well-conditioned team? Our work would seem effortless, and yet the church would continually accelerate in its goal to complete the Great Commission.

Throughout the Ephesian letter, Paul focuses on the incredible potential of the church to express God's "fullness" in the world. In Ephesians 1:19–23 Paul declares that God has made available to the church the power that raised Jesus from the dead so that the church, His earthly body, would express His fullness. In Ephesians 3:10–11 he tells us that it is God's eternal plan to reveal His manifold wisdom through the church and that He accomplished this by sending Christ Jesus our Lord.

Perhaps you are wondering how God can accomplish such a lofty goal through our church. The answer is that He gives the church gifted persons, who when they work together will cause the body to grow up in every aspect into Christ Jesus.

1. Unity is the foundation for kingdom service (vv. 1–6).

Paul begins with a plea for believers to live worthy of their calling. Since God sent His only Son to redeem us and to call us into community, it is incumbent on us to live worthy of that calling. Verses 2 and 3 remind us of the fruit of the Spirit. Paul is calling for behavior that manifests the character of Christ. Living in community is difficult because we come from diverse backgrounds, and we have different interests and tastes. But we are bound together by a great sevenfold cord which gives us incredible strength.

The first triad—"one body and one Spirit … one hope of your calling" (v. 4)—speaks of our calling and incorporation into the body of Christ through the ministry of the Holy Spirit by virtue of our redemption. The second triad—"one Lord, one faith, one baptism"—recalls the moment the believer confessed Christ as Lord and Savior and was incorporated through baptism into the church. The final triad is a reference to the triune God, whose oneness is the basis for our unity. In the great high priestly prayer recorded in John 17:20–21, we discover that our unity will convince the world that the Father sent the Son. Too much is at stake for us to allow petty differences to divide us. Unity is the necessary foundation for the exercise of diverse gifts within the body.

2. The exalted King gifts His church (vv. 7–11).

The emphasis on Christ as the giver of the gifts is unique to this letter. Paul is demonstrating that the all-sufficient Christ has, by virtue of His resurrection and glorious ascension, made His church sufficient for every task. But how does He empower His church? The answer is simple but profound. He gives gifts (abilities) to men and women and then He gives them to His church, placing them in it as He desires (cf. 1 Cor. 12:18). This single truth should shake us from the lethargy of playing church as if it is a spectator sport. We are saved to serve the King through His body, and He has redeemed and gifted us for this task. It is both our calling and our privilege.

3. Gifted leaders equip gifted members for service (vv. 11–12).

The New Testament church had no artificial distinctions, such as "clergy" and "laity." Some persons were gifted with leadership abilities—apostles, prophets, evangelists, and pastors/teachers—so that they could equip the saints for the work of service.

Paul's emphasis on leadership and declaration gifts in this letter was prompted by the historical situation that led to the writing of Colossians and Ephesians. A heresy was spreading throughout pro-consular Asia that was threatening the church. It questioned the uniqueness of Christ (see Paul's defense in Col. 1:15–20) and thus, in turn, the uniqueness of the church. If Jesus is not the one and only Savior, then the church is little more than one of the other mystery religions that dominated the landscape of Paul's day. But since Jesus is uniquely God's Son and our Redeemer, His church stands apart from every other earthly gathering. It is designed to advance His Kingdom until His return.

While leadership gifts are stressed, it is clear that every member has received a gift of grace (v. 7) that enables him or her to serve in essential and effective ministry. Every member is bound to Christ and to fellow members by our giftedness. We are a team and we need each other if the church is to fulfill its kingdom purpose. There are no spectators!

4. Gifted teamwork builds up the church (vv. 12–16).

Have you ever wondered what it would look like if we put all our petty differences aside and joined hands by employing our unique gifts at the King's direction?

In verse 12, Paul tells us that it would result in "the building up of the body of Christ." In other words, God has chosen to use His gifted people to accomplish His kingdom work through the building up of His church. This is not merely numerical growth; it is a multifaceted growth that will impact every area of the church's life. The results are enumerated in verses 13–15.

> a. "Until we all attain to the unity of the faith, and of the knowledge of the Son of God, to a mature man:" we will experience unity and grow in knowledge of Christ so that we express the "fullness" of Christ (v. 13).

b. "As a result, we are no longer to be children" (v. 14). We will grow in doctrinal knowledge and have stability.

c. "But speaking the truth in love, we are to grow up in all aspects into Him" (v. 15). Church growth is a work of God through every member and it impacts every facet of the body. Don't miss the concluding description of the growth of the church. All growth flows from the Head—Christ. But the power is applied in our church and through our church through the "proper working of each individual part" (v. 16).

Conclusion

We are the parts through whom God has chosen to manifest His supernatural power on earth through the growth of His church. Too much is at stake for us to play church! Do you know your place in His body and are you serving according to your giftedness?

Date: September 11

Suggested Title: The Church as Gifted Community

Scripture: Romans 12:1–8 NASB

Contributor: Ken Hemphill

Sermon Starter

Introduction

Remember elementary school days when we would choose sides for our recess activity? It was an awkward time for everyone as the two biggest guys or best athletes took turns selecting players for their team. Maybe your greatest fear was being the last one to be chosen. Do you ever feel like the last one out in terms of your ability to make a difference for the kingdom of God? If so, Paul has a word for you.

The Roman letter was written by Paul to a community he did not found. He planned to go to Rome so that he could be encouraged by the believers and, in turn, encourage the believers and participate in the expansion of their ministry (Rom. 1:12–15). Further, Paul hopes they will provide assistance as he expands the gospel to Spain (Rom. 15:24). In the first eleven chapters, Paul provides them with a detailed expression of the gospel as he declares it. In chapter 12 he turns his attention to some practical issues that flow from the gospel. The first one mentioned is the functioning of the gifted church.

1. The twin foundation for gifted ministry (vv. 1–2)

a. The presentation of the body. God always rewards availability. Make yourself available to God with no conditions attached, and He will place you in His gifted body as He chooses (cf. 1 Cor. 12:18). God designed you for Himself and for His church. The presentation of yourself as a "living and holy sacrifice" is our reasonable or spiritual act of worship. It is a gift that flows from our understanding of the "mercies of God." Good news—God has already declared your gift to be acceptable!

b. The renewal of the mind. We will either be conformed to the world or transformed by the renewing of the mind. The renewing of the mind means that we view our world and ourselves from God's perspective as created and gifted for ministry to Him.

2. The five principles of spiritual giftedness (vv. 3–8)

a. Sound judgment. The two most common problems when it comes to gifts are overevaluation and underevaluation. Some persons seem to think that gifts prove them to be spiritually elite. Gifts prove nothing about the possessor but everything about the giver. Others "humbly" argue they have no gift to offer. Such is contrary to the clear teaching of God's Word.

b. All are gifted. "God has allotted to each a measure of faith" means that all are empowered for ministry. Our apportioned faith allows us to discern and accomplish the will of God. Notice that verse 6 begins with the premise that all are gifted.

c. Unity through diversity. We have many members but all do not have the same function. It takes diversely gifted body members for the body to work appropriately (cf. the body imagery in 1 Cor. 12).

d. Interdependence. "We are … members one of another" (v. 5). Our gifts make us both dependent and interdependent. We cannot function appropriately apart from the body.

e. The common good. Gifts are not given for our amusement; they only find meaning when they are employed for the advancement of the kingdom.

Conclusion

Do you know your place in God's family? Have you thanked God for your giftedness by serving Him through the church?

Date: September 18

Suggested Title: The Bold Church

Scripture: Acts 3:11–16 NIV

Contributor: Ralph West

Full Sermon Outline

Introduction

The book of Acts talks about an early church that astonished the people of Jerusalem with a Demonstration and Declaration.

The church demonstrated radically changed lives and declared a blunt but benevolent personal message about the crucified and resurrected Lord Jesus Christ. It is amazing to witness the response of the people to biblical historical authoritative preaching. When the people heard Peter's first sermon, they were "cut to the heart" (Acts 2:37), and they asked Peter and said to the other apostles, "Brothers, what shall we do?"

A heterogeneous crowd in Jerusalem heard Peter's first sermon, and their response to his message was not to see who could beat the other person to the front line of the Bistro or Denny's or some other Sunday after-church destination. No, the Holy Spirit moved, and they were touched in their hearts. Their sincere response was, "What shall we do!"

Something was happening powerfully with the proclamation in that church. Also something was happening powerfully with the demonstration within that church. After the life of the lame man at the temple gates was radically changed as a result of a miracle, the people in town who had passed him at the gate of Beautiful for forty years saw him standing on his own two feet, and they were filled with wonder and amazement at what had happened to him. The very words suggest an impact that left people dumbfounded with amazement. They were beside themselves with the power evident in the proclamation and the demonstration of that bold church. No one could ignore the church.

On the other hand, the element of astonishment is missing from churches today. An honest interpretation of the book of Acts would suggest in comparison much of what we do in church is the ordinary, routine, and predictable. Our churches are admired, congratulated, or ignored, but we seldom astonish. When you compare the church in Acts with the church today, you see the contrast. Some things in Acts cannot be duplicated today: the wind, the fire, and the tongues belonged to unique beginnings. But the astonishing quality of the Christian fellowship should be duplicated today. God desires our church in its demonstration and declaration to be a fellowship of astonishment.

What are we to make out of this bold, amazing, and astonishing church and, in comparison, what we see in the typical church today? I suppose there are some conclusions we can reach. First, we could say God only wanted this to happen two thousand years ago in the Jerusalem church: it was the sovereign providential intention of God that the Jerusalem church would be a bold church, but thereafter, we would be ordinary, routine, predictable, and comfortable.

Or, you could conclude that God wants a bold, astonishing church. He wants the church to be a bold fellowship.

There is ample biblical and historical and contemporary evidence that supports the claim that God desires many churches to be bold churches, by our Demonstration and Declaration, to cause astonishment at the power of the name of the Lord Jesus Christ.

Demonstration

Things happened in the earliest church that caused astonishment: "Amazed and perplexed, they asked one another, 'What does this mean?'" (Acts 2:12).

This church had nothing that we have: no building, no budget, no staff, no real program, and no establishment. This church was in its very initial, embryonic stages. It had no credentialed ministry, it had no standing, and yet, because of what it did have, people were amazed and perplexed. What makes a church like that?

A bold church creates an attraction: "all the people were astonished and came running to them" (3:11).

Now you have two preachers standing in the courtyard and the once-lame man is standing on his own two feet with them.

The people came out of the inner court of the temple and the Jewish worshippers poured out onto Solomon's Colonnade, so-called because it was built on some of the remaining pillars of Solomon's temple. As the people left the ordinary, routine, predictable liturgical service, all of a sudden they saw this man with his radically changed life standing there beside the two preachers, and they thronged them. They mobbed them, because they saw the evidence of a changed life in the presence of the preacher.

A forty-year-old man lame from birth had been miraculously healed (3:1–10). In the very presence of the messenger stood an undeniable demonstration of a powerful message. They did not have to promote. They did not use any gimmicks. They were standing there with two preachers and beside them, an astonishingly changed life. No amount of advertisement substitutes for the reality of a changed life. This was in the same location, the temple. Yet the same worshippers in the same old place suddenly turned into a fellowship of astonishment.

Declaration

The preaching and testifying of an astonishing church was direct and startling. Such preaching immediately connected the listeners with the crucifixion of the Lord Jesus; it put in their very hands the hammer that nailed Him to the cross.

An astonishing church confronts the city with the disowning of Christ. Peter did not hesitate to confront the city with their denial of Jesus. Two times he emphasized the baseness of it. Pilate had declared Jesus innocent and desired to let Him go, yet Jesus stood face-to-face with Pilate and demanded the cross. Peter forced them to take responsibility for the cross (Acts 2:23). He puts the hammer in their hands. An astonishing church is willing to tell the city "You crucified Him." If the people of any congregation really told their city, "You nailed Him to the cross," there would be an astonishing reaction.

An astonishing church confronts the city with the dishonoring of the Christ. We must present the contrast. The city wanted Barabbas rather than Jesus (3:14). When the city could have chosen the very best, it chose instead something else. The astonishing church confronts the city with choosing everyone or anyone other than Jesus. The ultimate contradiction is stated in the words, "You killed the author of life" (v. 15). How can you put to death the Source and Prince of life itself?

An astonishing church confronts the city with the dignifying of Christ: "God raised Him from the dead" (v. 15). God reverses the verdict of the city. What God does more than undoes the rejection of Christ. God vindicates Christ, exalts Him, and makes Him Lord over all.

Conclusion

An astonishing church claims without flinching that Jesus Christ is Lord over the city now. We want to be able to say without hesitation that God has reversed the verdict of our city on Jesus Christ, just as He reversed the verdict of Jerusalem.

Date: September 18

Suggested Title: The Unstoppable Church

Scripture: Acts 4:1–22 NIV

Contributor: Ralph West

Sermon Starter

Introduction

A person with a testimony is never at the mercy of a person with an argument. When you present a radically changed life as exhibit A, it demonstrates to everyone and to anyone who speaks about the theory of change versus actual change. And so continues Acts 4. This is the same day when a man who had been lame forty years had been suddenly and dramatically made completely whole in the name and in the power of the Lord Jesus Christ.

A Living Faith Versus a Lifeless Religious

In this passage, you find a living faith versus a lifeless religious form. Look at the identification of the parties, look at the reaction of lifeless religion, and consider the precaution they took which was to no avail.

This lifeless religious form confronts Peter and John, these two Galileans. After their confrontation, we read their reaction: they were "greatly disturbed" (Acts 4:2). The word in the Greek New Testament is a picturesque, vivid word, which refers to someone who had been picking up and moving heavy stones. It is also a word that carries within it the idea of the pain caused by moving heavy stones. It means these men were dead weight to the priests, the temple police, and the materialistic, rationalistic Sadducees, who were the aristocratic religious element in Jerusalem. They were pained.

In every generation of the Christian church, God has been at work powerfully somewhere in a living faith. At the same time, there have been those involved in a lifeless religion that did not recognize *living faith* and at worst opposed it with *lifeless religion*.

But, look how ineffective a lifeless religion is: "But many who heard the message believed; so the number of men who believed grew to about five thousand" (v. 4). If there were five thousand men that believed in spite of what was happening, there were at least ten thousand people (including women and children).

The Unexplainable Acts of God Versus the Explainable Accusations of Humans

The next day the rulers, the elders, and the teachers of the law met in Jerusalem (vv. 5–6). When Jesus was in the synagogues in Galilee, He confronted the Pharisees. They were religious conservatives, the pietists who were hypocrites. After the resurrection of Christ, they waned. Now in the capital of Jerusalem it is the rationalists, the materialists, the religious liberals that encounter the gospel and Jesus.

The Indomitable Conquest of God Versus the Pitiful Opposition of Man

In the aftermath of this, Peter and John were confronted by the overwhelming undeniable when they saw their courage.

The word in the New Testament language means the bold freedom of speech. A kind of natural boldness as a friend would use when speaking to a perfect friend. They had not been to certified academic schools. They were unschooled. They were ordinary men, plebeian men. They belonged to the mass of people. They were not accredited, religious teachers. They must have remembered what people said about Jesus. They had never heard anyone "speak like this man." They spoke with authority.

Conclusion

God is at work in living faith when people hear the message of Jesus Christ and believe.

Date: September 25

Suggested Title: The Blessed Church

Scripture: Acts 2:42–47 NIV

Contributor: Ralph West

Full Sermon Outline

Introduction

Every sincere believer wants to belong to a church that God blesses. What is the church that God blesses? Is it the church that we invent? Is it the church that the community decides we ought to be? Or is there really a biblical mandate that in any given generation and in every location that expresses what an authentic church must embody?

Several chapters of Acts reveal the principles that God uses to bless His people as only He can. The ideals of the early church reflect God's eternal standard for His people. What kind of church can God bless?

The early church was devoted to:

- the apostles' teaching
- fellowship
- a close interrelationship to one another in the breaking of bread
- prayerful supplication

Focus on that word *devoted* in Acts 2:42; it is a word of intensity and continuity, which means they had adhered with all of their strength to these four things. The word translated "devoted" was also used in athletics to speak of someone who stretched himself out as he moved toward the end of the race. Scripture says they adhered with all of their might. They would allow nothing to impede their devotion to the apostle's teaching, fellowship, the breaking of bread, and prayer. They did this with continuity. They did not allow anything to interfere with it.

1. A sacred mentality

First, they devoted themselves to apostolic proclamation; the word for teaching underscored both the work of teaching and the content of the teaching. They honored the office of the pastor-teacher, and they absorbed the content of his teaching. God can only bless a people with a teachable spirit.

Remember the historical situation in Acts 2—the church exploded in size. When Jesus ascended, He could number only about five hundred followers. On one occasion, the risen Christ appeared to five hundred in one place (1 Cor. 15:6). He told the disciples that when He left, those who believed in Him would do greater things than He ever did (John 14:12). On the day of Pentecost three thousand "God-fearing Jews from every nation under heaven" (Acts 2:5) responded to the preaching of Peter. Jesus had never had three thousand people commit to His Lordship on any recorded day of His ministry. "Greater things" had already begun to happen!

These three thousand people did not even know the rudiments of the Christian faith. Can you imagine this number of new believers who did not even know the basics of the Christian faith? Because of that, the apostles gave themselves to teaching the rudiments of the faith. You may say, "Why the apostles?" Because they were the eyewitnesses, we believe in apostolic Christianity.

2. An engaged community

The second aspect that God blesses: they devoted themselves to fellowship. They allowed nothing to impede the *koinonia*, the fellowship. It was the apostolic proclamation that created the fellowship. The early church fellowship was based on the teaching of the risen Christ. A church only experiences authentic fellowship when it places emphasis on teaching the word of God.

Why use that word *koinonia*? We might think of *fellowship* as an event we have after church: "you bring the chips, I bring the dips." When we think of impeding fellowship, we think of someone forgetting the chips. However, that is not what the word means in the New Testament. We should not mix it up with having a fellowship meal; instead *fellowship* is the community that emerges from the teaching of the Word of God.

3. A joyful hospitality

The third thing is that they gave themselves to relationships around the table. They devoted themselves to the breaking of bread. Was this a communal meal or was it the Lord's Supper? Some biblical scholars, including F. F. Bruce (1910–1990), said it was both. The early church took meals together. Then, when the fellowship meal was over, they would clear off the table and one of the apostles would pick up a piece of the bread and say, "I give to you what was also given to me: how the Lord Jesus took bread, broke it, blessed it, gave it" (cf. 1 Cor. 11:23–24). So, they were a church that also shared the Table.

Throughout His ministry Jesus enjoyed ministry around a table. Frequently, he would sit at a table with sinners and share with them truths about the kingdom. After His resurrection, He ate with the men on the road to Emmaus and with the disciples on the seashore. Of interest is that the only miracle recorded by all four Gospels is the feeding of the multitudes (Matt. 14:13–21, Mark. 6:30–44, Luke 9:10–17, and John 6:1–15). Biblical fellowship should be a characteristic of the church today.

4. A praying community

They devoted themselves to prayer. One of the four navigation points and anchors of this first church was prayer. Following the first pair of priorities there is a second pairing. The church adhered to the priorities of worship and prayer. This was expressed in the breaking of bread and in both public and private prayers. The church gave itself to the ordinances and practice of worship. The result was that "the Lord added to their number daily those who were being saved" (v. 47). When churches cease to worry about their "public image" and give themselves to God's appointed priorities, the public image will take care of itself.

Conclusion

God blessed the early church because they were more interested in His priorities than their own mechanics.

Date: September 25

Suggested Title: The Empowered Church

Scripture: Acts 1:4–5; 2:1–4

Contributor: Ralph West

Sermon Starter

Introduction

What do you think they were doing all together that day spoken of in Acts 2? It was an encounter with God.

It Happened Suddenly

In Acts 2:2 the word that leaps from the page is *suddenly*. There were days of preparation; but when God did it, He did it *suddenly*. It was like a thunderclap, like a lightning bolt. It was like a flash flood. God is able to do that. God is able to do it *suddenly*. It was that way with the Exodus. Centuries of slavery and *suddenly* God intervened. It was that way for decades as Israel worshipped Baal and then when Elijah called down fire on Mount Carmel, it happened *suddenly*. It was that way in the resurrection of the Lord Jesus: *suddenly* there was resurrection.

Today, where the people would dare to be together in one place in totality, in unity and in repentance and pleading with Him on the basis of His promises that the Spirit would come in, it could happen *suddenly*.

A Real External Location

When it happens, the Holy Spirit comes in a certain external situation. There are eternals and there are externals. There was an external situation here. Scripture says these were real people in a real place. It says they were all together in one place. The place is not identified, but surely it was not the temple for that was too open and too public. Tradition gives the location as the Upper Room where they shared the Last Supper with the Lord Jesus, where He washed their feet, where He had breathed on them and told them they would receive the Holy Spirit.

That room was filled with intimate associations of the presence of the risen Christ, so they stayed there. The last place they had seen Him was the most likely place they would meet Him again.

A Place of Union

The Upper Room was not only an external place of location, but also of union. They were all together. The word *homothumadon* means they were of one heart; like one heart beating in the breast of the 120 people. There they were: the eleven, (now minus Judas), Matthias, the women, the mother of Jesus, all of them gathered together in one place. In that external situation, with unity of mind, the Spirit of God came.

Conclusion

Where was that external situation when the Spirit of God came for you? Was it with the Word of God in a certain place in your house or in your garden? Was it with a certain Christian friend? Was it in your church? Was it in a prayer meeting? The last place you met God in power is the most likely place you will meet Him again.

OCTOBER

The Harvest Is Plentiful

Date: October 2

Suggested Title: God Invades Our Life

Scripture: Luke 8:26–39 ESV

Contributor: Andy Lewis

Full Sermon Outline

Introduction

God loves us enough not to leave us alone. He invades our life with His truth, light, and grace. God comes not just to forgive our sin but also to convict us of our sin. In the end God invades our lives to liberate us from the sin that so easily enslaves us. In this passage of Luke, we see a man changed and restored to health. It reminds us that the power of God is greater than our sin, shame, and struggles. There is no one who cannot be healed by God. There is not a sin that He cannot put to death. And there is not one heart that He cannot tame. Our God is a powerful God who has come to invade our lives.

Sin Has Captured Us (vv. 26–33)

This scene opens with an invasion. Jesus comes ashore in enemy territory. The region of the Gerasenes was not a place where good little Jewish boys went to play. It was a Roman area filled with all kinds of nonkosher things like pig farmers and demon-possessed men. Jesus, however, came to seek and save the lost, and He invaded these shores with His power. As soon as Christ got out of the boat, He was met by the possessed man. The man was quite a sight to behold: naked and homeless. And yet, when he saw Jesus he fell down before Him and recognized His power and authority.

Before we move on in the text we should note a presupposition. Most of us probably feel as though we can't relate to this scene. It is good to note that no one plans to be homeless, naked, and not in a right mind.

Sin captures us. A common Christian saying is that sin always takes us further than we want to go and keeps us longer than we want to stay. Maybe we don't look like this man, but sin has affected us as well. Sin isn't just something we do; rather, our sinful nature affects everything—our physical, emotional, and mental health, our relationships, propensities, and affections.

This man sees the power of Christ. That makes sense because James 2:19 tells us, "You believe that God is one; you do well. Even the demons believe—and shudder!" The question is whether or not we see the power of God. Are we willing to let Jesus invade our lives? Will we be willing to bend the knee and say, "What have you to do with me, Jesus, Son of the Most High God?" (v. 28) Or will we remain captured by our sins that secretly erode our joy and freedom? What sin has captivated you? We can be free in Christ. Christ goes on to conquer the demons of this man by sending them into a nearby herd of pigs. If Jesus can conquer these demons then He can overcome our sins, including our pride, selfishness, lust, gossip, and greed.

Christ Restores Us (vv. 34–37)

After Jesus conquers this man's demons, we see an altogether new man. Before this he was without clothes, home, or companion. He lived in isolation among the tombs because no one knew what to do with him. But when Christ invades his life, he is described as sitting, dressed, and restored.

While sin seeks to conquer all of us, the grace of Christ wants to restore everything that we have lost. This once naked man is now clothed. When Christ invades our lives, He clothes us with His righteousness. No longer do we have to hide in our shame like Adam and Eve did in the garden. The robe of Christ's righteousness covers over our sin and shame. We also see that the man is sitting at the feet of Jesus. Christ settles us down. No longer do we have to run around trying to find joy or seek approval. The power of Christ allows us to sit and worship. Finally, the man is restored "in his right mind" (v. 35). Before, this man's mind was warped. But the truth of Christ helps him to gain sanity and think correctly.

When the people of town saw what Jesus had done with this man "they were afraid" (v. 35). It is a scary thing to put ourselves in the hands of a living and powerful God. Make no doubt, He wants to change you. C. S. Lewis put it this way:

> He will make the feeblest and filthiest of us into a god or goddess, a dazzling, radiant, immortal creature, pulsating all through with such energy and joy and wisdom and love as we cannot now imagine, a bright stainless mirror which reflects back to God perfectly (though, of course, on a smaller scale) His own boundless power and delight and goodness. The process will be long and in parts very painful, but that is what we are in for. Nothing less. He meant what He said.[1]

We Return with Joy (vv. 38–39)

The man healed by Jesus begged Jesus to let him go with Him. Interestingly, Jesus denied this request. Instead He sent the man away with these words: "Return to your home, and declare how much God has done for you" (v. 39). God puts this man on a mission to proclaim to the world what has been done for him. Evangelism is not a duty that we should feel constantly guilty over. Instead, when proclaiming the gospel we are testifying to what we have already seen God do in our lives.

Conclusion

As we "return home," we aren't trying to simply win an argument. We are seeking to let people know that Jesus has landed on the shores. God invades our lives to liberate us from our sin. He wants to change us—all of us. Once we are restored by Christ, it will be easy to proclaim throughout the city what God has done for us. Allow Him to invade and conquer your sin so that you can testify to His power and greatness.

Note

1. C. S. Lewis, *Mere Christianity* (New York: HarperCollins, 2001), 205–6.

Date: October 2

Suggested Title: The Clear Call to Follow Christ

Scripture: Matthew 4:18–25 ESV

Contributor: Andy Lewis

Sermon Starter

Introduction

During the fall season, it is always good to remember the harvest that God desires. Jesus has called us to follow Him into this world proclaiming His kingdom. Although it may have been years since you remember giving your life to follow Him, a study of Matthew 4 reminds us of Christ's intention for our lives.

The Call Interrupts Normal Life

The future disciples are normal guys going about their work. God interrupts the ordinary with the extraordinary. While Jesus was walking along the sea, He saw two brothers casting their nets. "Follow me, and I will make you fishers of men," Jesus declared (v. 19). There isn't much wiggle room in this statement. The words *follow me* demand action. At times we can go in and out of church, life, work, and responsibilities and forget that Jesus has come to interrupt our normal routine with an opportunity to follow Him. Perhaps you don't need more information or investigation of Christ. It may just be time to follow Him.

The Call Is Incarnational

This call is also incarnational. The incarnation refers to Jesus coming in the physical body. In other words, Christ comes to where we are. Christianity is the only world religion where God comes to man rather than making man work our way to God. Christ calls these disciples to follow Him, saying that He would make them fishers of men. Have you ever thought about the fact that Jesus wasn't a fisherman? Simon and Andrew were the professional fisherman. But Christ, knowing how to relate, tells them that they will be part of a greater harvest of men.

The Call Is for a Kingdom

The disciples immediately follow Christ into a greater kingdom. Jesus takes them throughout Galilee teaching and proclaiming the "gospel of the kingdom." (v. 23) In this new kingdom people are healed and restored. This is a great reminder that God is not just a polite hobby for the weekend. God wants to usher in His kingdom. When we follow Christ, we are a part of a spiritual kingdom being implemented on this earth.

The Call Is to Make His Name Great

As the young disciples followed Christ "his fame spread" (v. 24) and "great crowds followed" (v. 25). Our call in life as disciples is to glorify and honor Christ. Our lives are given to make His name great.

Conclusion

Wherever God takes us, His call is clear. We are to follow Him, become incarnational with others, speak of a kingdom, and make His name great. Napoleon famously said,

> I know men; and I tell you that Jesus Christ is not a man. Superficial minds see a resemblance between Christ and the founders of empires and the gods of other religions. That resemblance does not exist. Everything in him astonishes me. His spirit overawes me, and his will confounds me. Between him and whoever else in the world, there is no possible term of comparison. He is truly a being by himself.[1]

The call to follow Christ is to witness to His greatness.

Note

1. "Napoleon's Testimony to Christ at St. Helena," *Stem Publishing*, accessed March 4, 2015, http://www.stempublishing.com /magazines/bt/BT17/1889_319_Napoleons_Testimony.html.

Date: October 9

Suggested Title: God Initiates in Our Life

Scripture: Luke 19:1–10 ESV

Contributor: Andy Lewis

Full Sermon Outline

Introduction

Life is about relationships. If you have all of the toys and riches in life but you don't have people to enjoy them with, then life really isn't that good. On the other hand if you have troubles, poverty, and struggles in life but are surrounded by friends and family who love you—then life isn't really that bad. Relationships, not circumstances, make or break enjoyment of life. The Proverbs say something similar: "Better is a dinner of herbs where love is than a fattened ox and hatred with it" (Prov. 15:17 ESV).

Life is about relationships, and our God is a relational God. The Bible says, "And the Word became flesh and dwelt among us" (John 1:14 ESV). God is not aloof or distant. He desires to make His dwelling among us. God wants to be where we are. It is His presence that gives us joy in difficult circumstances.

God begins a relationship with us by initiating. In the garden, God comes to Adam and Eve. In the Old Testament, God pursues His people. He urges Moses, comforts Elijah, calls Samuel, and anoints David. In the New Testament, God initiates with the incarnation. He breaks into the humdrum of this world as a baby in Bethlehem. He challenges the Pharisees and teachers of the law. He asks Peter, "Who do you say that I am?" (Mark 8:29 ESV).

We see God initiate in this passage. God walks up to the tax collector and calls him by name, "Zacchaeus, hurry and come down, for I must stay at your house today" (v. 5). We see God initiating a relationship with a reluctant sinner. It reminds us that the gospel works and should convict us that many people are waiting for someone to tell them the gospel.

The Drama of the Gospel

Jesus was just "passing through" (v. 1) when He interacted with Zacchaeus. Who was Zacchaeus? His name means pure or just. His parents were probably hoping that he would be an upstanding citizen. He took a different path. He was the chief tax collector and the job made him rich. Most likely he was skimming a little off the top. He was also a man of small stature, so he climbed up in a tree in order to see Jesus.

I've wondered what motivated Zacchaeus to go see Jesus. With all of his riches, power, and prestige, somehow Zacchaeus seemed to be longing for more. Right before Jesus came to town He healed a blind beggar (Luke 18:35–43). Maybe Zacchaeus wondered why someone with such a following would humble Himself so drastically. Perhaps Zacchaeus was lonely. After all, who would want to be friends with a man who collects your taxes and becomes rich doing it? He may have struggled with never living up to his own name of being pure and just. Regardless, Zacchaeus was looking for the gospel. He was longing for a relationship, so he went to see Jesus.

What happened that day was dramatic. It shows the glory of the gospel. Zacchaeus climbed up in a tree so he could see the glory of Jesus. However, soon it would be Jesus who was crucified on a tree so all could see His glory. Jesus, the Son of God, stooped so low in the incarnation that He looked up to a sinful, despised, lonely little man in a tree. Christ called him by name and went to his house. Most of us, like Zacchaeus, are probably content to see God from a distance. The Son of God however wants to enter our homes, our hearts, and our workplace. Zacchaeus "received him joyfully" (v. 6), and the gospel began to thaw his heart.

The Tragedy of the Gospel

This passage also shows the tragedy of a hardened heart. While Jesus and Zacchaeus were dining and talking, others in the crowd "all grumbled" (v. 7). They said, no doubt in judgmental tones, "He has gone in to be the guest of a man who is a sinner" (v. 7). Here we see the tragedy of a heart that doesn't understand the gospel. Surely they were wondering how Jesus could be kind to Zacchaeus. You can just imagine them saying, "He is a rich, godless tax collector, but we are the ones that have been faithful. Why didn't Jesus come to our house? Why would Jesus go to a sinner's house? Jesus owes me because I have been faithful to Him." The grace of God will sometimes reveal our self-righteousness. We must ask ourselves if the grace of God to others makes us joyful or makes us grumble. If it makes us grumble, we probably don't love grace as much as we love ourselves.

The Comedy of the Gospel

Lastly, we see the comedy of the gospel. After a meal, Zacchaeus reemerges and announces that he will give back anything defrauded and half of his net worth to the poor. The grace of God has made this swindler generous. Zacchaeus is finally rich. It must have brought a smile to Christ to say, "Today salvation has come to this house" (v. 9). Once again the gospel of grace takes hard hearts and makes them new creations. Jesus reminds us that this is the reason He came. Verse 10 tells us that "the Son of Man came to seek and to save the lost."

Conclusion

As God initiates with Zacchaeus, we see Zacchaeus initiate restoration with others. Understanding the grace of God changed his heart. Zacchaeus was probably the last person expected to interact with Jesus, but that is how the gospel works. It is sometimes unexpected, but always glorious.

The questions for us are simple. Are we grumbling because others experience grace? Are we willing to share a meal and the grace of God with others who desperately need to know God? Christ has come to seek and save the lost—and that, my friends, is still the mission of the church.

Date: October 9

Suggested Title: The Hope of God in Christ

Scripture: Ephesians 1:15–23 ESV

Contributor: Andy Lewis

Sermon Starter

Introduction

Christmas shopping begins earlier each year. Your family may exchange names and lists at Thanksgiving. We ask each other what we want for Christmas, but have we thought about what God may want for Christmas? What are His desires for the church? This passage in Ephesians shows us God's Christmas list for the church in Ephesus. Not surprisingly, it revolves around the glory of Christ.

Revelation of Christ (vv. 15–18)

We serve a God of revelation. Paul's prayer is for God to "give you the Spirit of wisdom and of revelation in the knowledge of him" (v. 17). God doesn't hide in the corner or keep things from us; He desires for us to know Him. First, God has revealed Himself in natural creation—His world and everything in it. Secondly, He reveals Himself in special creation—the incarnation of Christ.

Now that Christ has been revealed, Ephesians tells us that the eyes of our hearts have been enlightened (v. 18). This is an important phrase for the times we live in because it affirms that Christianity is an open-minded religion. Christianity has been charged in recent times for being close-minded, intolerant, and antiquated, but the opposite is true. Christianity enlightens our minds by showing our sin, our purpose, and Christ's glory.

Knowledge of Christ (vv. 18–19)

Now that our eyes have been opened to God's revelation, what do we see? First, we know that we are called to hope in Christ. We could say that this world of cynicism, skepticism, and doubt needs hope more than anything. Perhaps that is why these words ring true: "The thrill of hope, a weary world rejoices, for yonder breaks a new and glorious morn."[1]

Second, we see the "riches of his glorious inheritance"(v. 18). Maybe you've never received an inheritance, but you can imagine that it changes your life. The knowledge of future financial stability would dissipate present worries. This is how we are to live in Christ. We have a glorious inheritance in Him. Therefore, our present sufferings are mitigated by this future hope.

Third, we know the "greatness of his power toward us who believe" (v. 19). At times we focus on the meek and mild nature of Jesus so much that we forget He is powerful. He can take our sin and sorrows. He conquers death, hell, and the grave. We are following a living, active, and powerful God.

Experience of Christ (vv. 20–23)

The revelation and knowledge of Christ lead us to experience Him as He is now: raised, seated, and with all things under His feet. In these final sentences we see a flurry of beautiful phrases describing our glorious God. And even more, we are raised with Christ and our lives are hidden with Him!

Conclusion

As you begin to prepare for Christmas, focus more on what God wants than what you want. His desires are for our benefit. He wants us to know the revelation, knowledge, and experience of Christ in all of its beautiful fullness. Christ is the gift that continues to give.

Note

1. John S. Dwight, "O, Holy Night!" in *The Hymnal for Worship and Celebration,* ed. Tom Fettke (Waco: Word Music, 1986), 148.

Date: October 16

Suggested Title: The Feast of Firstfruits

Scripture: Leviticus 23:9–14

Contributor: Ken Wilson

Full Sermon Outline

Introduction

We can see that the Old Testament Jewish calendar has a number of fascinating seasonal celebrations that are full of spiritual meaning and significance.[1] Too often we skip over these seasonal festivals and feasts, presuming they are outdated or irrelevant, and miss the rich principles imbedded in them.

Tucked away in the book of Leviticus is a chapter that deals with a number of these seasonal celebrations. Leviticus 23 addresses three of these celebrations associated with harvesttime.[2] The first of these is the Feast of Firstfruits in Leviticus 23:9–14, which we will discuss here.

1. Dependence

Faithful worshippers acknowledge their dependence on God by giving Him the first portion of their income (vv. 9–11).

The offering of firstfruits was a spring festival associated with the barley harvest. The placement of this offering at the beginning of the harvesting season is important. The barley crops were the first to be brought in, and this provision in the spring was a token of God's provision that would come during the summer and fall harvests ahead. By giving an offering out of this "first" harvest, the faithful worshipper was acknowledging the current blessing of the Lord but also anticipating future provision to come. This offering required faith. The family making this offering would be giving up what was already in hand and trusting that God would continue to provide as the year continued. They gave before the full provision was made.

The context of this offering connects it closely to the Passover and the Feast of Unleavened Bread (cf. Lev. 23:1–8, 14). While the Passover and Feast of Unleavened Bread reminded them of their suffering and redemption, the Festival of Firstfruits was a more joyful part of their worship that same week. The waving of the sheaf of barley by the priest that we read about in verse 11 would have been celebrative and communicated their acceptance by the Lord.

Our offerings are also given in the context of remembering what God has done and celebrating that He accepts us. But our offerings also cause us to look forward to provisions that God will make as we offer Him a portion of what He has already provided.

2. Dedication

Faithful worshippers bring their offerings to the Lord as a part of their worship and devotion (vv. 12–13).

The offering of firstfruits is to be done in connection with two other sacrifices. The Whole Burnt Offering (Lev. 1:1–17) celebrated the worshipper's full acceptance by God as an entire animal was fully burnt on the altar. The Meal Offering (Lev. 2:1–16) demonstrated dedication to God and opened the way for the worshipper to then express his dependence on God through the giving of firstfruits.

Understanding that we are accepted by God and dedicated to Him leads naturally to showing our dependence on Him for all our future provision.

3. Demonstration

Faithful worshippers demonstrate by the priorities of their lives that God will meet their needs (v. 14).

The final instruction related to this offering is easy to skip over, but it should not be. Passover has already taken place and now for seven days the worshipper was not allowed to eat any bread or even roasted grain.

By denying yourself and offering the best to the Lord, you are demonstrating that you know the best belongs to Him and that He will provide for your needs in the future.

Conclusion

We no longer live in a culture that revolves around the harvest calendar. We live in a day and age when paychecks are delivered at more regular intervals. This allows us to practice the principle in this passage on a much more consistent basis. Faithful worshippers today will regularly demonstrate their dedication to God and acknowledge their dependence on Him by presenting the first of their income as an evidence of their devotion. In the Old Testament this offering was taken at the beginning of the harvest season in the spring—before the full harvest was brought in. This calls for believers today to live by faith that God will provide for our needs. This demands that we give our offerings in anticipation of His provision and not only after it has been fully received.

The next time you are giving your offering, remember God's blessing in the past and anticipate His provision in the future. Does your giving demonstrate that you are dependent on Him? What would change if it did? How much more would our churches flourish if we gave the best to God first and trusted Him for the future?

Notes

1. The Jewish calendar is based on the lunar cycle. This means it does not sync with our calendar that is based on a solar cycle. While we add an extra day every leap year to catch up, the Jewish calendar adds an extra month periodically to keep the harvest festivals near the actual harvests. *The Baker Illustrated Bible Dictionary*, (Grand Rapids: Baker, 2013), s.v. *calendar.*
2. Allen P. Ross, *Holiness to the Lord: A Guide to the Exposition of the Book of Leviticus* (Grand Rapids: Baker, 2002), 415–28.

Date: October 16

Suggested Title: The Fulfillment of Firstfruits

Scripture: 1 Corinthians 15:20–23

Contributor: Ken Wilson

Sermon Starter

Introduction

What possible connection could the feasts of the Old Testament have to the work of Christ? The regular sacrificial system of the Jews, as well as the Passover and Day of Atonement, seems easy to connect to the work of Christ. But what about the feasts? In looking at the meaning of the feasts in their Old Testament context, we find rich symbolism, deep significance, and clear personal application related to each feast. These same feasts of the harvest are connected to Jesus. These typological feasts do not immediately point to Jesus but they ultimately find their fulfillment in Him.[1]

In making the connection to Christ, Scripture does not open the door to free association as a method of interpretation. Rather, the New Testament itself will be our sure and certain guide as we make the connection to Christ and His finished work of redemption and anticipate His coming again to reign.

1. Timing

Christ fulfilled the Feast of Firstfruits by being raised on the very day the feast was celebrated (Matt. 28:1; Mark 16:2; Luke 24:1; John 20:1).[2]

> a. Christ was put to death on the night of Passover as our Passover Lamb (1 Cor. 5:7).
> b. Christ was raised from the dead on the first day of the week (Matt. 28:1; Mark 16:2; Luke 24:1; John 20:1).

2. Principle

Christ is the firstfruits of resurrection in anticipation of the believer's resurrection (vv. 20–23).

> a. Christ has been raised from the dead (v. 20).
> b. Believers will be raised from the dead (vv. 21–23).

Conclusion

The work of Christ is just the beginning of what is in store for believers. His resurrection is the first part of the harvest. It is a token of a greater harvest to come.

The full harvest of the summer and the final harvest of the fall have been guaranteed by the resurrection of Christ. After His resurrection, Jesus ascended to be seated at the right of God, taking His rightful place in perfectly restored fellowship. He bore our sin and was somehow separated from the Father but now is forever in intimate relationship with Him. Our sins have been borne by Christ on the cross, and we anticipate following Him in resurrection. At that moment, we will take our rightful place as children of God in perfect fellowship with Him for all eternity.

Notes

1. J. Scott Duvall and J. Danny Hays, *Grasping God's Word: A Hands-On Approach to Reading, Interpreting, and Applying the Bible* (Grand Rapids: Zondervan, 2005), 195–97.
2. Harold Hoehner, *Chronological Aspects of the Life of Christ* (Grand Rapids: Zondervan, 1977), 65–73.

Date: October 23

Suggested Title: The Feast of Pentecost

Scripture: Leviticus 23:15–22

Contributor: Ken Wilson

Full Sermon Outline

Introduction

Placing your money in an offering plate during a church service can be seen from a number of different perspectives. First, the offerings meet the needs of the church. This may not seem like a very spiritual point of view, but it is one that is as real as priests being able to eat the meat that was sacrificed during the Peace/Fellowship offering (Lev. 7:11–21). Writing your check from week to week is also an act of worship as we offer to God a portion of our income because He is worthy. Setting up your electronic funds transfer is an act of pure stewardship for some as we recognize that God is the owner of all we have and we are honored to be His stewards and manage what He has entrusted to us. Let us look at our worshipful stewardship as an expression of gratitude.

Leviticus 23 presents three celebrations associated with harvest. In the October 16 outline, we looked at the Feast of Firstfruits in Leviticus 23:9–14. This week we will explore the meaning of the Feast of Pentecost in its Old Testament context.

1. Gratitude

Faithful worshippers show their gratitude to the Lord by presenting an offering of what His blessing has produced (vv. 15–17).

The Feast of Pentecost took place fifty days after Passover (Lev. 23:4–8) and the Feast of Firstfruits (Lev. 23:9–14). During that fifty-day period, spring turned into summer and more harvests were brought in from the fields. The summer harvests were the grain harvests that included wheat. At the beginning of the harvesting season, barley was brought in as a firstfruit of God's blessing. Now, in the middle of the summer, the abundant blessing of God is more clear and the offering changes from a sheaf to a loaf. Rather than a token of the harvest, the offering is now the produce of the harvest. The loaf of bread is to be baked with fine flour and leaven and then brought before the Lord. The gratitude of the worshippers is seen in their recognition that the abundance of the grain harvest has enabled them to eat the bread that sustains them. Thus, a token in the form of a prepared loaf of bread is brought before the Lord and accepted by Him.

Believers today must see beyond the limits of giving the minimum amount of financial resources and recognize that the blessing of God produces abundance in our lives. We drive cars and live in houses that should all be offered to the Lord and used by Him for His purposes. In this way, we offer back to Him what His blessing has produced.

2. Thanksgiving

Faithful worshippers remember their redemption and are thankful for the Lord's full provision that allows them to enjoy fellowship with Him (vv. 18–21).

The simplicity of the firstfruit offering at the beginning of the season is now in the past. The grand offerings of multiple lambs, bulls, and rams might seem excessive were it not for the fact that this is the high point of the harvest season. The regulations for these offerings are presented in detail in the first seven chapters of Leviticus.[1] The point here is that the worshipper is experiencing God's abundant provision. They are now celebrating with the offerings that atone for sin, express dedication, and culminate in the celebration of peace/fellowship with God. The offerings that make fellowship with God an experiential reality are made because God has blessed them with the sacrifices that are given back to Him. Our redemption is costly, but God is the One who makes the provision necessary for the sacrifice.

The observance of a sacred assembly when no work is to be done adds to the festive mood of the occasion. After the intense days of harvest and bringing the animals to the sanctuary for sacrifice, this requirement is more gift than burden. When we have a clear understanding of God's provision, not only for our daily sustenance but especially for our very redemption, our worship will be more thankful and less obligatory.

3. Provision

Faithful worshippers trust God for His provision by making provision for the poor and foreigners in their midst (v. 22).

Once again, the final verse of the section seems at first to be an add-on. However, the consistent pattern of God is that when the Lord is worshipped, the poor are taken care of and outsiders experience grace. Allen Ross notes that, "The evidence of true gratitude is generosity."[2] The regulation for gleaning is set forth in other passages (Lev. 19:9–10; Deut. 24:19–20) and is exemplified in the magnanimous character of Boaz, who allows Ruth to glean from the corners of his field (Ruth 2:1–23) before he extends the protection of kinsman-redeemer to her in marriage. When we truly worship with a grateful heart, our worship extends outside the walls of the church and leads to a generous lifestyle that contributes to the redemption of others.

Conclusion

Imagine what it would be like if the times we take the offering in church were more a grateful celebration than an obligation. What would happen to our hearts if we fully embraced the idea that we are only giving back to God out of the abundant provision He has already made for us in the first place? Finally, how attractive would our churches be if our gratitude overflowed to include provision for the poor and paths for unbelievers to experience grace? We need those kinds of churches filled with grateful worshippers.

Notes

1. Allen P. Ross, *Holiness to the Lord: A Guide to the Exposition of the Book of Leviticus* (Grand Rapids: Baker, 2002), 73–193.
2. Ibid., 423.

Date: October 23

Suggested Title: The Fulfillment of Pentecost

Scripture: Acts 2

Contributor: Ken Wilson

Full Sermon Outline

Introduction

Every Christian familiar with the New Testament knows that the Day of Pentecost was a big deal. It was the birthday of the church. Three thousand people got saved. Dramatic miracles took place. What is not so widely known is how the work of Christ, which gave birth to the church, is a fulfillment of the Feast of Pentecost.

The Feast of Pentecost is not a prophecy. It is typology. Grant Osborne is helpful in making the distinction: "Typology differs from direct prophecy in that the latter texts are forward-looking and directly predict the New Testament event, while typology is indirect and analogously relates the Old Testament event to the New Testament event."[1] In the Old Testament a prophecy feels predictive when you read it. It has a future tense embedded in it. Typology, on the other hand, is not seen as predictive until the New Testament authors, under the inspiration of the Holy Spirit, make the connection. The Old Testament Feast of Pentecost is a type fulfilled on the New Testament Day of Pentecost (v. 1).

1. Timing

Christ fulfilled the Feast of Pentecost by gloriously producing the church on the very day the feast was celebrated (v. 1).

  a. The Old Testament Feast of Pentecost brought the product of God's blessing and offered it to the Lord (Lev. 23:15–22).

b. The New Testament Feast of Pentecost brought the product of Christ's work—the body of Christ—and offered it to God (vv. 1–47).

2. Principle

Christ inaugurates the blessings of the New Covenant on the Day of Pentecost (vv. 16–21).

a. New Covenant blessings come with the advent of Messiah (Jer. 31:31–34; Ezek. 36:24–32, Joel 2:28–32).[2]

b. New Covenant blessings were inaugurated on the Day of Pentecost (vv. 16–21).

Conclusion

The church is the body of Christ. The church is the bride of Christ. The church is also the Pentecost offering of Christ. As the two loaves that were offered at Pentecost represented the blessing of God and the product of that blessing, the church itself is the product of the work of Christ. The New King James Version translates Acts 2:1: "When the Day of Pentecost had fully come," reflecting the use of an unusual Greek (*symplēroō*) word at that point.[3] It does seem that Luke is trying to call out that this is a very special and perhaps even climatic fulfillment of the Day of Pentecost. What a wonderful way to live out our new life in Christ. We are His Pentecost offering to God.

Notes

1. Grant Osborne, *The Hermeneutical Spiral: A Comprehensive Introduction to Biblical Interpretation, rev. ed.* (Downers Grove, IL: InterVarsity, 2006), 328.
2. Darrell L. Bock, *Acts: Baker Exegetical Commentary on the New Testament,* (Grand Rapids: Baker, 2007), 94–96.
3. Johannes P. Louw and Eugene A. Nida, eds., *Greek English Lexicon of the New Testament Based on Semantic Domains,* (New York: United Bible Societies, 1988), 638.

Date: October 30

Suggested Title: The Feast of Trumpets

Scripture: Leviticus 23:23–25

Contributor: Ken Wilson

Full Sermon Outline

Introduction

How can we ever get church to start on time? I have heard it all. More coffee! Less coffee! Quiet music! Loud music! Dim the lights! More cowbell! May I suggest, more trumpets? Perhaps more on target would be a service worthy of blowing trumpets to gather people together for worship. When God's people gather, the mood is critical. Worship includes repentance, confession, adoration, prayer, singing, offerings, hearing from God, and responding to His Word.[1] A church service that includes all of that as it brings glory to God, exalts Jesus Christ, and is guided by the Holy Spirit would be worth blowing some trumpets.

Leviticus 23 presents three celebrations associated with harvest. In the spring, the Feast of Firstfruits (vv. 9–14) started the offerings after the barley was harvested first from the fields. The provision of the early harvest as well as the offering itself was a token of more to come. In midsummer, the grains were being harvested and the abundant provision led to the joyful celebration of Pentecost (vv. 15–22). In the fall, the harvests were completed and the nation gathered to worship and celebrate a new year that began with the Day of Atonement. The Feast of Trumpets gathered the people for the celebration of their pardon and redemption.

1. Gathering

Faithful worshippers gather as a sacred assembly of God's people (vv. 23–24).

The Feast of Trumpets concluded the harvest festivals and gathered the congregation together to begin a new season of worship. In later Judaism, the Feast of Trumpets became known as Rosh Hashanah—the Jewish New Year.[2] The religious calendar began with Passover, but the civil and agricultural calendar began with The Feast of Trumpets. At the end of the harvest, when God's provision was fully manifested, all Israel was called once again to gather in Jerusalem for a sacred assembly that would lead directly into the celebration of the Day of Atonement (vv. 26–32) and the Feast of Booths (or Tabernacles) (vv. 33–43).

The blowing of the trumpet recalls the meeting of God with the nation on Mount Sinai (Ex. 19:16–19). The trumpet blasts called the people to the mountain where God would speak to them and deliver the Ten Commandments through Moses (Ex. 20:1–17). When the trumpet sounded, God's people gathered to hear Him speak and committed themselves to follow Him.

The purpose of the grand ingathering of people in the fall, announced by the trumpets, was to bring the harvest year to a close with offerings and begin a new year which started with the removal of sin (the Day of Atonement nine days after the blowing of the trumpets) and the remembrance of God's provision in the wilderness (the Feast of Booths five days after the Day of Atonement).

When we gather as Christians, our time should be worthy of trumpet blasts. It should include offerings that recognize the fullness of God's provision. The community of God should gather to hear from God, remember His accomplishment of redemption, and celebrate His provision in the future.

2. Renewal

Faithful worshippers gather to remember their redemption and renew their commitment to the Lord (v. 25).

The call to come hear God and remember His work is, at the same time, a call to cease from the regular mundane activities of daily living. In our world where we are connected and networked at every turn, it is more important than ever to pull away from the regular routines of life and make time to enter into a sacred assembly of God's people to refresh and refocus. Leviticus 23 begins with a discussion of Sabbath (v. 3). Sabbath is a time of cessation of work and separation to God.[3] The Lord blesses the work of man's hands with abundant harvest. God's people recognize this blessing by giving offerings, but they also take a break from the hustle and bustle of life and gather together for sacred purposes. This time of Sabbath is not an intrusion but a gift from a loving God who invites us to rest in His presence on a regular basis until He calls us permanently into that rest.

On the first day of the seventh month, Nehemiah gathered the exiles that returned from captivity and read the Law, making it clear to them (Neh. 8:1–12). Bruce Waltke commented, "Remarkably, 'all the people' tell Ezra to bring out the Book of the Law … In their encounter with the law, the people are united, eager, attentive, enthusiastic, and worshipful. Revival is in the air."[4] This is the mood our services can have if we gather in sacred assembly to hear the voice of God.

Conclusion

Why do we gather? Is it worthy of trumpets? Do we approach it as a sacred assembly? Is the voice of God heard clearly? Is it an obligation and intrusion or is it a gift? How we approach the gathering of God's people makes all the difference. If we come away from a week of work and look back to see God's provision not only through the week, but through the year, we will enter into His presence with joy and celebration. If we come to hear His voice, remember His work, embrace His grace, and commit ourselves more deeply to Him, then the gathering will be more worthy of the God we worship. Perhaps it would be worthy of trumpet blasts.

Notes

1. Daniel I. Block, *For the Glory of God: Recovering a Biblical Theology of Worship* (Grand Rapids: Baker, 2014).

2. *The Baker Illustrated Bible Dictionary* (Grand Rapids: Baker, 2013), s.v. "festivals."

3. Abraham J. Herchel, *The Sabbath: Its Meaning for Modern Man* (New York: Farrar, Straus and Giroux, 1986).

4. Bruce K. Waltke, *An Old Testament Theology: An Exegetical, Canonical, and Thematic Approach* (Grand Rapids: Zondervan, 2007), 792.

Date: October 30

Suggested Title: The Fulfillment of Trumpets

Scripture: 1 Corinthians 15:51–57; 1 Thessalonians 4:16–17

Contributor: Ken Wilson

Sermon Starter

Introduction

Worship wars! We are all tired of them. Most of us are either over them or avoid them. But the questions still remain. Is it really worship if there is no organ or piano? Does the guitar drive the music or should the drums? Do I want to hear the voices or feel the bass? All the debate will come to an end one day with a trumpet blast. That's right! The trumpet of God signals His final judgment and His final gathering of people to Himself. Paul tells us it is a "mystery" (1 Cor. 15:51–52), and he also says we should comfort one another with these words (1 Thess. 4:13–18). Let's look at the mystery and find some comfort.[1]

1. Timing

God's people are gathered to Him at the end of the age (1 Thess. 4:16–17).

> a. The Old Testament Feast of Trumpets brought the harvest to a close and ushered in a new year for God's people (Lev. 23:23–25).
> b. The New Testament Feast of Trumpets will bring the current age to a close and usher in a new age in the plan of God (1 Cor. 15:51–57; 1 Thess. 4:16–17).

2. Principle

Christ will come with the sound of trumpets to gather His people to Him and celebrate the fullness of God's blessing (1 Thess. 4:16–17).

a. Trumpet blasts signal a time of judgment and bring the harvest of believers to an end (Rev. 8–11).

b. Trumpet blasts signal a time of reunion and refreshment as believers are gathered into the presence of God (1 Thess. 4:16–17; 1 Cor. 15:51–57).

Conclusion

The early feasts of Israel (Passover, Unleavened Bread, and Firstfruits) were all fulfilled at the first coming of Christ in His death and resurrection. Pentecost was fulfilled with the beginning of the church. The fall festivals (Trumpets, Pentecost, and Booths) will be fulfilled at the second coming of Christ. Trumpets will gather us to Him. The final Day of Atonement will remove all sin from our midst. Finally, the coming of the kingdom will fulfill the Feast of Booths. Trumpets called God's people together for special events. Trumpets were blown on the first day of every month in Israel. Trumpets were blown to signal the beginning of the Fall Harvest Festival. Trumpets gathered God's people for revival in the days of Nehemiah (Neh. 8:1–12). Trumpets will gather us together at the end of the age. "Even so, come, Lord Jesus" (Rev. 22:20).

Note

1. This message has been intentionally written to avoid any specific eschatological perspective. Whatever your view is on end-time events, you can use this message as is and avoid the specifics or you can adapt it and put your perspective in the delivery.

NOVEMBER

The Attitude of Gratitude

Date: November 6

Suggested Title: The Lost Virtue

Scripture: Romans 1:18–25

Contributor: Tim Hawks

Full Sermon Outline

Introduction

From *The Book of Virtues* to Plato's four virtues, one virtue is missing: gratitude.[1] Though lost, gratitude is arguably the most important virtue. Researchers McCullough and Emmons demonstrated that gratitude, considered the parent of all other virtues by Cicero, actually improves psychological, relational, cognitive, and spiritual well-being.[2] When gratitude is missing from the fabric of our lives, we are diminished. A clip from the *Andy Griffith Show* shows Andy and Opie discussing his allowance—the amount, the work required, and the increase of work with increase in pay. Opie finds the whole concept is "just kind of depressing."[3] Like with Opie, gratitude eludes us.

What Is Gratitude?

Gratitude is "the appreciation of benefits received." Gratitude is not happiness, a fleeting feeling from a particular circumstance. Gratitude is not conditional. I get; therefore, I am thankful. I do not get; therefore, I am not thankful. Gratitude is not guilt. The story of starving children somewhere else in the world might create guilt but not necessarily gratitude. Gratitude is not a mind game, a psychological trick to vanquish difficult situations. Gratitude is a mentality that recognizes a benefit, its value, and its source.

Where Did We Lose It? (vv. 18-25)

Romans 1:18-25 explains some foundational concepts in our understanding of God and the human situation, and gratitude is right in the midst of it. Here we see a perfectly loving God displaying His wrath because of "godlessness," the absence of God, and "wickedness," a result of the rejection of God's moral values that actually make life good. People, in fact, push down God's truth while creation clearly communicates the reality of God's power and divine nature. From the solar systems and the systems of the human body to our own pull toward altruism and civilization, God's power, moral excellence, and divine nature are plain. Yet, "Although they knew God, they did not glorify Him as God, nor were thankful" (v. 21). Man began to trivialize God and idolize His creation. They failed to give glory and failed to give thanks.

The term *glory* often creates ideas of dazzling beauty, the display of glory. In Hebrew, *glory* means "heavy," implying weighty and significant. For example, your opinion about our country's foreign policy is "light," without much weight; however, our President's opinion is "weighty," having significant impact on our country's actions. Giving God glory means weighing God into life as the most important factor to our priorities, values, and attitudes. Failing to give God glory means to give weight to something or someone else, making decisions and shaping priorities by it. It becomes our idol, and we diminish God's value, God's influence, God's glory. That damages us.

We also fail to give thanks, viewing God's gifts in our circumstances and relationships as entitlements. We expect them. Without them, we become frustrated and dissatisfied. Our lives are diminished. Thankfulness is not for God's fulfillment; it's for us. Gratitude infinitely improves our lives.

What Do We Really Lose?
1. Without gratitude, we lose our sense of wonder.

Life becomes mundane. Our First World problems of slow smartphones or delayed flights reveal our sense of entitlement. While discovery of a heart defect or brain tumor happens with a machine—without even an incision—we lose the wonder of the remarkable quality of that and are unhappy if our "things" don't work. Where's the wonder?

2. Without gratitude, we lose our sense of value.

Gratitude elevates worth. During a simple haircut, appreciating rather than ignoring the effort of the stylist to learn her trade and employ it with difficult customers elevates her value. Students, do you realize in your irritations with your parents, your lack of expressing thanks devalues their role in your life? Spouses, we do the same thing. Without gratitude, value is lost.

3. Without gratitude, we lose our sense of rest.

Ungratefulness for God's daily provisions drives us away from God. Never at rest, we idolize what we don't have, creating dissatisfaction and a striving to acquire what won't satisfy. Melody Beattie, a guru of codependency, writes:

> Gratitude unlocks the fullness of life. It turns what we have into enough, and more. It turns denial into acceptance, chaos to order, confusion to clarity. It can turn a meal into a feast, a house into a home, a stranger into a friend. It turns problems into gifts, failures into successes, the unexpected into perfect timing, and mistakes into important events. It can turn an existence into a real life, and disconnected situations into important and beneficial lessons.[4]

4. Without gratitude, we lose sensitivity of heart.

Ingratitude is a heart-hardening habit. We should tell our children, "You are becoming today who you will be tomorrow." Our daily habits shape our character over the long haul. If we tell the truth today and again tomorrow, we become people of integrity. Likewise, if we express thanks today and tomorrow and again the following day, we not only experience the benefits of wonder, value, and rest but also are changed in our character. If we complain today, blame tomorrow, and grouse the following day, we become grumpy people no one enjoys.

Conclusion

Grumpy or grateful—it's your choice. Gratitude begins when we truly understand the grace of life. We deserved death for our sin and received life by God's grace.

Notes

1. William J. Bennett, ed., *The Book of Virtues* (New York: Simon and Schuster, 1993), 9; Plato, "The Republic," Book 4.

2. Robert A. Emmons and Michael E. McCullough, "Counting Blessings Versus Burdens: An Experimental Investigation of Gratitude and Subjective Well-Being in Daily Life," *Journal of Personality and Social Psychology*, 84 no. 2 (2003), 377–89. More extensive studies are summarized in Robert A. Emmons and Michael E. McCullough, eds., *The Psychology of Gratitude* (Oxford: Oxford University Press, 2004).

3. "Opie's Allowance," *Andy Griffith Show,* YouTube, https://www.youtube.com/watch?v=MPMbo-WyiEM.

4. Melody Beattie, *The Language of Letting Go: A Meditation Book and Journal for Daily Reflections* (Center City, MN: Hazelden, 2003), August 1 entry.

Date: November 6

Suggested Title: Be the One

Scripture: Luke 17:7–19

Contributor: Tim Hawks

Sermon Starter

Introduction

Deborah Norville wrote in a book about the science of gratitude: "Practicing gratitude, acknowledging the blessings in our lives and making it a point to recognize the good things can change us positively. We'll sleep better and exercise more. We'll feel more optimistic. We'll be more alert and active."[1]

Gratitude is a gift from God, given for our benefit. A parable and a story juxtaposed in Luke 17 show us that gratitude expressed truly changes the trajectory of our lives.

A Parable: The Unworthy Servant (vv. 7–10)

This parable captures normal interaction or a "transactional approach" to life. The servant obeys, performing his responsibilities, then receives the benefits. Additional benefits are unexpected. Then, in verse 10, Jesus gives a jarring command regarding our attitude, urging humble obedience with a sense of duty, which counteracts our individual heart's tendency toward entitlement. In a "transactional approach," we tend to want more, feel we are owed more. His warning protects us from an entitlement mentality, the enemy of happiness.

A Story: The Ten Lepers (vv. 11–19)

Next, we read of the healing of the lepers. Nine of the ten take a "transactional approach" to life, calling to Jesus for help and obeying His instructions. As they obey, they are healed, receiving the benefits of their response. One of them, however, takes a "transcendent approach." He returns to express gratitude and praise. Gratitude moves him into a significant relational encounter with much greater benefits. His faith, Jesus says, has made him "well," the Greek word being *sozo*, meaning "saved." Gratefulness brought more than his body being saved; his entire life was saved through a relationship with Jesus. Gratitude creates a bond with the person to whom it's expressed, a bond giving a quality of life greater than the benefits earned.

Barriers to Expressing Gratitude

What are barriers to expressing gratitude seen here?

- Adopting an entitlement mentality.
- Hurrying to the next Big Thing in our full lives.
- Downplaying the significance of help we have received.

Conclusion

This week, take concrete steps to shift from a transactional approach to the far better transcendent approach to life. Write a letter of gratitude to God, thanking Him for what He has done for you. Additionally, actually write out a letter of thanks to an individual who deserves to hear your gratitude, planning a time to read it aloud to him or her in a personal, relational encounter. Face-to-face, eye-to-eye—it will not only change someone's life; it will change yours.

Note

1. Deborah Norville, *Thank You Power: Making the Science of Gratitude Work for You* (Nashville: Thomas Nelson, 2007), 7.

Date: November 13

Suggested Title: Consider the Alternative

Scripture: Hebrews 12:18–29

Contributor: Tim Hawks

Full Sermon Outline

Introduction

Broccoli, school, exercise, work—honestly, we just aren't thankful for many things that are good for us. We know the things of God are good for us. We need them. Nevertheless, often we are more bored than "blown away" with gratitude. Let's consider the alternative.

Hebrews 12:14–29 compares the alternative to the benefits of life in Jesus Christ. Written to believers desiring to return to their Jewish roots because of severe persecution, the book of Hebrews explains that going back to Judaism is not only impossible but inferior to the true and superior way of Jesus. Verses 14–17 warn: Don't miss the peace and unity. Don't let sexual sin or, like Esau, the appeal of immediate gratification hinder you from bigger blessing. Consider the alternative by comparing two mountains—Mount Sinai, representing the law and Judaism, and Mount Zion, representing Christianity and Jesus Christ.

The Dread of an "Earn It" Future (vv. 18–21)

A look at Mount Sinai reminds us of the fear-filled experience of the Israelites. Amid smoke and fire, God spoke as the God of judgment (cf. Ex. 19:17–19; 20:18–19). Mount Sinai represents an "Earn it" faith with an "Earn it" future. Obedience led to right standing before God. Disobedience brought condemnation. Their future depended on performance. The alternative to Jesus Christ is the dread of standing before God with the impossible load of earning our future.

The Anticipation of an Unbelievable Future (vv. 22–24)

In contrast, Mount Zion anticipates an "Unbelievable Future," not of dread and distance but welcome and invitation. Christ-follower, here is your future:

1. Living at God's house (v. 22)

The place you will arrive is God's place, reflecting His excellence, majesty, mercy, and love. The Architect of all beauty has crafted this city in magnificent perfection, flawlessly capturing His character.

2. Over the top with joy (v. 22)

Approaching, you hear angels rejoicing. What makes angels celebrate? They celebrated at creation (cf. Job 38:7). They exulted at the incarnation (cf. Luke 2:13–14). And they rejoice here at your arrival.

3. Your name in His book (v. 23)

But will they let the likes of you in? Ancient cities kept a roster of citizens for their assembly. Here *ecclesia*, translated "church," refers to the assembly of heavenly citizens. Believers in Jesus, you can approach with confidence that you are a part of this heavenly citizenship with your name on God's roster (cf. Rev. 20:11–15).

4. A pardon from the Judge (v. 23)

You come now before the "Judge of all." Facing the judgment of God at Mount Sinai created the dread of condemnation. Here, you come before the Judge with a full pardon. You enter with no fear, no regrets, no baggage, no pain.

5. Hanging with Daniel (v. 23)

You also approach "the spirits of righteous men made perfect," referring to the Old Testament saints. In addition to Jesus, you will be hanging out with Daniel—and Moses, David, Elisha, and others, hearing their stories firsthand.

6. Hosted by Jesus (v. 24)

Then, you will come to Jesus, "the Mediator," your host. If you have ever been navigated through an extravagant buffet at an elegant restaurant and made to feel at home, you've had a perfect host. In your heavenly home, Jesus will be your perfect host.

7. Good word: grace (v. 24)

Finally, you come to "the blood of sprinkling that speaks better things than that of Abel." Abel's blood speaks a word that calls for judgment of sin (cf. Gen. 4:10). Jesus' blood speaks a better word, *grace*, not giving what you deserve but what you don't deserve—forgiveness, access to God, a future in heaven.

The Response to Our Unbelievable Future (vv. 25–39)

How then do we respond? Not turning away but recognizing the things of God will never be shaken, we give thanks. In thanksgiving, we worship God in an acceptable, reverent, awe-filled way. True worship flows out of gratitude.

Conclusion

1. An ungrateful Christian is an oxymoron.

"Airline food," "government organization," and "ungrateful recipients of God's grace" are all oxymorons and self-contradictory.

2. Choosing ingratitude is choosing an inferior life.

Like choosing to return to the law was choosing a lesser life, choosing ingratitude is choosing an inferior life.

3. Gratitude is the avenue to experiencing God.

When we choose to give thanks we are ushered into the presence of God who is the source of life and all blessings.

Date: November 13

Suggested Title: A Life of Gratitude

Scripture: 1 Thessalonians 5:16–18

Contributor: Tim Hawks

Sermon Starter

Introduction

A favorite *Andy Griffith Show* episode shows Andy extinguishing a rag fire followed by Gomer's overreaction of appreciation. He brings fresh fish for Andy's breakfast, washes and repairs his car, and pledges to fix the fence, trim the hedges, sweep the garage, and literally carry Opie to school, "the firstborn child of the man that saved my life." Andy, conversely, downplays his role.[1]

Which is it? Is gratitude some kind of arduous, frantic payback for what God does for us? Or is it no big deal—what God does, it's in His nature? Why get all worked up with gratitude?

A key idea is that gratitude is God's gift to enrich our lives and enhance our relationships. Matthew 11:28–30, John 10: 7–11, and Romans 8:31–32 show God's heart for us. God is for us, for our good. The objection that God is for His glory rather than our good is a false dichotomy. His glory is always for our good; they are compatible.

Gratitude Is God's Will for You: Three Clear Characteristics

1. Joyful in every circumstance

As opposed to happiness—transient delight in momentary circumstances—joy is a state of mind that focuses on the bigger perspective of God's goodness (cf. Heb. 12:2).

2. Prayerful in every moment

"Pray continually" implies uninterrupted communication with God. Like a cell phone that we never turn off, we are never to disconnect from God.

3. Thankful in every situation

Rating every event "good" or "bad," we label each day based on the sum of the ratings, failing to recognize that the negatives highlight and give value to the positives. Ingratitude in the process diminishes the value of the gift and of the Giver.

Gratitude Is Cultivated: Four Practical Applications

1. Repent: of the sin of entitlement

Charis or *grace*, meaning a benefit I didn't deserve, is the root of the Greek verb "give thanks" (Gk. *eucharisto*). Thankfulness is the acknowledgement of that benefit. Entitlement takes it for granted, cultivating dissatisfaction and discontentment.

2. Pause: gratitude grows in the pause

Busyness in life is a barrier to reflection on God and His good gifts and, therefore, a barrier to the expression of gratitude for those gifts.

3. Capture: built-in reminders

Our cultural and spiritual traditions offer us built-in reminders for gratitude. Take advantage of cultural days (e.g,. Labor Day, Memorial Day, Fourth of July, Martin Luther King Jr. Day, and Thanksgiving) or spiritual celebrations (e.g., Advent and Christmas, Lent and Easter, and our weekly gathering for worship or "Resurrection Day") to develop a lifestyle of gratitude.

4. Model: pass on to the next generation

Children often feel entitled rather than grateful. If spiritually minded adults don't model gratitude, where will our children learn it?

Conclusion

Whatever our circumstances are today, we do know this: Jesus loves us and died to take away our sin and secure our place in His kingdom. That gift alone is worth our gratitude. We should all commit today to become a person of gratitude. We will be thankful we did.

Note

1. "Andy Saves Gomer," *Andy Griffith Show*, YouTube, https://www.youtube.com/watch?v=PYmSGT_ltQ8.

Date: November 20

Suggested Title: From God's Hand

Scripture: 1 Chronicles 29:16

Contributor: Rick Fisher

Full Sermon Outline

Introduction

Just before his death, King David had called the people to make sacrificial gifts for the building and furnishing of the temple that would be built under the leadership of his son Solomon. With the gifts assembled and the people gathered, David prayed and praised God for blessing them and enabling them to do this great work. As part of his prayer, David spoke these words, recorded in 1 Chronicles 29:16: "O LORD our God, all this abundance that we have prepared to build You a house for Your holy name is from Your hand, and is all Your own."

David realized an eternal spiritual truth—if it were not for God's practical involvement in our lives, we would have nothing of value and blessing. The resources for life come from God's hand because everything belongs to Him. That realization should affect our perspective and shape our attitude about life and toward God for all that comes to us from His hand.

Two significant provisions from God's hand profoundly affect us and call us to a place of great thanksgiving and praise to God.

1. Grace from God's hand

"For by grace you have been saved through faith, and that not of yourselves; it is the gift of God, not of works, lest anyone should boast" (Eph. 2:8–9). What is grace? It is everything that God does for us even though we don't deserve it; God giving us what we need, not what we deserve. The first and greatest work of grace is the working of salvation through the ministry of the Holy Spirit, drawing us to Christ and imparting to us a righteousness that is not our own. Paul declared in Philippians 3:9 that his passion was to "be found in Him (Christ), not having my own righteousness, which is from the law, but that which is through faith in Christ, the righteousness which is from God by faith."

There is no purpose or meaning apart from God's grace. God, out of His marvelous love, comes to us from the place of grace. Apart from the love relationship we have with God through faith, we are destined for guilt, fear, bitterness, worry and regret. In the love relationship, guilt is replaced with forgiveness, fear with trust, bitterness with compassion, worry with confidence, and regret with hope.

2. Transformation from God's hand

We were given life for a reason. There is a purpose and a plan for each of us according to God's words to us in Jeremiah 29:11. God's plan is good, even as He takes the hurts and failures in our lives and works them together to bring good, to bring His purpose for our lives into reality (see Rom. 8:28).

And God works constantly within us by His Spirit to bring His power to bear on our hearts and minds, shaping us and changing us in ways that we could never do in our own strength and best thinking. Paul said it this way: "For it is God who works in you both to will and to do for His good pleasure" (Phil. 2:13). God not only plants within us the knowledge of His plan, along with an inner desire and passion to live out His plan; He also places in our lives the power to accomplish it.

In 2 Corinthians 3:18, Paul states clearly the position of every follower of Christ (those of an "unveiled face") in relation to living out the plans and purposes of God in our lives: "But we all, with unveiled face, beholding as in a mirror the glory of the Lord, are being transformed into the same image from glory to glory, just as by the Spirit of the Lord." We should be thankful that God loves each one of us and His love is so personal that He has a plan and purpose for our lives. His love moves to transform us increasingly into His likeness, enabling us to live out our God-authored purpose for His glory.

Conclusion

The great drama and message of the Bible rests on the truth that God is always at work, and one of His great desires is to bring good and blessing to His people. His activity in our lives is essential if we are to live with any measure of peace, joy, and purpose in the midst of the swirling winds of daily life that surround us.

The great news is that God does have a plan for us—a plan in us and through us as we live in a love relationship with Him. From God's ever-working hand, we receive the gift of grace that brings eternal hope and present peace. From God's ever-working hand, we experience His transforming power, shaping us into His likeness, bringing glory to Him and blessing to our lives.

From God's hand, we know and experience abundant life!

Date: November 20

Suggested Title: Expressing Our Gratitude

Scripture: Psalm 63:3, 5; 2 Corinthians 2:14–17

Contributor: Rick Fisher

Sermon Starter

Introduction

To help children develop an attitude of thankfulness, both to God and to those God places in their lives, we must intentionally work with them to verbalize thank-yous and also, when appropriate, write a thank-you note to the person who has blessed them in some way. We also have the same opportunity in our relationship with God that children have with those who give them gifts. God blesses us in a myriad of ways and we have the wonderful privilege of saying thank-you. We express our thankfulness in two significant ways.

1. With our lips

The tongue is a powerful muscle, and the words that come from our lips have great power, influence, and impact on others (Prov. 13:3). Just as God's Word to us is "living and active" (Heb. 4:12), so do our words have a life of their own—with the power to bring unity or division, to soothe or to offend, to praise or to accuse and abuse.

 a. Our words reflect the position of our hearts before God (Luke 6:45).

 b. Our words are expressions of worship and thanksgiving to God (Ps. 63:3–5).

 c. Our words bring either cursing or blessing to others (James 3:10).

2. With our lives

In Colossians 1, Paul expresses his heart toward brothers and sisters in Christ by sharing how he prays for them. In verses 9–10, Paul shares, "For this reason we also, since the day we heard it, do not cease to pray for you, and to ask that you may be filled with the knowledge of His will in all wisdom and spiritual understanding; that you may walk worthy of the Lord, fully pleasing Him, being fruitful in every good work and increasing in the knowledge of God." Paul brings a clear focus to the importance of our "walk," that we live in ways that are "worthy of the Lord," with actions that are "fully pleasing" and "fruitful."

> a. Our actions are prepared in advance by God to bring Him glory (Eph. 2:10).
> b. Our actions are intended to bring blessing to others (Matt. 25:31–46).
> c. Our actions are to spread the aroma of Christ to all people (2 Cor. 2:14–17).

Conclusion

When receiving a compliment, instead of deflecting the compliment by a false humility or by changing the focus of the conversation, the best way to complete the gift and to bring joy to the one who spoke the complimentary words is by simply saying thank-you. Perhaps that is the way we complete God's gifts to us and bring Him the greatest joy—when we simply and intentionally say thank-you with our lips and with our lives.

Date: November 27

Suggested Title: The Impact of Gratitude

Scripture: 1 Thessalonians 5:16–18

Contributor: Rick Fisher

Full Sermon Outline

Introduction

When we hear the word *gratitude*, most likely our minds are drawn to the more common choices of appreciation or thankfulness to define the word and the emotion. However, we should sometimes consider a deeper need, to stop and consider not only the way we express gratitude to God and others but also the impact God intends for the emotion and character mark of gratitude to have on us.

In 1 Thessalonians 5:16–18, Paul exhorts us to be people of gratitude, giving thanks in the midst of all life circumstances, relationships, and experiences. He reminds us that it is God's will and God's purpose for us to live as people of joy, prayer, and thanksgiving. Perhaps Paul knew that one of the great blessings of being people predisposed to gratitude is the positive impact on our own lives, not just those to whom we express our thankfulness and appreciation. The experience of life each day is profoundly affected by the gratitude at work in our hearts.

1. A grateful spirit slays our pride.

We live in a culture driven by performance; we pay great sums of money to sit in arenas, stadiums, and auditoriums to be entertained by the performance of specific skills. We assign great importance, bestow lofty platforms, and grant great influence to those who perform at the highest levels. And while this is certainly characteristic of our culture, it is also increasingly an issue within the body of Christ. Could it be that we find it much easier in contemporary Christian circles to perform acts of ministry than to engage in personal acts of praise and worship, content to perform for God versus living out of a grateful heart, which is the overflow of our love relationship with Him?

This performance mentality tends to tilt our thinking away from reliance on God and recognition of our need for His leadership, His purposes, and His resources in our lives. We become arrogant and prideful as we succumb to the temptation that our thoughts and ways are best and that success is somehow of our own making and dependent on our efforts (Isa. 55:8–9). Pride robs us of a willingness to consult the thoughts and ways of God. Pride robs us of a grateful spirit, separates us from a humility that is necessary for godliness to take root and grow, for we have remade God in our image, captive to our best thinking and efforts. Gratitude is the personal declaration of our dependence on Almighty God for every aspect of life, and it slays our pride, puts it to death, and realigns our heart with the heart and mind of God.

2. A grateful spirit orders the actions of our lives.

Gratitude and daily living are essential companions if we are to be in right relationship to the plans and purposes God has for our lives. Paul encourages us in Colossians 3:17: "And whatever you do in word or deed, do all in the name of the Lord Jesus, giving thanks to God the Father through Him." Scripture teaches us that an orientation toward giving thanks in all things will shape the way we see life (life will be lived in light of the name and character of the Lord Jesus) and the way we live daily (whatever we do) toward others. Apart from a deep and personal understanding that life is to be lived in light of who God is and in relationship to what Jesus has done and is doing within us, our vision of life's priorities and actions will be skewed and out of step with God's plans for us.

The ultimate impact of gratitude is seen in the action of our lives. In John 13, Jesus spent time with the disciples, and in a very profound and impactful way He showed them the connection of gratitude with the priorities and actions of life. Kneeling before them, one by one, Jesus performed the act of a common servant, washing their feet. John records the teaching:

> So when He had washed their feet, taken His garments, and sat down again, He said to them, "Do you know what I have done to you? You call Me Teacher and Lord, and you say well, for so I am. If I then, your Lord and Teacher, have washed your feet, you also ought to wash one another's feet. For I have given you an example, that you should do as I have done to you. Most assuredly, I say to you, a servant is not greater than his master; nor is he who is sent greater than he who sent him. If you know these things, blessed are you if you do them." (John 13:12–17)

The ultimate fruit of a grateful spirit is service to others. Jesus teaches us the importance of a proper and right perspective toward life and then drives home the reality that our perspective toward life will shape every word and action. Gratitude will order the actions of our lives.

Conclusion

A barometer is a scientific instrument that measures pressure in the atmosphere, and the barometric pressure assists meteorologists in predicting weather patterns. As goes the barometric pressure, so goes the expression of weather in a specific region of the nation.

The presence and level of gratitude in our lives exert a pressure on our lives, affecting the way we view ourselves, the way we view people, and the way we live toward God and others. Paul encourages us to be people who are always thankful, people of gratitude in all things, allowing the presence and pressure of gratitude to slay our pride and order our actions, for "this is the will of God in Christ Jesus."

Date: November 27

Suggested Title: Give Thanks!

Scripture: Psalm 150

Contributor: Rick Fisher

Sermon Starter

Introduction

Thanksgiving Day has a long-standing tradition among our national holidays. One year after the Plymouth colonists had set foot on and settled in the new land, a celebration of thanksgiving was held to thank God for His sustaining presence and provision during those first difficult months. Not only did our national ancestors make the giving of thanks to God a priority, but also Scripture is filled with the words of thanksgiving and praise offered to God by our spiritual ancestors.

- 1 Chronicles 16:8
- Psalm 100:4
- 2 Thessalonians 5:18
- Hebrews 12:28

In Psalm 150, one of the Bible's great passages of praise and worship, the writer is filled to overflowing with thanksgiving, offering praise to God with every breath and word of the song. The psalmist's heart of praise calls us to the place of worship and thanksgiving, setting a great example for us as we give thanks.

1. The focus of our thanks (v. 1)

If we are to live in ways that honor the image of Himself that God placed within us, we must keep our lives centered on Him. Praise assists in moving the focus of our lives from being man-centered to God-centered.

2. The motivation of our thanks (v. 2)

- The character of God became the motivation for continued praise and thanksgiving.
- The psalmist praised God for His mighty acts and His excellent greatness; the psalmist praised God for who He is and what He does. There is no one or no thing as great as God and no one or no thing can do what God does (see also Eph. 3:20–21: "exceedingly abundantly above all that we ask or think").

3. The method of our thanks (vv. 3–6)

- With joy and celebration—for example, we can dance and play instruments.
- With intentionality—the people were encouraged to use whatever was in their hands to honor and worship and praise the Lord.
- Everyone that has breath—all of us and each of us have abundant reason to praise the Lord. No believer is exempt from or has sufficient excuse—we are all called to praise the Lord.

Conclusion

We are all cut from the cloth of thanksgiving, in our spiritual ancestors and in our national ancestors. May thanksgiving be on our lips and in our lives today, tomorrow, and all year long!

DECEMBER

Give Me Jesus This Christmas

Date: December 4

Suggested Title: Authentic or Inauthentic Worship This Christmas?

Scripture: Matthew 2:1–12 ESV

Contributor: J. Kie Bowman

Full Sermon Outline

Introduction

Are you ever fooled by anything that appears real and then turns out not to be? It happens all the time in the movies because of CGI, computer-generated imagery.

When you go to the movies, you expect them to fool you a little bit. But when it comes to other things in life you don't want to be fooled. You don't want any CGI when it comes to your spiritual life—you want only what's real. When Jesus was born two thousand years ago, some people came to worship Him with a genuine, pure motive, and some people's motives were not authentic.

We don't know everything there is to know about the Magi, but we know they didn't come to Jerusalem to look at a star; they came to worship "he who has been born king of the Jews."

Authentic Worshippers Desire Worship (v. 1)

The Magi left everything to pursue worship. Worship ought to be the priority of our lives, and when we place anything else at the center of our lives, it is an insufficient substitute.

The Magi said, "We saw his star ... and have come to worship him." It was natural for them to come to Jerusalem. After all, Jerusalem was the city of the Jewish king. But Jesus wasn't born in Jerusalem. He was born five miles south on a back road in a place called Bethlehem, a little, insignificant city. David was born in Bethlehem, and so Joseph, his descendant, and Mary had to make their way to Bethlehem because the Roman emperor had decided to tax the empire. The Magi didn't know all that. So they showed up to Jerusalem expecting to find the newborn king since Jerusalem was the city of the king.

The Magi were astrologers who thought somehow the stars have significance over our everyday lives. Yet even after the long trip these men essentially said, "We don't care about the star. Just show us the baby that the star is pointing to because we have come to worship the king."

This word for *worship* means "to kiss toward." It's a word that describes a culture in which everyone bows to royalty. If the royalty extends a hand, you kiss it, showing humility, service, and obedience. Worship means when we come into the presence of God, we desire Him. Worship means, "I come into His presence and I bow before Him, thank Him, and offer myself in willing service, humility, and obedience before Him." Worship is the innate desire of the Spirit-filled believer to come into the presence of God and say, "I love you, and I'm here to serve you." That's authentic. It doesn't mean it's perfect, but it's authentic.

Inauthentic Worshippers Deceive in Worship (vv. 3–8)

After Herod learned about the Old Testament prophecy of the birth of Christ, he hatched a plot. "Then Herod summoned the wise men secretly and ascertained from them what time the star had appeared. And he sent them to Bethlehem, saying, 'Go and search diligently for the child, and when you have found him, bring me word, that I too may come and worship him'" (vv. 7–8).

You cannot tell the story of the Magi without bringing Herod into the story. These stories are inextricably linked. One is a story of authentic worship, and the other is the story of inauthentic worship. Of the twelve verses of this story Herod is mentioned eight times directly and the Magi are mentioned eight times directly. Herod was a ruthless, bloodthirsty killer with a pathological paranoia. He was a poser seated upon the throne of the Jews, and he knew instinctively that the baby was more than just a newborn king threatening his crown. This was actually the

Son of God. In his paranoia he planned to kill Jesus while pretending to worship Him!

Any time that I think that I can disobey God and yet continue to pretend that I'm a follower, I am deceiving myself. If I only pretend to worship, I am inauthentic.

You can cover yourself with every kind of disguise, but God will look closely at your heart. Any time I step out of the blessings and the plan of God and do things my own way I'm just displaying that ancient old spirit of Herod and inauthentic worship.

Whenever I put myself in a position of controlling my own footsteps and my own agenda—in clear opposition to what God has said—I'm displaying inauthentic worship.

Authentic Worshippers Delight in Worship (vv. 9–11)

There ought to be something in us that says, "I don't worship because I have to. I worship God because I *love* to worship God."

The Magi famously brought three expensive gifts: gold, frankincense, and myrrh. There's only one explanation why they brought these gifts, and verse 11 tells us. They "fell down and worshiped him." Verse 10 says they rejoiced "exceedingly with great joy." The Magi came into the presence of God with the kind of spirit we need when we come into the presence of God—with exceeding great joy! Worship was the purpose of their visit, and they didn't waste it. They came with exceeding great joy and fell down and worshipped Him.

Conclusion

When it comes to worship, is your motive pure? You're the only one that can answer that. Is your worship authentic or inauthentic?

Date: December 4

Suggested Title: The God of the Impossible This Christmas

Scripture: Luke 1:26–38 ESV

Contributor: J. Kie Bowman

Sermon Starter

Introduction

Do you believe the supernatural is possible? Even in our skeptical age, Christmas is the reminder that with God nothing can be impossible!

1. God accomplishes the impossible in unexpected places (v. 26).

If there is nothing supernatural then there is no God. If there is no God then the Christmas story is at best a fable or at worst a complete fraud. The Christmas story, however, is the miraculous story of God's intervention in the world.

Mary was from a town so insignificant it wasn't even mentioned in the Old Testament. One of Jesus' disciples would later ask if anything good could come out of Nazareth (John 1:46). One of the miracles of Christmas involves how God locates otherwise insignificant places to do significant things. The angel went to the tiny "city of Galilee named Nazareth" to do the impossible.

Do you believe God can do the impossible where you are right now? He has done the impossible in the most unlikely places before. Your town is not too small for the miraculous intervention of God. Your city is not too large for miracles either. No matter how overwhelmed you might feel by the unimpressive size of your town or the intimidating powers around you or the limited resources you have, remember that nothing is impossible with God.

2. God accomplishes the impossible in unexpected people (vv. 32–37).

Mary was a virgin, and that fact was not lost on her when she received the news about the birth of Jesus. She wanted to believe it, but how could it be possible? The angel informed her that "nothing will be impossible with God" (v. 37). While God does not promise more virgin births, the miracles He is able to perform through you might be just as unlikely. Telling God you're too young or too old, too sick or too busy to expect the impossible are only expressions of a faithless point of view. God always does the most unexpected things through the most unlikely people. He chose the older woman when a younger woman was more likely to succeed (Gen. 18:10–12), the younger son when tradition favored the older (Gen. 27), and the virgin to bear the Son of God.

You may be tempted to think, "Yes, God did the impossible in their lives, but I'm not them." True, you're not them, but God is still God and He hasn't changed a bit. He still delights in doing the impossible through unlikely people.

Conclusion

Regardless of where you are or who you think you are, God can do the impossible right now, right here with you. The only question is, "Will you believe and receive the impossible?"

Date: December 11

Suggested Title: God's Christmas Presence

Scripture: Matthew 1:18–25

Contributor: J. Kie Bowman

Full Sermon Outline

Introduction

Have you ever been around anyone and wondered if they were really there at all? Here's an example: in a conversation, someone mentioned he didn't think the new boss liked him. When asked how he could tell, he replied, "I could sense the absence of his presence." That's a good description for some relationships.

In a close relationship, however, the exact opposite is true. For instance, even in our spiritual lives we desire an intimacy with God. We need that close spiritual relationship with Jesus. In fact, that's what Christmas is all about: the presence of God. The goal of every believer, at Christmas and throughout the year, is to live in the presence of God.

The four Gospels are obviously filled with stories about Jesus. Fittingly, it's the story of a miraculous intervention of God in the lives of two ordinary people living lives of faithfulness to God. Suddenly God miraculously intervened. The first news we receive about Jesus is in this little narrative from Matthew's Gospel.

> But as he [Joseph] considered these things, behold, an angel of the Lord appeared to him in a dream, saying, "Joseph, son of David, do not fear to take Mary as your wife, for that which is conceived in her is from the Holy Spirit. She will bear a son, and you shall call his name Jesus, for he will save his people from their sins." All this took place to fulfill what the Lord had spoken by the prophet:

"Behold, the virgin shall conceive and bear a son, and they shall call his name Immanuel" (which means, God with us). (vv. 20–23)

This is a well-known part of the Christmas story. Almost everybody knows something about the details. Joseph is a working-class, single adult living in a little town called Nazareth, just west of the southern point of the Sea of Galilee, up in the mountains on the way to nowhere. He's engaged to be married to a young woman, and she surprises him with the news that she's going to have a baby. He's 100 percent certain that it's not his child. While he's thinking it over and deciding what he's going to do, an angel of God tells him the child has been conceived by the Holy Spirit. The angel tells Joseph that the baby will be called "God with us." Here's the truth that leaps off the page: God has gone to extraordinary lengths to have a relationship with you.

In the busyness of this season, what does Christmas really mean? It's simple. All the decorations, all the songs, all the celebrations are about one thing: God has come near to you and me. Christmas is simply this: God is here with us now. Jesus is "God with us." How is this true?

God Promises His Christmas Presence (v. 22)

An angel explains that the unexpected baby is God's plan, and the only way for Joseph to understand it is to remember the prophecy made by Isaiah the prophet centuries earlier. He said, "All this took place to fulfill what the Lord had spoken by the prophet" (v. 22). The unexpected news was part of a plan after all. God had predicted these events (Isa. 7:14). God has always had a plan to send Jesus. The miraculous events of that first Christmas were part of God's eternal plan.

Christmas is a miracle or it's nothing at all. It is the miraculous story of God intervening in human history. God has stepped into our experience. His eternal story becomes part of our story here and now. Here's the promise God made to Joseph and to you and me: God is with us in the person of Jesus Christ.

God Personalizes His Christmas Presence (v. 23)

"'Behold, the virgin shall conceive and bear a son, and they shall call his name Immanuel' (which means God with us)." That's personal. God didn't send just a prophet or a priest or a pastor. God sent His own Son. God is with us.

Here's the real power of Christmas. God has entered the human story. God has come into our lives in order to solve our biggest problem. Our biggest problem is not the economy. It's not the weather. It's not global terrorism. It's not cancer. Our biggest problem is this: sin. We have sinned against God. Our sin problem is so serious God had to come and handle it Himself. That's what the Bible says. "She will bear a son, and you shall call his name Jesus, for he will save his people from their sins" (v. 21). God had to come and deal with the sin problem because the problem of sin in your life and my life is so terrible God had to deal with it on His own. God got personal on that first Christmas. Jesus is God in person, dealing with the problem of sin (v. 21).

Conclusion

Here's what Christmas is all about; in fact, here's what *life* is all about: that we may know Him, the only true God, and Jesus Christ whom He has sent. It is extremely personal. Christmas, and ultimately our life itself, comes down to this, living in the presence of God. As a result of Christmas, believers can know God because Jesus is "God with us."

Date: December 11

Suggested Title: Where the Christmas Miracle Leads

Scripture: Matthew 1:18–25 ESV

Contributor: J. Kie Bowman

Sermon Starter

Introduction

Do you believe in miracles? In our culture it's easy to be skeptical. We live in an age of false claims. Have you ever seen an ad in print or on TV and thought, "That is just too good to be true"? At some point it's hard to remain gullible when so many outrageous claims are made every day.

No wonder we're all so skeptical. But we have to remember the first Christmas is unapologetically presented to us as a miracle. God became a man!

The Christmas Miracle Can Lead to Forgiveness of Sin (vv. 20–21)

Nearly everybody knows the story of Joseph and the Virgin Mary. They were planning to be married. Then Joseph received the news that she was going to have a baby that wasn't his. One night while he was praying about it, he fell asleep. An angel of the Lord appeared saying, "That which is conceived in her is from the Holy Spirit" (v. 20).

Think of how many questions you might have if you were Joseph. The angel didn't explain everything—but he was emphatic on one thing: he said, "You shall call His name Jesus." Why? "For He will save His people from their sins" (v. 21).

If Jesus had not been born of a virgin, you would have never heard of Him at all. But Joseph was not his father; God was His father. The angel said to name Him Jesus. Why? Because the Hebrew name *Jesus* means

"The Lord saves." The miracle of Christmas leads to the forgiveness of sin.

We are surrounded with problems of all kinds, but our biggest problem isn't economic, political, or psychological. Our biggest problem is spiritual. We have a sin problem. God dealt with that problem by becoming a man like every other man with one exception: He never sinned. It was His sinless life that made His death so important. His miraculous birth gives meaning to His death. The cross only makes sense in light of the miraculous birth of Jesus.

You've probably never heard of James Wolfe, a British army officer who was leading a battle. As his army was winning, he was shot and killed. A large memorial was erected in Westminster Abbey in his honor, and inscribed there are these words: "Slain in the moment of victory."[1]

The same thing could be said about Jesus Christ because it was on that cross that the miraculous baby of Bethlehem grew up and died to secure our victory. He was slain in the moment of victory. He died to bring salvation, forgiveness, and eternal life to a lost world.

Conclusion

Jesus' birth, death, and resurrection are miraculous, and as a result your faith, forgiveness, and salvation bring glory to God and life to your soul.

Note

1. http://www.westminster-abbey.org/our-history/people /james-wolfe/.

Date: December 18

Suggested Title: Christmas Surprises from God

Scripture: Luke 2:8–11 ESV

Contributor: J. Kie Bowman

Full Sermon Outline

Introduction

Christmas is a time for surprises. Under Christmas trees are gifts wrapped so the contents can be kept secret. Part of the tradition of Christmas includes surprises. The surprise that occurred two thousand years ago to a group of shepherds outside Bethlehem may be the greatest surprise of all time. That surprise back then can remind us that God is still able to surprise you with what He wants to do in your life today.

For the shepherds around Bethlehem, life was predictable. They worked hard for low pay. They worked long hours. They even had the night shift. But God surprised them. He intervened in a way they could never have predicted. God can still do things in your life you cannot predict. You need to live believing that at any moment God can do what you didn't expect.

God's Surprises Remind Us that He Can Appear at Any Time (v. 8)

God's surprises remind us He can appear at any time. "And in the same region there were shepherds out in the field" (v. 8). In those days, Bethlehem wasn't on the way to anywhere in particular. It was a small shepherds' town. What is remarkable about this passage is the reminder that God can "show up" at any moment!

These men were living on the outskirts of town in a place called Shepherd's Field. The shepherds may have been half asleep. In the midst of this calm, predictable routine, a night just like any other night, "an angel of the Lord appeared to them" (v. 9).

This wasn't a prayer meeting. They weren't in church. They weren't in the temple. Yet there was a sudden, unexpected appearance of God. "And the glory of the Lord shone around them" (v. 9). The word *glory* in the Greek New Testament is the word *doxa*. We get our word *doxology*, which we know as a hymn of praise, from *doxa*. The word *doxa* in the Greek New Testament, however, is a word that refers to the brightness of the sun or the splendor of the moon or the stars. Picture that dark night in Bethlehem's Shepherd's Field when all of a sudden the lights came on! The phrase "shone around them" is one word in the New Testament made up of two words, *perilampo*. *Peri* means "around" (like our word *periscope*). *Lampo* means to shine or to cast a light. We get our word *lamp* from it. *Perilampo*, the lamp of God, the light of God, the glory of God suddenly burst onto the scene, on a dark night, all around Shepherd's Field.

For the shepherds God made Himself obvious. Suddenly everything changed because God got involved. God changes things! And the God that intervened in their life can intervene in your life. When God does intervene, don't expect your life to be predictable, safe, and boring. Nobody ever stays the same after God shows up.

God's Surprises Remind Us that He Can Assure Us at Any Time (vv. 9–11)

> And an angel of the Lord appeared to them, and the glory of the Lord shone around them, and they were filled with great fear. And the angel said to them, "Fear not, for behold, I bring you good news of great joy that will be for all the people. For unto you is born this day in the city of David a Savior, who is Christ the Lord. (vv. 9–11)

We do not need to be afraid. God does not want us to live in fear. The words "filled with fear" in the Greek New Testament make a phrase consisting of two words: *megas phobias.* We get our word *phobia* from it. They had mega phobia! The angel said, "Fear not." In Scripture, "Fear not" is a frequently repeated command. God gives us abundant reminders and assurance that we do not have to be afraid.

God's assurance, however, goes beyond the absence of fear. The angel also said, "I bring you good news of great joy" (Gk. *mega chara*). They had *mega phobia,* but God replaced the mega fear with mega joy! When God is doing a work in your life, you do not need to live with fear; you can have joy. How? The same way they had it two thousand years ago. "And the angel said to them, 'Fear not, for behold, I bring you good news of great joy that will be for all the people. For unto you is born this day in the city of David a Savior, who is Christ the Lord'" (vv. 10–11). The Savior is our hope! Jesus is our joy.

In our world, terror is a strategy. Fearmongering has been honed to a science. You also have a spiritual enemy, and his greatest weapon today appears to be fear. The Christian responds to the problem of fear with faith. You can refuse to live in fear if you're saved and if your fears have been replaced with the joy of the Lord. Faith is the opposite of fear.

Because a "Savior has been born," you must not live in fear any longer. Jesus is God's assurance that fear will fail as a tactic against you. Let your faith in the "Savior born to us" overcome every fear.

Conclusion

When God surprises His people, it is always for our good and His glory, so His surprises at Christmas are the best surprises of all!

Date: December 18

Suggested Title: Anna: Spiritual Disciplines at Christmas

Scripture: Luke 2:36–38 ESV

Contributor: J. Kie Bowman

Sermon Starter

Introduction

Do you have a spiritual mentor? Every believer benefits from the spiritual leadership of godly mentors. One of the best examples of spiritual leadership is a woman often overlooked in the Nativity story.

When Jesus was taken to the temple as a newborn, He and His family were met by an elderly Jewish prophetess named Anna, one of the lesser-known personalities in the Christmas narrative. Appearing only once in the New Testament, her personal commitment to the spiritual disciplines serves as a model for all of us!

You Need the Spiritual Discipline of Worship at Christmas (vv. 36–38)

> She was advanced in years, having lived with her husband … and then as a widow until she was eighty-four. She did not depart from the temple, worshiping with fasting and prayer night and day. And coming up at that very hour she began to give thanks to God and to speak of him to all who were waiting for the redemption of Jerusalem. (vv. 36–38)

When we review the spiritual practices of Anna, we discover some essential disciplines of Christian devotion. For example, Anna had a *place* for worship. She was a regular at the temple. She was also *persistent* in worship as evidenced by the fact that she worshipped "night and day" (v. 37). While you are not expected to live at church, your regular participation in worship services is part of a godly tradition worth emulating.

Do you have a visible *passion* for worship? Anna did. She fasted as a way of life. Jesus would later encourage all of His followers to fast (Matt. 6:16–18). Giving up meals for the purpose of seeking God is an ancient and excellent way to passionately pursue God.

In addition, no one grows deep in the things of God without *prayer*, and Anna was a role model in prayer. The word used for prayer (Gk. *deomai*) in verse 37 comes from a Greek word meaning "to lack" and implies a humble prayer of admitted need. Prayer admits our need for God.

Finally, in worship, *praise* should epitomize the Christian life. Anna gave thanks when she saw Jesus. Shouldn't you?

You Need the Spiritual Discipline of Witness at Christmas (v. 38)

When we think of spiritual disciplines, evangelism might be too easily overlooked. Anna was an evangelist as well as a prayer warrior. As soon as she saw Jesus, she began to "speak of him to all" (v. 38). Her example is powerful and persuasive. She didn't know about the future: the cross, the resurrection, or Pentecost, but she told everyone about Jesus. With all you know now, this Christmas you should be even more willing to tell the whole story of Jesus.

Conclusion

With a healthy blend of worship and witness, this might be the most spiritual Christmas you've ever had.

Date: December 25

Suggested Title: The Name Above Every Name at Christmas

Scripture: Matthew 1:18–22 ESV

Contributor: J. Kie Bowman

Full Sermon Outline

Introduction

What names come to your mind when you hear the word *greatness*? Maybe in sports you think of Hank Aaron or Vince Lombardi or Michael Jordan. In politics, you might think of Abraham Lincoln or Nelson Mandela. If you think of a humanitarian, a great name comes to mind: Mother Teresa. In the field of science you might think of Albert Einstein. In the study of literature great names include Voltaire or Shakespeare or Charles Dickens. In different fields, throughout history, there have been some great names, but the Bible says there is one "name that is above every name" (Phil. 2:9). It's the name of Jesus.

Jesus is better known today and followed by more people than ever before in history. Some people have estimated eighty two thousand people a day worldwide come to faith in Jesus Christ. In every way, His name is above every name! Even at Christmas His name is above every name. How is this true?

The Name Above Every Name Comes to Us by the Spirit (v. 18)

What do we learn about the name that is above every name? "Now the birth of Jesus Christ took place in this way. When his mother Mary had been betrothed to Joseph, before they came together she was found to be with child from the Holy Spirit" (v. 18). This is a fact of the Christmas story that we dare not overlook. Jesus was born of a virgin as a result of the power of the Holy Spirit of God. The child conceived in her is "from the Holy Spirit" (v. 18). In the Greek New Testament it literally says that the child is *ek pneuma hagios*: "out of the Holy Spirit." *Hagios* means holy. *Pneuma* means spirit. *Ek,* like our word *exit* above a door, means "out of." This phrase teaches us that the birth of Jesus was *ek* Holy Spirit, "out of" the Holy Spirit. Jesus comes directly from the presence of God Himself. That's important for two reasons.

First, Jesus is the only person ever born who is qualified to be your Savior. He had God as His Father. He was virgin-born. That means He was able to live a sinless life and die a perfect death so that He could be the satisfaction for all of our sins. When God sent Jesus, He didn't just send any person; He came "in person" because Jesus is the fulfillment of Isaiah 7:14 (ESV): "The virgin shall conceive and bear a son, and shall call his name Immanuel." *Immanuel* means God with us (v. 23). Jesus is God with a body because He was conceived out of the Holy Spirit.

Second, everything about the Christian life is initiated by the Holy Spirit. Even the Christmas story wouldn't be possible without the Holy Spirit. Your soul would not be saved without the Holy Spirit. Even Jesus would not be here if it were not for the Holy Spirit.

The Name Above Every Name Confronts Us with Our Sin (v. 21)

In the twenty-first century we might be tempted to describe the Christian faith in purely psychological terms. There are psychological issues in life to be sure, but our main problem is not psychological. Our main problem is a sin problem. At the core of every human being is a twisted part of us that tends toward that which is not pleasing to God. As a matter of fact, the Word says: "for he will save his people from their sins" (v. 21). The Greek word for *sin* here means "to miss the mark." It's like when an archer completely misses the target when he releases the arrow from the bow and the trajectory of the arrow is wrong.

We have sinned against God. We are "off target." You cannot fix your sin problem any more than you can pick up a bathtub if you're sitting in it. We need a Savior. We've *sensationalized* Christmas. We *sentimentalized* Christmas. We've *secularized* Christmas. Jesus, however, wants to *save* us at Christmas!

The Name Above Every Name Comforts Us with Salvation (v. 21)

The name *Jesus* was not an uncommon name. It's the Hebrew *Yeshua* and it means "Yahweh is salvation." You see, you can't even say the name *Jesus* without saying God is all about salvation. You cannot mention Jesus without talking about salvation. Our problem is sin; our solution is Jesus and the salvation that He brings. The Bible says, "You shall call his name Jesus, for he will save his people from their sins" (v. 21). The word *save* means to rescue. It's a word that describes somebody in trouble, and someone else helps this person out of trouble. Salvation is the Greek word *sozo*. We get our English word *soteriology* (the doctrine of salvation) from this word. It means to deliver, to rescue, or to save.

We say a lot of things about Christmas, but as the church of Jesus Christ, we must insist upon this: "Jesus saves." The Bible says, "Everyone who calls on the name of the Lord will be saved" (Rom. 10:13 ESV). It doesn't say you have to know everything the Bible teaches. It doesn't say you have to be a Baptist or a man or an American. It doesn't say you have to be white or black. The Bible says "everyone"—man, woman, young, or old. "Everyone who calls on the name of the Lord will be saved."

Conclusion

This Christmas only one name can meet our needs—the name above every name—the name of Jesus!

Date: December 25

Suggested Title: Worship: The Purpose of Christmas

Scripture: Matthew 2:1–12 ESV

Contributor: J. Kie Bowman

Sermon Starter

Introduction

What is God's purpose for your life? If God has a purpose for your life, then wouldn't that purpose be eternal and unchanging like God Himself? When Jesus was born the wise men came for one purpose. They came to worship Jesus, and by doing so they blazed a trail for us to follow their example. We were made for worship.

Christmas Puts Your Worship to the Test (vv. 1–2)

It seems reasonable that the priests and religious leaders should have been gathered around the baby Jesus to worship, but they were absent. Instead, Gentiles from a foreign country came as soon as they could. Assuming their home was in Persia or Babylon, we know the Magi paid a price in time and effort to come hundreds of miles across the desert to give the Lord the worship He deserved. When they arrived in Jerusalem, Herod was already king. But they weren't looking for a political king; they were looking for a newborn King! They were willing to bypass the powers that be in order to seek instead the presence of God.

Are you willing to seek Him first even if you have to become oblivious to earthly powers and invest time and energy just for the sake of giving Him praise?

Christmas Calls You to Worship Like the Rest (v. 2)

Sometimes it is necessary to stand alone in our commitment to Christ. At other times we need to join with the throngs who owe our

Lord praise and worship. The Magi represented the political powers of a foreign kingdom. They spoke a foreign language, held different customs, and were schooled in a different religion. Yet they said, "Where is he who has been born king of the Jews … for we … have come to worship him" (v. 2). The wise men weren't Jews. They were coming to a worship service no one knew they were invited to attend, but that little detail didn't stop them. When it comes to worship, we have to set aside sectarian bias and secondary differences because Christmas is a reminder to all of us that Jesus deserves our worship.

Christianity is not small or localized. Christianity cannot be contained by one church or denomination because Jesus is bigger than all the members of His church combined. Through the ages God has used different kinds of Christians for one purpose—to give our Lord praise. If it takes a group of anonymous Persian astrologers who were nothing like us to teach us that our Lord deserves our worship, then we should be ready to learn this Christmas.

Conclusion

The purpose of Christmas is the worship of the One bigger and more important than anything in our lives. The purpose of Christmas is the real purpose of life—to worship Jesus!

SPECIAL OCCASION REGISTRIES

Baby Dedication

Infant's Name: _____

Significance of Given Names: _____

_____

Date of Birth: _____

Date of Dedication: _____

Siblings: _____

_____

Maternal Grandparents: _____

Paternal Grandparents: _____

Life Verse: _____

Notes: _____

_____

_____

_____

_____

_____

_____

_____

Baptisms & Confirmations

Date   Name   Notes

_____

_____

_____

_____

_____

_____

_____

_____

_____

_____

_____

_____

_____

_____

_____

_____

_____

_____

_____

_____

_____

_____

_____

Funeral Registration

Name of Deceased: _____

Age: _____

Religious Affiliation: _____

Survivors:

     Spouse: _____

     Parents: _____

     Children: _____

     Siblings: _____

     Grandchildren: _____

Date of Death: _____

Time and Place of Visitation: _____

Date of Funeral or Memorial Service: _____

Funeral Home Responsible: _____

Location of Funeral or Memorial Service: _____

Scripture Used: _____

Hymns Used: _____

Eulogy by: _____

Others Assisting: _____

Pallbearers: _____

_____

_____

_____

Date of Interment: _____ Place of Interment: _____

Graveside Service: Yes: _____ No _____

Funerals Log

Date	Name of Deceased	Scripture Used

Marriage Registration

Bride: _____

    Religious Affiliation: _____

    Parents: _____

Groom: _____

    Religious Affiliation: _____

    Parents: _____

Date of Wedding: _____

Location: _____

Ceremony Planning By: _____ Minister _____ Couple

Others Assisting: _____

_____

Maid/Matron of Honor: _____

Best Man: _____

Wedding Planner: _____

Date, Time, Location of Rehearsal: _____

Reception: _____ All Wedding Guests _____ Invitation Only

Reception Location: _____

Photography: _____ During Ceremony _____ After Ceremony

Date of Counseling: _____ Date of Registration: _____

Miscellaneous: _____

_____

_____

_____

_____

Marriages Log

Date	Names of Couple	Scripture Used

Sermons Preached

Date   Text   Title/Subject

INDEX

Index